ADVANCES IN SOCIAL COGNITION
VOLUME III

Content and Process Specificity
in the Effects of Prior Experiences

D1296458

ADVANCES IN SOCIAL COGNITION, Volume III

Content and Process Specificity in the Effects of Prior Experiences

Edited by
THOMAS K. SRULL
ROBERT S. WYER, JR.
University of Illinois, Urbana—Champaign

LEA LAWRENCE ERLBAUM ASSOCIATES, PUBLISHERS
1990   Hillsdale, New Jersey   Hove and London

Lawrence Erlbaum Associates, Inc., Publishers
365 Broadway
Hillsdale, New Jersey 07642

LC 89-643539
ISSN 0898-2007
ISBN 0-8058-0700-4
ISBN 0-8058-0714-4 (pbk.)

Printed in the United States of America
10 9 8 7 6 5 4 3 2 1

Contents

Preface

The present volume is the third issue in the series of *Advances in Social Cognition*. The purpose of the series, from the beginning, has been to present and evaluate new theoretical advances in all areas of social cognition and information processing. An entire volume is devoted to each theory, thus allowing it to be evaluated from a variety of perspectives and its implications for a wide range of issues to be considered.

The series reflects the two major characteristics of social cognition: the high level of activity in the field and the interstitial nature of the work. Each volume contains a target article that is chosen because it is timely in its application, novel in its approach, and precise in its explication. The target article is then followed by a set of critical commentaries that represent different theoretical persuasions, different subdisciplines within psychology, and occasionally separate disciplines. We believe that the dialogue created by such a format is highly unusual but, if done with care, extremely beneficial to the field.

Public debates are interesting and informative but they require a special group of people if they are to be productive. In this respect, we want to thank the many people who agreed to participate in the project. Most of all, we owe a considerable debt to Eliot Smith. In many ways, Smith is swimming against the tide of most current work in social cognition. But he swims with grace, strength, endurance, and an overall strategy. This is indeed a rare combination and we believe that Smith has produced a treatise that is exemplary in its concinnity. We are pleased to have it and we thank him, both for the months he spent writing and for those he spent waiting.

The commentators have played an equally important and difficult role. They were asked to prepare chapters that were critical but fair, and ones that were detailed but well reasoned. Readers will find that each of them is insightful, thought provoking, and an important contribution in its own right. We want to extend our sincere appreciation to each of the commentators for being so analytical and clear.

And, as before, we want to acknowledge the contributions of Larry Erlbaum. He is an endearing and encouraging publisher. And a good friend.

Thomas K. Srull
Robert S. Wyer, Jr.

1 Content and Process Specificity in the Effects of Prior Experiences

Eliot R. Smith
Purdue University

Something about John, whom she has just met, reminds Mary of an old boy-friend; this influences Mary's actions toward John.

Sam needs to hire a clerk for his organization. One applicant is a member of an ethnic minority group and Sam wonders whether the applicant will have the skills and education for the job.

After they watch a movie involving violent and aggressive themes, Susan interprets a remark by her companion as hostile, even though he denies hostile intent.

These everyday examples illustrate the types of effects on which I focus in this article: *the effects of prior experiences and social knowledge on a person's current perceptions or reactions.* The social cognition literature offers many examples of such phenomena, including priming effects on social categorization, effects of stereotypes on person perception, effects on an accessible schema on attention and memory for schema-consistent or inconsistent information, effects of practice on the efficiency and content of social judgment, and effects of scripts on story processing and event memory (e.g., Bodenhausen & Wyer, 1985; Carver, Ganellen, Froming, & Chambers, 1983; Higgins, Rholes, & Jones, 1977, White & Shapiro, 1987).

As these examples suggest, prior experiences or knowledge can affect social judgment and behavior in a variety of ways. Theorists and researchers in social cognition seek to identify the mechanisms underlying these effects. Two main themes underlie their treatment in this article, and a third will emerge as a number of empirical results are discussed. First, over time our theories in social cognition are growing more adequate and hence more complex. There is no reason to think that the mind is simple! Our theories are coming increasingly to

1

reflect that fact as the field's empirical data base, stock of conceptual tools (e.g., the language of information representation and processing), and methodological sophistication grow. An outstanding recent example of theoretical complexity (Wyer & Srull, 1986) includes 23 propositions and a variety of theoretical constructs like schemata, Storage Bins, and a Goal Specification Box. As social cognition becomes more integrated with other areas and with cognitive psychology in particular (cf. Ostrom, 1984; Smith, 1984), the tendency toward increasing complexity will be reinforced. In the future, then, we will have an increasing variety of theoretical constructs to invoke as mediators of effects of past experiences on current processing, perhaps including schemata or other representations of abstract constructs, episodic memories or traces left by specific experiences, and cognitive procedures.

The second theme is that in order to decide what particular mediator is responsible for any given effect of a prior experience on current responses or judgments, one can examine the pattern of specificity of the effects. Each mediator has its own characteristic pattern of specificity, and these "signatures" can be used to make inferences about mediation, much as police can sometimes identify a particular criminal by detecting known patterns in the *modus operandi* of a crime.

I view the first theme, the increasing theoretical complexity in the field, as self-evident. The second, the usefulness of specificity as a clue to mediation, is supported by detailed arguments in this chapter. A third theme will emerge from a consideration of relevant research in social cognition with an eye to identifying patterns of specificity. It is not so much an empirical claim as a suggestion that social cognition may have devoted a disproportionate amount of attention to one class of mediators: schemata and other abstract, generic knowledge structures. Many phenomena appear to depend on other types of mediators, particularly memory traces of specific experiences and procedural knowledge. If this suggestion proves correct, we have an exciting new set of research issues before us that have barely begun to be explored.

SPECIFICITY AS A METHODOLOGICAL PRINCIPLE

The specificity of effects of prior experiences on later performance is of empirical and practical interest. That is, it is often useful to know how broad or narrow and how long-lasting the psychological effects of a particular event may be. One central theme of this article, though, is that patterns of specificity are also theoretically significant. Theory and empirical findings can support generalizations concerning the patterns of specificity that are expected from different types of cognitive mediators. *Therefore, investigating the patterns of specificity for a given effect can yield evidence concerning how the effect is mediated.* Applications of this methodological principle to diverse empirical phenomena occupy much of this paper.

Four dimensions of specificity can be distinguished, of which the first two receive the most attention here. These dimensions answer questions of the form, "*What* information (content) is processed *how* (process), *where* (context), and *when* (time)?" To illustrate the dimensions concretely, assume a priming paradigm (Higgins et al., 1977).[1] For example, a person might read the word "punch," which is related to the concept of hostility. Then (in an ostensibly unrelated study) the person reads that John insults Bill and rates John on the dimension of hostility. Research like this has shown that the earlier exposure to the prime can influence this "category accessibility" measure. Compared to unprimed controls, people who have encountered information related to the trait category rate ambiguous target behaviors higher on the trait. The four dimensions of specificity are as follows.

Content Specificity

How similar are the content of the priming information and the target stimulus? A prime might influence interpretations only when prime and target are the same behavior (i.e., category accessibility might be influenced only for the target stimulus "John punches Bill"). This would represent a highly specific effect. Alternatively, the priming might shape the interpretation of behaviors that are similar to the prime (e.g., kicking) or even dissimilar (but still potentially hostile) behaviors like insulting. Content specificity refers to the question: Does a prior experience (for example, reading a priming word) have broad effects on processing of a wide range of target stimuli, or are the effects specific to targets that are identical or highly similar to the prime?

Process Specificity

How similar is the processing accorded to the priming information and to the target stimulus? One possibility is that priming influences the person's response to the target only when the same process is applied to both (e.g., inferring hostility based on a behavior). Alternatively, performing one process on the priming stimulus (just reading the word, or counting the number of syllables in it) might have effects even when a *different* process (for example, a trait inference) is applied to the target. Process specificity asks: Does a prior experience influence only those later performances that involve the same process that was used on the earlier occasion, or can it have broader and more general effects?

---

[1]In this paper, for clarity I use the term *priming* in a theory-neutral way, to refer to the manipulation of presenting information to perceivers. Usage of this term in the literature is often confusing because it is used both in this concrete, operational sense and to indicate endorsement of a particular theoretical model of the manipulation's effects, that they arise from the "priming" of constructs or schemas in memory. I use the term *activation* (of declarative knowledge structures) to refer to a proposed theoretical mechanism.

Context Specificity

How similar are the contexts in which the priming and target information are encountered? A priming effect might be highly context-specific, occurring only when the prime and target are encountered in the same setting, with the perceiver in the same internal state, etc. Or it might be more general, so that a prime administered in a laboratory might influence someone's behavior later outside of the laboratory. Context specificity refers to the question: Does a prior experience in a particular situation and setting influence later judgment or behavior in a wide range of contexts, or is its influence restricted to the same or a closely similar context?

Time Course

How close together in time are the encounters with the prime and the target information? "Priming" effects with time scales from milliseconds to years have been demonstrated in the literature. Of course, this fourth dimension of specificity corresponds to the question: How long-lasting is the effect of the earlier experience?

Summary

Because different psychological mediators will show different patterns of specificity in their effects, specificity may be viewed as a methodological principle, allowing empirical tests of hypotheses regarding the mediation of the effects of past experiences. Effective application of this principle depends, of course, on the researcher's knowledge or assumptions about the patterns of specificity that would be expected due to theoretically plausible mediators. This means that the inferences drawn from observed patterns of specificity—as from any empirical investigation—are inevitably theory-dependent. I draw on Anderson's ACT* theory (1983, 1987; cf. Smith, 1984) as the general framework for interpretations in this chapter. Readers who prefer other frameworks, such as Wyer and Srull (1986) or Rumelhart and McClelland (1986), will find that both the list of potential theoretical mediators and the set of properties of each mediator will differ in some cases. The principle that specificity of effects can yield evidence as to mediation, however, will still be applicable.

Within ACT*, the two fundamental classes of cognitive mediators are *declarative* and *procedural* representations in memory. Declarative knowledge can be encoded as images, serial strings, or in other formats, but I will generally focus on propositional representations. In ACT*, propositions are represented in long-term memory by links among nodes encoding concepts, and activation spreads along links from currently active nodes. In the absence of external input, activation is short-lived, decaying in a few seconds. The level of activation determines the momentary accessibility of a memory representation, and short-term memory is assumed to contain the most highly activated materials in memory (see Anderson, 1983, ch. 2-3 for more detail). In ACT* there is no distinction between separate "semantic" and "episodic" memory systems (cf. Anderson & Ross, 1980; Tulving, 1983). Instead, general knowledge and knowledge about specific events are stored in the same way.

Procedural knowledge is represented as *productions*, if–then (or condition–action) pairs. Productions provide the active component of the cognitive system, matching and operating on the contents of declarative memory. When the pattern or condition of a production matches activated information in memory, the production becomes a candidate for execution, in competition with other productions that also match. The actions of the production that is chosen for execution are carried out. They may activate information in memory, deposit new representations into memory, or perform motor actions (see Anderson, 1983, ch. 4, 6; 1987). Productions change with use in several ways, as described on p. 28; the most important change is *strengthening*, which makes a procedure that has been used (practiced) execute more quickly on future occasions. The strength of a production decays very slowly over time.

To illustrate the methodological principle of specificity within this theoretical context, consider that any processing episode, considered as a prime, could have multiple effects. For instance, seeing John punch Bill and inferring that John is hostile may (a) temporarily activate declarative knowledge structures including those related to punching, hostility, John, and Bill (Higgins et al., 1977); (b) create a new memory trace encoding this specific incident; (c) use and therefore strengthen relatively specific productions involved in inferring hostility from punching; or perhaps (d) strengthen general productions that underlie inferences of traits from behaviors. Each of these effects of the priming episode could influence later information processing, but the pattern of specificity of the effects will give clues as to which mechanism is actually operative. Activation of general hostility-related knowledge structures like (a) should have short-lived but general effects, perhaps influencing the perceiver's later judgments of the hostility of other, unrelated target persons, or making the perceiver more likely to act in a hostile and aggressive way (Carver et al., 1983). Effects of a memory trace like (b) should be longer-lasting but more specific. For instance, such a memory trace may influence future judgments about John's hostility but should have little or no effect on judgments about other, unrelated target persons. Effects of strengthening a specific procedure like (c) will include facilitation of later inferences of hostility based on the behavior of punching, but not trait inferences based on other behaviors. The point is that the particular pattern of effects due to priming (their specificity as to process and content as well as their time course) can show what kind of cognitive representation mediates the effect.

CONTENT SPECIFICITY

Theorists and researchers in social cognition have elaborated the properties of abstract, general social knowledge structures and their role in explaining social judgment and behavior. Schemata and related notions (constructs, prototypes) have been central in theoretical explanations of category accessibility effects (Wyer & Srull, 1986; Higgins, Bargh, & Lombardi, 1985), stereotyping in person perception (Ashmore & Del Boca, 1981), attribution (Read, 1987b), attitudes (Fazio, 1986), and other areas. These knowledge structures have several significant characteristics. First, they are abstract and general. A schema is assumed to represent the typical characteristics of a class of objects or events, rather than the details of a specific experience (Alba & Hasher, 1983; Brewer & Nakamura, 1984; Rumelhart, 1984). For example, a stereotype might include information that members of a social category (such as fraternity members) typically possess particular attributes. These attributes or properties are themselves represented abstractly, at a semantic rather than a perceptual level of encoding (Alba & Hasher, 1983).

Because the information represented in schemata or other knowledge structures is abstracted from many experiences with objects in the relevant class, it will be slow to change. This property provides stability for social knowledge. In fact the resistance to change of some knowledge structures, notably social stereotypes, is notorious.

Finally, declarative knowledge structures can be accessed by diverse cognitive processes in diverse contexts (Anderson, 1983, ch. 3; 1987, pp. 201–202). Our general knowledge about the rules of basketball, for instance, can be used to answer questions, to referee a game, or to regulate our own behavior as a player. The knowledge that Ronald Reagan sold arms to Iran can be used to answer questions about Iran's sources of arms for its war with Iraq or about the correspondence between the Reagan Administration's words and its deeds, or to form an attitude toward Reagan. Processes that generate verbal reports are among those that can access these declarative knowledge structures. Thus, many studies of the content of people's schemata or stereotypes have used verbal reports (often attribute-listing tasks) to assess that content (e.g., Deaux & Lewis, 1984).

Schemata and other abstract knowledge structures have proven to be powerful theoretical constructs. Many of the theoretical explanations cited earlier have been well tested and empirically fruitful. Nevertheless, the focus on abstract knowledge and its properties may have obscured attention to the role of more specific cognitive mediators of social judgment and behavior. In this section I describe evidence concerning the role of memory for general, abstract information versus more specific, concrete records of particular experiences. If the effects of a prior experience are relatively specific to similar new experiences, rather than applying more globally, this content specificity points to specific declarative memories as mediators of the effect. For if an experience had effects only through its incorporation into some sort of averaged, abstracted representation, the effect would not be expected to be large or long-lasting. If we have seen 1000 red-haired people, encountering another one will not substantially change our memory representation of characteristics of the prototypical red-haired individual. *Thus, if a single experience has a notable effect on behavior or judgment on a future occasion, the effect must be mediated by a relatively specific memory of the prior episode.* This is the form in which the methodological principle of specificity is applied in many experiments described later.

The role of particular experiences in shaping a perceiver's reactions to new events should be distinguished from the strategic, planful use of analogies (cf. Anderson, 1983, pp. 226–230; Read, 1987a). My focus here is not on the conscious retrieval of a past experience or exemplar for use as an analogy, but on a more "nonanalytic" (Jacoby & Brooks, 1984), automatic process of memory retrieval and use. In particular, the retrieval and use of exemplars in many of the studies described in this section appears to occur without the perceiver's conscious awareness or control.

This section describes results related to the content specificity of effects of prior experiences in two domains: stereotyping, involving the social categorization of people in groups, and category accessibility effects, encompassing behavior-to-trait inferences.

Categorization of People into Social Groups

The categorization of people into social groups is a central issue in social psychology. Social categorization permits inferences about the target person's characteristics (via the application of stereotypes), and influences the perceiver's affect and possible behaviors toward the target (Fiske, Neuberg, Beattie, & Milberg, 1987; Zarate & Smith, in press). Social psychologists have studied how people categorize others by traits (Cantor & Michel, 1979), social stereotypes (Anderson & Klatzky, 1987), gender (Park & Rothbart, 1982), and other attributes. The importance of social categorization is also demonstrated by research under social identity theory (cf. Turner, 1987), which has shown that merely classifying a person as an outgroup member can influence judgment and evaluation even in the absence of objective group differences.

Most research has focused on the content of the knowledge associated with a social group; i.e., the affective, behavioral, or cognitive elements that are activated and made available when a target person is categorized (Fazio, 1986; Fiske et al., 1987). There has been much less attention to the categorization process itself. This lack presumably stems from the assumption that categorization is relatively unproblematic and straightforward. After all, it seems that many significant social categories (age, gender, ethnicity) are cued by visually salient, immediately perceptible attributes.

However, the implication that categorization processes are simple and straightforward cannot be accepted. First, many socially significant categories—concerning whose members people have definite attitudes and stereotypes—do not have immediately perceptible defining attributes. These include socio-economic level, marital status, occupation, sexual preference, and membership in political or social groups (such as the KKK or a fraternity). Second and even more important, every person can be multiply categorized (cf. Rothbart & John, 1985). A *Black person* is never just that, but is also young or old, male or female, a professor or a secretary, well or poorly dressed, tall or short, friendly or hostile, from the South or the North. Therefore the assumption that he or she can be easily categorized as Black begs the question: which category is used, when?

These considerations become even more compelling when we consider that stereotype researchers (e.g., Brewer, 1988; Weber & Crocker, 1983) have recently emphasized category subtypes, suggesting that most perceivers do not apply stereotypes at the level of broad social groups (like Blacks or females) but use more specific types, like militant Black, sexy woman, or grandmother (Brewer, Dull, & Lui, 1981). Obviously, the defining characteristics of subtypes will not be as easily perceptible as those of the broad categories.

In general, then, person categorization must depend on multiple attributes of the target, having differentially diagnostic and potentially conflicting cue relationships to several potentially applicable categories. The context of the interaction and the perceiver's goals and expectations may influence categorization in particular instances. Even the perceiver's own category membership may matter, for there is evidence that ingroup and outgroup members are categorized differently (Park & Rothbart, 1982; Zarate & Smith, in press).

Prevailing Theories.   The above arguments suggest that social psychologists, with notable exceptions like Rothbart and John (1985) and Lingle, Altom, and Medin (1984), have often simplified the issues involved in categorization. The general implicit assumptions seem to be as follows. (1) For many social categories (gender, race) there are defining—that is, necessary and sufficient—features that are easily perceptible and directly related to classification. Anyone possessing the defining feature(s) is considered to be a member of the category, corresponding to the "classical model" of Medin and Smith (1984). As noted before, this model is inadequate because it fails to deal with overlapping category memberships (e.g., race, gender, and age). (2) For other categories (including trait categories, subtypes, and social groups) a prototype model (Medin & Smith, 1984) is assumed. A representation of the average or typical category member, or (equivalently) information about the typical or expected ranges of attribute values for category members, is stored in memory. When a new instance is encountered, its attribute-by-attribute similarity to multiple category prototypes is assessed (weighed by the temporary or chronic accessibility of each one) and the instance is classified in the category to which it is most similar.

These assumptions of the prototype model carry several significant implications. (1) A single prototype is stored in memory for each category. This rules out the storage of several prototypes to represent the same concept as it is used in different contexts, for example. Therefore, categorization cannot be markedly context dependent. Prototypes (as abstract, general knowledge structures) should be accessible without regard to context. (2) Instance-to-prototype similarity is calculated by a weighted sum of similarities on the attributes, with the weights perhaps influenced by a stored indication of the category's variability on the attribute (Fried & Holyoak, 1984). This implies that correlated attributes play no special role. (3) The similarity of a new instance to a category prototype will govern categorization decisions; similarity to specific known instances of the category will have no effect if prototype similarity is controlled. (4) The prototype should change only slowly with exposure to new category instances, since it is presumed to have been either socially learned or abstracted from a large number of past experiences with category members. A single new instance from a category with which the perceiver has had considerable experience should make little or no difference. The following sections review research that examines the validity of these implications of the prototype assumptions concerning categorization, and the viability of an alternative model stressing the storage of specific exemplars and their use in categorizing similar new instances.

Nonsocial Categorization. Research examining these basic assumptions in the domain of social categorization is as yet uncommon, so I begin by reviewing research on nonsocial categories. Several researchers have presented subjects with stimuli exemplifying novel categories, and had subjects learn to classify them. Whittlesea (1987) used materials that were pronounceable pseudowords forming two categories centered on the prototypes NOBAL and FURIG. Subjects learned to categorize stimuli formed by changing one or two letters from the prototypes. Under study conditions that encouraged subjects to integrate the stimuli (e.g., pronounce them) rather than analyze them letter by letter, the results for both classification and perceptual fluency dependent variables suggested that performance was based on memory for the individual training stimuli rather than on the abstraction and use of the category prototypes. For example, both classification performance and the ability to identify a word presented in a brief flash were better for a new item that was similar to a specific old item (differing by only one letter) than for a new item that was more distant from old items but closer to the prototype. These categories appear to be represented in memory, then, as a set of learned instances rather than as an abstracted *typical* value. In contrast, other study conditions (e.g., having to copy individual prototypical letters from the stimulus instead of pronouncing each as a word) led to more reliance on prototypical values in categorization (cf. Jacoby & Brooks, 1984, pp. 23–24).

The Whittlesea studies deal with newly learned categories, where subjects carry no relevant knowledge into the experiment. Perhaps this constitutes an unfair test of prototype-abstraction versus instance-based classification theories, since people have little other than the newly learned instances on which to base judgments. However, other research has used familiar categories. Brooks and

Whittlesea (cited in Brooks, 1987) showed people a photograph of a cup—an instance of a highly familiar category. Later, photos of cups and other objects were displayed and response time (RT) to answer whether or not the photo showed a cup was recorded. The familiar prototypicality gradient was observed, with photos that pilot subjects had judged as more prototypical being classified faster than less prototypical cups. More important, both the old (previously seen) photo and other photos that were perceptually similar to it were classified very quickly—even faster than the most prototypical test photos. The facilitation of responses to the old photo and similar ones was maintained over 24 hr between training and test. Even for a well-learned category, then, specific recent experiences can have a notable effect on classification.

This last study has strong parallels with a study by Jacoby (1983), who showed that reading a word once increased subjects' ability to perceptually identify it in a brief flash 24 hr later. Obviously all Jacoby's subjects could read—just as all Brooks and Whittlesea's subjects could identify cups before they entered the experiment—but they still showed specific facilitation of later performance from reading the word on one occasion. Brooks (1987) refers to this phenomenon as the "rapid specialization of a well-practiced skill" (p. 147). The implication for categorization processes is that encountering and classifying a single category instance leaves a trace in memory that can facilitate later categorization of the same or similar instances. Our knowledge of a category and our ability to classify is (at least in part) *distributed* in memory across representations of a series of specific instances, rather than embodied in a single prototype representation.

Hintzman's (1984, 1986) simulations, in fact, have demonstrated that key findings concerning memory and categorization can be reproduced by a hypothetical representation using only exemplars, with no abstracted prototypes at all. However, it seems likely that both types of representation are psychologically real. On logical grounds, some have argued that a category-level (intensional) component as well as an exemplar-based (extensional) one is needed for category representations (Lakoff, 1987; Medin & Wattenmaker, 1987). The former is required to explain properties of conceptual combination (e.g., Osherson & Smith, 1981) as well as to set constraints on what makes sense as a category. Property inheritance too is probably best accounted for by the storage of category-level information. People can answer that birds have stomachs, information that is probably not stored with exemplars of the bird category but is deduced from general knowledge about animals. Finally, much learning about social and nonsocial categories takes place at the category level. We not only encounter particular police officers, but also are told or analytically infer that police officers have certain traits and properties. This information is presumably represented at the category level rather than stored with specific exemplars in memory.

Medin, Altom, and Murphy (1984) have tested a mixture model of categorization that assumes both types of representations are possible. In their category-learning experiment, people in different conditions were presented with both exemplars and category prototypes concurrently, exemplars only, or prototypes first and then exemplars. In the prototypes-first condition, the subjects learned the prototypes of the two groups before they started to categorize the stimuli. In contrast, in the exemplars-only condition, subjects learned group characteristics only through the presentation of group members. The authors predicted that these manipulations would influence subjects' relative reliance on exemplar and category-level information in categorization. The results supported the hypotheses. In classifying new instances, people who were given the prototypes before the exemplars relied more on the group prototypes than did those who saw only exemplars. In the latter condition, the subjects relied only on exemplars in classifying new instances, even though they could successfully abstract and report on group level information. In other words, they used exemplars exclusively for classifications unless they were specifically given the prototype.

Other research using nonsocial categories has raised additional problems for pure prototype models, involving such issues as the role of correlated attributes (Malt & Smith, 1984) and the effects of category structure on categorization performance (Medin & Schwanenfluegel, 1981; Wattenmaker, Dewey, Murphy, & Medin, 1986). Research on nonsocial categorization thus supports the generalization that specific category exemplars are stored and used in making category membership judgments. In some cases prototypes may also be stored in memory and used, but the evidence weighs against a prototype-only model of category representation. Without any reason to believe that social categories are unique in their representational format, we might expect that they too will often incorporate exemplars.

To illustrate the different representational possibilities, take police officer as an example of a social category. A category prototype might be represented propositionally (Anderson, 1983, ch. 3) as:

Police officers wear badges

Police officers stop speeders

Police officers carry guns

Knowledge about the category's typical characteristics is linked to the category name, constituting the prototype. Figure 1.1, panel *a* shows a schematic representation of this structure. An alternative exemplar-only representation could be written propositionally as follows:

John is a police officer   Mary is a police officer

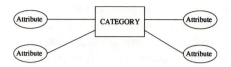

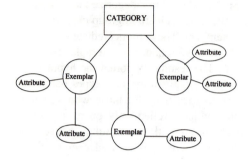

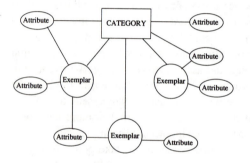

FIG. 1.1.   Three different memory structures representing a category. *a:* Category-level attributes only; *b:* Attributes represented with exemplars only; *c:* Mixed category-level and exemplar representation.

John wears a badge	Mary wears a badge
John hassles panhandlers	Mary stops speeders

Here, attributes are linked to each exemplar that they are known to characterize; parsimony or economy of storage is presumed not to be important (Fig. 1.1, panel *b*). No attributes are explicitly represented at the category level, though of course they could be inferred by reflecting on the attributes of the known exemplars. This type of representation could be formed in a so-called "memory-based" processing situation (Hastie & Park, 1986) in which the goal of making group-level generalizations is not given to the subject (or spontaneously adopted) when the exemplar information is learned.

Finally, a mixed representation (panel *c*) stores knowledge at both the category and the exemplar level.

John is a police officer	Mary is a police officer

Police officers wear badges   Mary stops speeders
John wears a badge

It is likely that (a) social learning and (b) the typicality or frequency of attributes across category members will influence what attributes are stored at the category level. Conversely, unusual or category-incongruent attributes may be particularly likely to be stored with exemplars (cf. Brewer, 1988). Representations like this could be formed on-line processing situations (Hastie & Park, 1986) in which the perceiver induces group-level generalizations as exemplar information is processed. As a corollary, note that either duplication or contradiction could exist between attributes represented at the category and exemplar levels. We would expect the two levels of representation to be somewhat independent (Judd & Park, 1988; Park & Hastie, 1987).

Considered this way, the assumptions of the mixed model appear consistent with the structures postulated by research on stereotyping and person memory over the past decade. But past research has focused almost exclusively on how group- and individual-level knowledge influence memory and judgments about a *particular* person, whereas my point is that the exemplars also function as *part of the category representation*. That is, as I argued with respect to Brewer's model (Smith, 1988b), stored exemplars may be used in categorizing new instances that are similar to them. Mary's characteristics as represented in memory may influence not only judgments about Mary but also categorization and other judgments concerning similar, newly encountered individuals.

Social Categorization.   To test the hypothesis that exemplars form part of the representation of social categories, we used an extension of the Medin et al. (1984) design in experiments with social stimuli (reported more fully in Smith & Zarate, in press). These experiments involved a category-learning phase in which perceivers learned about nine individuals described briefly in writing, five from group A and four from group B. After subjects could correctly classify those nine by their group membership, they were asked to categorize the same stimuli plus new ones, based on their just-learned knowledge. The learning and test items (Table 1.1) were designed in such a way that patterns of learning and categorization will differ depending on whether perceivers use an exemplar or a prototype approach. The stimuli also reflect realistic properties of social categories in that no single attribute is perfectly related to group membership; each group displays some variability on each dimension.

The design depends on the prediction that for pure prototype-based classification, test stimuli that are most similar to the group prototypes (i.e., those that have more of the typical attribute values for their group—1's for group A and O's for B) will be easiest to categorize. Similarity to specific group members will be irrelevant. On the other hand, for pure exemplar-based classification, test stimuli that are similar to specific known members of the group will be easiest to

TABLE 1.1
Stimuli and Category Membership (Smith & Zarate, in press)

| Exemplar | Dimension: | | | | Closest Neighbors |
	D1	D2	D3	D4	
A1	1	1	1	0	A2,B1,B2
A2	1	0	1	0	A1,A3
A3	1	0	1	1	A2
A4	1	1	0	1	B1
A5	0	1	1	1	B2
B1	1	1	0	0	A1,A4
B2	0	1	1	0	A1,A5
B3	0	0	0	1	B4
B4	0	0	0	0	B3
N1	1	0	0	1	A3,A4,B3
N2	1	0	0	0	A2,B1,B4
N3	1	1	1	1	A1,A3,A4
N4	0	0	1	0	A2,B2,B4
N5	0	1	0	1	A4,A5,B3
N6	0	0	1	1	A3,A5,B3
N7	0	1	0	0	B1,B2,B4

Note. Drawn from Medin et al. (1984). Dimensions D1-D4 refer to attributes of the stimuli, and values 0 and 1 refer to different values of the attributes (for example, a clumsy versus skillful person). "Closest neighbors" are A and B stimuli that differ from the given stimulus on only a single dimension.

classify, while similarity to the prototype will be irrelevant. For example, stimuli A4 and A5 should be relatively easy to classify as A's under a prototype model, since they each have three (out of four) dimension values that are typical for group A. On the other hand, if exemplars alone are used in categorization, these two stimuli should be relatively difficult to categorize, because each differs by only one feature from a category B member and is not that similar to any A. In other words, even though an instance may be closer to the A prototype, it could be classified as a B due to its greater similarity to individual category B members (cf. Sherman & Corty, 1984, pp. 237–245). Comparisons like this invoke the methodological principle of specificity. The predicted patterns of errors in learning as well as categorization of new test stimuli differ between exemplar-based and prototype-based processes, allowing an empirical determination of the process that people rely on.

In one experiment, as in Medin et al. (1984) we had some subjects learn the prototypical attribute values of the two social groups before encountering the training exemplars, while others were not given this information. We predicted that perceivers who learned the prototypes first would be more likely to categorize new instances based on the learned prototypes, while the other perceivers would be more likely to rely on exemplars. This is a meaningful manipulation in terms of social interaction. Since stereotypes are socially communicated, people often enter social interactions with prior expectations or stereotypes while at other times they learn groups' typical characteristics only through exposure to exemplars. Our hypothesis was supported, with the proportion reliance on exemplars estimated at .41 in the prototype-first condition and .74 in the exemplars-only condition.

Perceivers' strategies and processing goals could also favor the formation of prototype versus exemplar-based memory representation, leading to corresponding differences in categorization processes. For example, attempting to form impressions of individual group members should increase the probability that the perceivers would follow exemplar model predictions. Impression instructions should induce perceivers to organize the information by individuals, forming integrative links among the attributes of each stimulus person (Hamilton, Katz, & Leirer, 1980; Ostrom, Pryor, & Simpson, 1981). Whittlesea (1987) and Jacoby and Brooks (1984, pp. 23–24) have found that integrative processing of stimuli favors exemplar storage and use. Therefore, these exemplars should be used as reference points in the classification of new stimulus persons.

On the other hand, memory instructions should induce perceivers to form summary representations of the two groups; the fact that members of each group tend to share attribute values that are typical of the group will be more salient. In this condition, perceivers should be more likely to store and use prototypes rather than exemplars, summing up attributes rather than thinking about particular individuals. Though there were unanticipated interactions with the specific attributes used in the experimental materials, results of one study (Smith & Zarate, in press) generally supported this hypothesis, with the estimated proportion reliance on exemplars being 1.00 under impression instructions and 0.80 under memory instructions.

As I implied in the foregoing discussion, manipulations that produce on-line versus memory-based processing (Hastie & Park, 1986) should also influence the type of representation stored in memory and hence perceivers' categorization strategy. If subjects encounter exemplars without the goal (explicitly given or spontaneously adopted) of making category-level judgments, they should be left with only exemplars in memory (cg. Fig. 1.1b) on which to rely for categorization. Processing exemplars when category membership is salient and subjects expect to make judgments about the category, however, should result in more attributes being stored at the category level (Fig. 1.1c), as Park and Hastie's (1987) results suggest. A mixed or even a pure-prototype categorization strategy could then be used.

Finally, an intrinsically social determinant of exemplar-based versus prototype-based processing may be the perceiver's own group membership, for it has been proposed that in-groups are more likely to be represented as exemplars and out-groups in terms of prototypes (Judd & Park, 1988; Park & Rothbart,

1982). This hypothesis has the attractive property that it could account for the known tendency to view in-groups as more variable than out-groups (Park & Rothbart, 1982; Wilder, 1984). The single prototype representation of the out-group would serve as an anchor for judgments, reducing perceptions of variability.

These results and hypotheses suggest that exemplar-based social categorization can occur, to an extent that is influenced by socially relevant manipulations. Trying to form impressions of individuals, encountering group members without a prior stereotype of the group, as well as encountering in-group members, should lead to relatively exemplar-based memory and categorization processes. On the other hand, conditions like trying to remember individual's attributes, learning a group prototype or stereotype before encountering individuals, and dealing with out-group members, may lead to more reliance on prototypes in categorization. It is interesting to note that in three of the four conditions in Smith and Zarate's (in press) two experiments the use of exemplars greatly predominated. Even when prototypes were learned first there was some use of exemplars (41%), suggesting that in social cognition, memory storage and use of group-level information may almost always be supplemented by individual-level information.

The hypothesis that both exemplar and prototype information can be used under appropriate circumstances is also supported by other research using different dependent variables. Judd and Park (1988) and Park and Hastie (1987) both present evidence of the relative independence of judgments of various attributes (e.g., variability) at the level of groups and of individuals. The implication is that the group-level information is abstracted on-line and that information at these two levels is stored independently in memory (cf. Hastie & Park, 1986) as in Fig. 1.1c. If a single representation was used, either a prototype supplemented with variability information (Fried & Holyoak, 1984), or a set of exemplars, then one would expect substantial dependence between answers to questions about the group and about individuals because those answers would rely on the same representation.

The bulk of the evidence from both the nonsocial and social domains points to the conclusion that information about previously encountered exemplars is stored in memory and used in new categorization judgments, alongside (or even in place of) abstract representations of category prototypes. Our knowledge of categories is distributed across multiple exemplars rather than being completely captured in abstract, general context-free prototypes or rules (Brooks, 1987, p. 165). The methodological principle of specificity implies that stored information about specific exemplars is responsible for the observed rapid and accurate classification of new stimuli that are similar to familiar category members, even if they are not particularly close to the prototype (e.g., Whittlesea, 1987). The evidence also suggests that the conditions under which information about category members is acquired influences how it is stored and used. For example, individuating the category members can be encouraged by the perceiver's own membership in the category, by small members of stimuli to be learned, by impression-formation instructions, or by encountering the stimulus persons without prior stereotypic expectations. Individuation leads to greater use of exemplar-based strategies in classification (Jacoby & Brooks, 1984; Smith & Zarate, in press), compared to alternative conditions.

Effects of Exposure to Single Instances.   It seems, therefore, that a single experience with a member of a particular category can influence categorization of other individuals in the future. Such experiences can affect other types of judgment and behavior as well. Lewicki (1986) has performed a number of intriguing studies of the effects of social experiences on people's later behavior. In his paradigm, an encounter with a stimulus person is staged or manipulated through photographs. Then the perceiver's reactions to a target person who shares attributes with the previously encountered stimulus are assessed. In one study (Lewicki, 1986, p. 200), people encountered an experimenter who insulted them as they were filling out a questionnaire. Later the subjects were instructed to take their completed experimental materials to whichever assistant was not busy when they entered the room. When the subjects got there, both assistants were free, requiring an arbitrary choice. Subjects who had been insulted by the experimenter tended to avoid one assistant whose hair style resembled that of the experimenter. Control subjects who were not insulted by the experimenter showed no tendency to avoid the person with the similar attribute.

In another study, Lewicki (1986, p. 187) showed people three photographs of females paired with verbal descriptions which emphasized a specific ability (e.g., math, languages) in each case. The person described as high in math ability had a different type of hair style from the other pictured women. This was presented as preliminary "psychological training," used to relax the subjects for the main study. An unrelated questionnaire (described as the "main part of the study") followed. Subjects were finally asked in an ostensibly separate experiment to rate six new photos on a number of dimensions including math ability. General facial similarity and other characteristics that might be sterotypically associated with math ability were counterbalanced. In these conditions, the pictured woman with a hair style similar to the high-math-ability person was also rated significantly higher in math ability.

The effects identified by Lewicki are not dependent on the subject's drawing of a conscious analogy between the target person and the earlier experience, for the subjects generally denied that the earlier encounter had any effect on their later behavior. The effects appear to be content specific, limited to stimulus persons similar to the previously encountered person. If they were solely due to the activation of a general construct (such as unfriendliness or math ability), they would equally affect reactions to all the target persons at the choice point. The time duration of these effects is unclear, though at least a few minutes must have passed between priming and the dependent measure of both studies. This pattern of specificity points to mediation by specific episodic memories.

Looked at in another way, in these studies it is implausible to argue that the perceiver's prototypic representation of a unfriendly person or of a person with strong math abilities is changed in a lasting manner by a single experience. Instead, the results seem to call for the assumption that information about the specific experience—the encounter with the single individual—is stored and can influence judgment and inferences in the future (cf. White & Shapiro, 1987). Kahneman and Miller's (1986) norm theory gives one theoretical account of these effects, by postulating that an encounter with the person about whom a judgment is required triggers the automatic retrieval of similar exemplars. For instance, in the first study mentioned above, the subject has no strong basis for choice between the two assistants. Yet the one who has a feature similar to the unfriendly experimenter will call the experimenter to mind, eliciting a prediction or expectation that this person too might be unfriendly.

Theoretical Implications.   The evidence reviewed here implies that specific instances or exemplars may be included in the memory representation of some social categories, in addition to or even in place of more abstract category-level information. The mediating role of exemplars can be demonstrated by using the methodological principle of specificity: effects of a particular experience are most evident on similar targets, rather than extending to all category members. The relative balance of exemplar and prototype information may be influenced by social factors such as the perceiver's goals (e.g., impression formation versus memory), prior knowledge of a stereotype, or group membership.

The prevalence of exemplar-based social categorization means that specific experiences or knowledge about particular individuals may have major implications for future social judgment or behavior. Consider my friend Joe, who is quite different from the prototype of a chemistry professor—perhaps Joe is more like the prototype of a history professor—but is similar to Sam, a known chemistry professor. Reliance on prototypes versus exemplars would lead perceivers to categorize Joe differently. Since categorization mediates perceivers' assignment of stereotype traits to the target as well as their affective and behavioral responses (e.g., Fiske & Pavelchak, 1986; Zarate & Smith, in press), this difference could alter fundamentally the nature of the interaction.

It is also likely that under an exemplar model, specific similar exemplars rather than categories will be important bases for trait inferences and affective reactions. That is, if Joe is similar to Sam, a perceiver might attribute some of Sam's traits to Joe and react affectively to Joe in the same way as to Sam—rather than assuming that the (possibly somewhat different) typical properties of chemistry professors will characterize Joe (cf. Lewicki, 1986; White & Shapiro, 1987). Kahneman and Miller (1986) discuss the impact of similar exemplars retrieved from memory on trait, affective, attributional, and other social judgments concerning a target person or event.

Exemplar versus prototype models also have significantly different implications for the flexibility and changeability of stereotypes (including the formation of *subtypes*). An experience with a single group member will alter a perceiver's prototype very little if the prototype is based on encounters with hundreds or thousands of exemplars. Therefore, prototype models have problems accounting for long-lasting effects of single experiences with category members. Exemplar models, on the contrary, predict that the treatment of a new exemplar that is identical or similar to one previously encountered may be influenced by the properties of the old one, so that single experiences could have enduring effects (cf. Brooks, 1987; Lewicki, 1986; Logan, 1988).

Exemplar models predict that categories could also be flexible in a different way: sensitive to particular social contexts or to currently activated goals. Roth and Shoben (1983) have shown that the relative fit of different exemplars to nonsocial categories (such as bird) may change depending on contexts; for example, in "the bird walked across the barnyard," "chicken" is rated a better example of a bird than is "robin," though in most contexts (and when context is unspecified) the reverse is true. Barsalou (1987) has extended this demonstration by showing that people have systematic representations of concepts from different (social) *points of view;* e.g., a bird from the viewpoint of a Southerner, a Frenchman, a housewife. Social categories may show similar sensitivity to context and viewpoint. For example, the category of "good performer" in a school or organization might have different attributes in the context of evaluating minority and majority group members. And some research shows that the perceiver's own group membership, one sort of point of view, can influence social categorization: ingroup and outgroup members are often represented differently (Park & Rothbart, 1982; Zarate & Smith, in press). Exemplar-based social categories can show this kind of flexibility, because the set of exemplars that is retrieved and used to represent the category can be influenced by the perceiver's goals or the current context (perhaps through a spreading-activation mechanism; Kahneman & Miller, 1986).

It is important to note that exemplars that influence categorization need *not* be consciously accessible or reportable by the perceiver. Perceivers would not necessarily be expected to report "I thought Jim might be a Republican because he's short and bald like my Uncle Harry, who is a strong Republican." That is, dissociations between the effects of a past experience or instance on memory measures and on categorization and other judgments have often been demonstrated (Brooks, 1987; Jacoby, 1983; Jacoby & Witherspoon, 1982; Lewicki, 1986, Metcalfe & Fisher, 1986). Thus, judgments and behavior can be influenced by specific past experiences in ways that the perceivers are unaware of. A convincing theoretical explanation of such dissociations has been proposed and is discussed later after some related findings have been presented.

Categorization of Behaviors using Trait Constructs

We often learn about other people's "deeper" characteristics, such as their enduring character traits, by making inferences from their observable behaviors. For this reason, behavior-to-trait inferences are central to processes of impression formation and person perception, and they have been intensively studied within social cognition.

Prevailing Theories. An intriguing class of "category accessibility" effects that can alter behavior-trait inferences has been demonstrated by research in two paradigms. Srull and Wyer (1979) use "scrambled sentences" describing behaviors to prime a construct such as hostility. Under a cover story concerning "the way people perceive word relationships," people read sets of words like *leg break arm his* and underline three words that make a complete sentence. In the relevant experimental conditions, a large proportion of the sentences that can be created have content related to hostility, like the example. Next, believing that they are participating in an unrelated experiment, subjects read a paragraph describing a fictitious character's behaviors, which are ambiguously hostile. They rate "Donald" on several scales related to hostility, which constitute the dependent measure. The essential finding from these studies is that priming with hostility-related materials increases subjects' ratings of the target character's hostility, as much as 24 hr after the priming manipulation (Srull & Wyer, 1979).

One theoretical explanation is that priming increases the accessibility of the general concept of hostility in memory, putting the construct of hostility at or near the top of its "Storage Bin" in memory (Wyer & Srull, 1986). When the subjects read about Donald's ambiguous behaviors, the hostile construct is therefore more accessible and more likely to be used in interpreting them, because Storage Bins are searched from the top down until an applicable construct is located.

Higgins and his associates have used a related paradigm (e.g., Higgins et al., 1977; Higgins et al., 1985). Under a cover story these researchers expose subjects to trait words related to the target construct (e.g., reckless or adventurous). The subjects then read descriptions of a target character's behavior that are ambiguously related to the primed constructs and rate the target character. Category accessibility is influenced by priming in this paradigm also, though the effect has only been shown to last a matter of minutes, not 24 hr. Higgins et al. (1985) have developed a theoretical model in which constructs in memory are associated with an energy cell, whose charge increases with priming but decreases with the passage of time. The applicable construct associated with the highest charge is selected for use in interpreting behaviors.

Though the Wyer/Srull and Higgins models differ in many respects, their similarities are more significant for the purposes of this chapter. The models agree that (a) abstract representations of constructs are stored in memory (in the form of schemata or prototypes), and (b) priming influences some property of those representations (position in a Storage Bin, or charge of an energy cell). The effect of priming under these models is (c) automatic, not depending on the perceiver's processing the priming materials with some particular goal, (d) not content or context specific, and (e) not process specific. The reason is that the general concept of hostility (for example) that subjects use in the lab is presumably the same concept of hostility they use in other contexts. In addition, accessibility effects cannot depend on the identity of the specific trait-related words that were encountered and activated the trait construct. Because the construct represents a general semantic structure, any words with related meanings will activate it with similar effects. Finally, any task that activates the item's abstract representation in memory should produce similar priming effects. Wyer and Srull (1986) are explicit about this, postulating that constructs used *in any way* in processing are moved to the top of their Storage Bin. Effects of this increased accessibility cannot be process-specific: that is, they cannot depend on the similarity of processes used in the later tasks to those involved in the initial (priming) task.

Exemplar-based Memory and Category Accessibility. I have applied a computer simulation method to evaluate the plausibility of a theoretical alternative to these assumptions (Smith, 1988a). The goal was to investigate whether known properties of category accessibility effects can be reproduced using a simple model in which (a) no constructs or other abstract representations—only records of specific episodes—are stored in memory, and (b) the effect of priming is only to add new episodic records to memory, rather than to change the accessibility or other properties of existing constructs. The model is Hintzman's MINERVA (1984, 1986).

In Hintzman's model, each episode or experience is encoded and represented in memory by a number of features. A record of every experience is stored in memory, even if it is highly similar to previous experiences. Each memory trace therefore records a single episode. Forgetting under the model is a process in which randomly chosen features in LTM are changed to zero. Retrieval is a process in which a response is elicited from memory by a probe, which can be either a complete array of features or an array with a subset of features set to zero (indicating unknown). The former case describes recognition memory; the memory response can be used to judge whether or not an experience similar to the probe has already been stored. The latter case describes associative learning, for the information retrieved from memory may include values of the features that were unspecified in the probe. I used this aspect of the model to simulate learning and retrieval of behavior-trait relationships.

The model's generation of a response to a probe is described by a few equations (see Smith, 1988a). In effect, all stored traces are activated by a probe, to an extent depending on each trace's similarity to the probe (a function of the proportion of feature values that the trace shares with the probe). Each trace in

LTM contributes to the overall memory response, in proportion to the trace's activation level. Thus, traces that are similar to the probe will be more highly activated and will contribute more heavily to the memory response. If those traces include nonzero values for features where the probe had zeros, the memory response will include that information.

The Hintzman memory model as applied to the priming paradigm assumes that the effect of priming is simply to add episodic traces to memory, rather than to activate a preexisting abstract construct or schema. In fact, the model does not incorporate abstractions at all. Yet it is able to reproduce the major features of social priming or category accessibility effects. In the simulation there is an overall priming effect (one or more primes increase the use of the primed category compared to no primes) that is greater as more primes are used. This replicates Srull and Wyer (1979). Priming with behavior-trait pairs is more effective, and more resistant to forgetting, than priming with trait labels alone. This replicates Smith and Branscombe (1987). Finally, in the model the decrease in priming effectiveness due to forgetting is slower with a greater number of primes. This pattern was obtained with human subjects by Higgins et al. (1985). Thus, the exemplar-based model of priming can reproduce some of the major features of human performance in the category accessibility paradigm.

Content Specificity of Priming Effects.   The episode-only model of category accessibility effects not only matches several findings in the literature but also generates new predictions that differ from those of a schematic model. In the Smith (1988a) simulation, the similarity of a new instance (the ambiguous test stimulus) to old, stored instances (the primes) is crucial in determining its categorization. Priming should have the greatest influence on the categorization of test stimuli that are highly similar to the *primes*—independent of their similarity to the category prototype. Under alternative theoretical viewpoints, only the similarity of the test stimulus to the prototype should determine the magnitude of priming effects, since priming is said to operate by activating a representation of the category as a whole, not by storing specific representations of the priming stimuli. Put another way, the issue is whether the effect of a prime is content specific: Is it limited to stimuli that resemble the prime, or is it more general, increasing the accessibility of the primed category with respect to a wide range of test stimuli?

Whittlesea (1987) tested hypotheses like these using the categorization of letter strings as the dependent variable. Prior exposure to stimuli drawn from particular categories increased his subjects' ability to categorize similar stimuli. Whittlesea found that similarity of the test stimuli to previously encountered instances, rather than their similarity to the category prototype, determined the subjects' performance.

This hypothesis has not previously been tested for the trait category accessibility dependent variable. For an initial investigation I used pilot subjects' ratings to select, for each of 25 traits, three behaviors that exemplify the trait. An example behavior for the trait *careless* is "left his friend's camera out in the rain." For the study or priming manipulation, each subject saw five traits with behavior 1, five with behavior 2, five with 3, five with the trait word alone, and five were not studied. (Of course, the individual traits were counterbalanced so that each occurred in each study condition across subjects.) The study list was presented as an investigation of how people complete words given different kinds of hints. Subjects wrote the trait word after reading the related behavior plus the trait word's first few letters, or the initial letters alone. After a 2-min delay filled with an irrelevant verbal task, subjects were given a list of 25 behaviors (behavior number 1, 2, or 3 for all the traits) and told to write a trait that was suggested to them by each behavior. This questionnaire was presented as a pilot, to prepare materials for a future, related study. Thus, the design is 5 (study format, within subject) by 3 (test format, between subject). The dependent measure is the probability of given the target trait as an inference for each test behavior.

The exemplar model predicts an interaction: The largest priming effect should be seen when prime and target behaviors are identical, next largest when they are different, and the smallest when the trait word (rather than a behavior) was the priming stimulus (as in Smith & Branscombe, 1988). In contrast, the prototype or construct activation model could accommodate main effects for the prime and target behavior factors (because the three behaviors might differ in their priming effectiveness or their sensitivity to the activated construct) but could not predict an interaction. This is because the fact that the general trait construct is activated carries no information about what activated it, so the effect of its activation could not be larger for identical than for different prime-target pairs.

The results (N = 33 subjects) showed a highly significant priming by test condition interaction. Summarizing the means (Table 1.2), for a given behavior on the category accessibility test subjects produced the target trait 72% of the time when the same behavior had been studied, compared to 56% when a different behavior had been studied, 50% when the trait word alone was studied, and 40% when the trait had not been studied. The effect is highly specific, in that the appearance of the identical behavior on the study and test lists leads to a much

TABLE 1.2
Percentage of Target Traits Given on Category Accessibility Test
with Different Study and Test Behaviors

| Test | Study Condition | | | | |
	Behavior 1	Behavior 2	Behavior 3	Trait Alone	Not Studied
Behavior 1	73	62	60	44	42
Behavior 2	42	64	51	47	38
Behavior 3	56	65	78	60	40
Mean	57	64	63	50	40

Note. Column main effect has MANOVA $F(4,27) = 5.66$, $p = .002$. Row main effect has $F(2,30) = 2.53$, $p > .05$. Interaction effect has MANOVA $F(8,54) = 2.83$, $p = .01$.

higher likelihood of the primed trait being produced, compared to the different-behavior condition. The word-alone priming may have its effect through the activation of a general trait construct. However, construct activation cannot explain the content specificity of the effect: its greater magnitude when identical (versus different) behaviors are used at study and test. Thus, this study supports the prediction generated by the exemplar-based model of category accessibility (Smith, 1988a).

Theoretical Implications. It seems clear that the accessibility of memory representations can be increased for a short time in an automatic way by activating the representations (e.g., Anderson, 1983, p. 104; Neely, 1977). A related automatic activation process probably underlies the priming effects on category accessibility demonstrated by Higgins (e.g., Higgins et al., 1985). Evidence for this interpretation is the fact that priming is effective under conditions where elaborative processing should be minimal (e.g., when the primes are presented as distractors whose meaning is irrelevant), the broad range of dependent variables that are affected by this type of activation, and the relatively short time over which these effects last (seconds rather than hours or days).

However, the evidence just outlined suggests that in some cases the storage of specific experiences in memory, and their retrieval by related cues encountered later, may also influence category accessibility. The presence of a memory trace consisting of a particular behavioral exemplar, together with its category (trait) label, may suffice to influence the categorization of the same or a similar behavior later. This is by definition a type of "implicit memory" (Schacter, 1987): an influence of past experience on a present performance that occurs without explicit instructions to remember the past experience. As with many other types of implicit memory reviewed by Schacter, category accessibility effects can be dissociated from explicit measures of memory (e.g., recognition) for the priming material (Higgins et al., 1985; Smith & Branscombe, 1988). Thus our past experiences can effect us in ways of which we are not consciously aware (cf. Lewicki, 1986). Theoretical explanations for dissociations of this type generally invoke *process* specificity (e.g., Roediger & Blaxton, 1987), to which I turn shortly. In essence, the argument is that the type of processing that was performed on the exemplar when it was initially encountered will control its relative influence on different processes (categorization, recognition memory, etc.) later.

It is interesting to speculate on another form of specificity with respect to category accessibility effects: context specificity. The accessibility increase due to activating a general construct or schema, though short-lived, should be general across contexts because of the nature of general knowledge structures. People use the same general concept of hostility, for instance, in the lab as they do in nonlaboratory environments, so if that concept is made more accessible its effects should be similar regardless of context. On the other hand, the retrievability of episodic memories of specific past experiences is markedly context-dependent. Therefore category accessibility effects mediated by such traces should display slower decay but also greater context sensitivity than those mediated by schema activation. No research has as yet tested context sensitivity of such effects, and such tests may be difficult to frame in practical terms.

Content Specificity: Overall Conclusions

It is often said that the information-processing perspective in psychology, among whose great early landmarks are Miller (1956), Miller, Galanter, and Pribram (1960), and Newell and Simon (1972), is based on a computer metaphor. Indeed, the development of digital computers gave scientists ways to think abstractly about the representation and transformation of information—concepts that are at the core of modern cognitively oriented psychology. Yet the computer metaphor may be misleading, *not* because it ignores affect and other human qualities in favor of cold, logical cognition (see Isen & Hastorf, 1982 and Clark & Fiske, 1982 for arguments against this position), but in another way. Current computers are memory-limited: easily accessible memory is always insufficient to store all relevant information. As a result, economizing on memory storage is an intrinsic part of programming methodologies and of our thinking about information processing. This implies the use of abstraction. If we see a hundred dogs and each has four legs it just seems like common sense to "store that information only once," i.e., induce a dog *schema* and store only the individuating characteristics of dogs we have known, together with a pointer to the schema containing generic information. To change our thinking and consider memory storage as virtually unlimited is not easy, and it is this type of change that is called for by exemplar models of categorization. Significantly, such a change in perspective is also advocated by Rumelhart and McClelland (1986) and other researchers who work with distributed memory models inspired by the properties of the nervous system.

The storage and retrieval of information about specific experiences can influence categorization and other judgments in ways that are quite different from the effects of general schemata or other abstract representations. The influences will be *flexible, changeable,* and *responsive to particular recent experiences*, because recent experiences will tend to be more accessible than comparable older ones. These properties contrast with those of schemata, which should be slow to change in response to a few experiences. The effects of specific experiences on judgment and behavior will often be *outside of the perceiver's awareness*, in contrast to abstract, generic knowledge, which is usually consciously accessible and verbally reportable. The mediation of any particular effect of past experience on present performance can be investigated by looking at its pattern of specificity, and influences of specific exemplar storage and use will generally be content and context specific.

The research reviewed earlier suggests that specific exemplars can constitute part of the representation of social categories, with the result that categorization, judgments, and affective reactions to a target person may depend on the observer's specific experiences with another individual who is similar to the target in some way (e.g., Lewicki, 1986). Person categorization and stereotyping may depend on similarity to specific individuals rather than membership in abstract categories. Trait inferences from behaviors may also be influenced by specific experiences, memory traces of behaviors that are similar to the target. Thus, an observer's impression of someone who performs a particular behavior may depend on what behaviors the observer has witnessed in the past, not just on the accessibility or activation of general trait categories in the observer's memory.

Pure exemplar models for the representation of social categories probably will not, however, prove adequate. First, as Medin and Wattenmaker (1987) note, representation of the intension (semantic meaning; criteria for inclusion) as well as the extension (set of exemplars) of a concept is probably required in most cases. Medin and Wattenmaker discuss this in terms of the perceiver's *theory* that links together and makes sense out of a set of exemplars. Without a theory, a set of instances (e.g., a golden retriever, the number 39, and the graphics board in my computer) does not hang together and form a coherent concept or category. Further research and conceptual development are required to apply this insight to social categories. Perhaps a theory that links the content of a stereotype (the particular traits involved) to a social group is necessary before perceivers will apply the stereotype to the group; mere encounters with several group members who share the stereotype traits may not suffice in the absence of such a theory.

Second, much of what we know about key social categories is learned at the category level: we may be told that "Hoosiers like basketball" rather than having to induce that category-level regularity by reflecting on our experience with individual category members. In fact, interesting discrepancies could exist between exemplar-level and category-level knowledge, because of their potentially different bases in concrete personal experience versus social learning (cf. Judd & Park, 1988). Theories of social categorization will have to be powerful and flexible indeed to account for the diverse and potentially contradictory effects of specific exemplars and abstractly represented category-level knowledge on classification and judgments concerning new exemplars. The Medin and Schaffer (1978) model and its generalization by Nosofsky (1987), based on their success in experiments on nonsocial categorization, appear to be adequately powerful. Some hint of the necessary complexity comes from the research and theories outlined above, which suggest that the balance between exemplar and prototype influences depends on (among other things) the way the perceiver processed the original exemplars, the order in which exemplar and prototype information is learned, and even the perceiver's own group membership and the resulting ingroup/outgroup dynamics.

PROCESS SPECIFICITY

It sometimes seems that the content of information to which the perceiver is exposed is the most crucial determinant of later performances. For example, someone may read a list of words and later attempt to recall them; knowing what particular words were present on the list naturally appears to be the key to analyzing the recall performance. But this is an oversimplification, for it ignores issues of *process*. Not only what information the perceiver confronts, but how he or she deals with it, can shape later performances. There are several powerful demonstrations of this fact (Jacoby, 1983; Kolers & Roediger, 1984), but it has not yet been fully appreciated by researchers or theorists within social cognition. In our field, efforts are often made to identify the content of people's knowledge structures in order to explain their performances. However, without explicit assumptions about the processes that access and apply the knowledge, predictions are bound to be loose and informal at best (Anderson, 1976, pp. 10–13; Locksley, Stangor, Hepburn, Grosovsky, & Hochstrasser, 1984). This section discusses some effects of prior experiences on performance that depend on the nature of the process that was applied in the prior (study) context, not just on the content of what was studied or learned.

Practice Effects on Social Judgments

Prevailing Theory. The fact that practice improves performance is one of the most widely known principles of psychology. Surprisingly, the social cognition literature reveals little attention to the effects of practice, probably because of the general focus on the content of knowledge representations rather than the processes involved in their use. Even in studies of expertise, the emphasis has been on explaining expert-novice differences with reference to differences in the amount or organization of their static knowledge (Fiske, Kinder, & Larter, 1983; Fong & Markus, 1982). One exception to the general neglect of processing variables is Pryor and Merluzzi (1985), which showed that despite generally equivalent knowledge content, experts and novices differed in the speed with which they could access and use their knowledge in a domain.

One theoretical construct within social cognition that could be applied to explaining practice effects is cognitive accessibility (e.g., Higgins & King, 1981). Fazio's work on attitude accessibility provides an example: Repeatedly accessing one's attitude toward a particular object increases the efficiency (speed) of access and can even lead to automaticity of access, in that the attitude may be accessed upon encountering the object even without any explicit demand for an attitude report (see Fazio, 1986, for a review). Higgins and King (1981) and Wyer and Srull (1986) have made increased accessibility of recently or frequently used information the cornerstone of their theoretical structures, and (at least in the case of Higgins' model) RT dependent measures have been used to test predictions (e.g., Bargh & Tota, 1988).

The accessibility of declarative knowledge inevitably produces *content-specific* changes in efficiency. That is, the accessibility of a stored representation will influence the speed and likelihood of its future use, but is irrelevant for processing that does not use that representation. Furthermore, the predicted increases in efficiency will not be process specific. The accessibility of the information will increase for any process that uses it, not just for the particular process that was practiced. The studies to be described here set out to test these predictions against the alternative that practice effects are process specific but not content specific.

Effects on Efficiency of Judgment Processes.   My theoretical viewpoint is that cognitive processes may usefully be represented as productions (Anderson, 1983, ch. 4). A production is a condition-action or if–then pair, which triggers particular actions when certain conditions are met. Productions are widely used to represent process components in theories of nonsocial cognition (e.g., Hunt & Lansman, 1986; Thibadeau, Just & Carpenter, 1982) but have been little used in social cognition. Wyer and Srull (1986, p. 354) mention the possibility that a production-based procedural component could be added to their model of social cognition, but do not detail specifically how this could be done and do not present any examples of predictions from their model that depend on the procedural component.

Productions are assumed to follow certain postulates, including an increase in strength with practice (Anderson, 1983, ch. 6; Pirolli & Anderson, 1985). Increased strength increases the speed with which the production will apply on a future occasion when its pattern matches information in memory, as well as the probability that the strengthened production will actually be selected for execution in competition with other productions that also match. Production strength is a long-lasting property, decreasing only very slowly as a power function of time. Increases in procedural strength and efficiency will be distinguishable from increases in accessibility of declarative knowledge by the methodological principle of specificity. Content specificity will not be observed, because a strengthened production is able to operate faster on any data, not just the data with which it was practiced.[2] The effect will, however, be process specific because only tasks that involve the strengthened production will show speedups from practice. Even other processes that access the same declarative knowledge will not benefit from procedural strengthening.

The effects of practice on the efficiency of cognitive processes are obvious in everyday life and easily reproducible in the laboratory (Anderson, 1987; Newell & Rosenbloom, 1981). For example, in one study of a high-level, complex skill (problem-solving in computer programming), McKendree and Anderson (cited in Anderson, 1987) found that subjects increased their accuracy from 58% to 85% over 4 days of practice, while decreasing their average time from over 18 sec per problem to 10 sec. Such powerful effects of practice, and the related issues of differences between experts and novices in various domains,

---

[2]Processes that create specialized productions that are specific to the data they operate on necessitate some qualification of this statement; the issues are discussed below.

have attracted a good deal of research attention within nonsocial cognitive psychology.

To test the prediction of process specificity, McKendree and Anderson used conditions in which subjects practiced tasks that used the same knowledge in different ways: *evaluating* the result of a particular combination of LISP functions, or *coding* combinations of LISP functions that would achieve a desired result. The relevant declarative knowledge in both cases is knowledge of the result computed by each primitive function and of how functions may be combined in LISP. Subjects who practiced evaluation for 4 days increased greatly in their speed and accuracy at the evaluation task—but did not improve at all in the coding test even though it involves the same knowledge. The *process of using knowledge* in a particular way is what becomes more efficient with practice, as opposed to the accessibility of that knowledge in general.

In several studies (Smith, in press; Smith, Branscombe, & Bormann, 1988; Smith & Lerner, 1986) my colleagues and I have investigated the content and process specificity of the effects of practice on social judgments. One experiment (Smith et al., 1988, Experiment 2) illustrates our general approach. People made 250 judgments concerning whether or not a particular behavior implies a trait. A sample judgment would be, "Is hitting friendly?" The behavior stimulus word, presented in a computer screen, was different on each of the 250 trials (except for systematic repetitions of behaviors, to be described later). The target trait was fixed for the first 200 trials and then was changed. Someone might judge the friendliness of different behaviors for 200 trials, for instance, and then judge intelligence for the remaining 50 trials.

The dependent variable is the time to make each judgment. In this paradigm, because the judgments are subjective it is impossible to fully check on subjects' accuracy, but several arguments persuade us that speed-accuracy tradeoff is not a problem in these studies (see Smith, in press and Smith et al., 1988). This design permits us to answer several questions. (a) Do people speed up as they practice making the judgments? They do; over 250 trials the typical reduction in RT is from the initial 2400 to about 1000 ms, approximately 2/3 of the way down to the estimated asymptotic value, 500 ms or so.

(b) How long does the speedup last? Smith (in press) had subjects return to the experiment 24 hr after the first session and resume their work at the task. Their speed was about what it had been at the *end* of the first session, rather than at the beginning, demonstrating that the increased efficiency lasted without notable loss for at least a day.

(c) Is the speedup specific to the practiced target trait, or does it transfer to the new target introduced after 200 trials? The answer is that approximately 3/4 of the benefit is not content specific, but helps people when they perform the practiced process even with a new target. Figure 1.2 shows results from Smith et al. (1988), plotted as the average speed per trial. The results appear close to a completely general speedup (100% positive transfer to the new target at trial

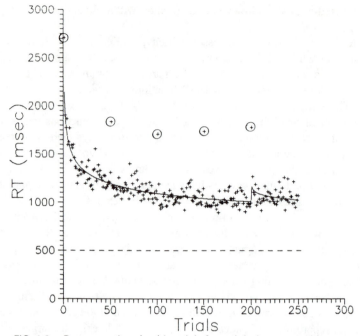

FIG. 1.2.   Response time (ms) by trials for trait judgments, with target trait changed at trial 201. A power function fit is shown, which ignores the first trial of each block of 50 trials (circled data points). From Smith et al. (1988). Copyright (c) 1988 by the American Psychological Association, Inc.

201), but the times for the last 50 trials are perceptibly above the continuation of the trend line from trials 1-200, showing some degree of specificity. The results differ dramatically from zero transfer (i.e., complete specificity of the practice to the practiced target), which would make the last 50 trials look just like the first 50. On the other hand, Smith (in press) shows that practicing one task (e.g., trait judgments) does not help people when they transfer, not just to a new judgment target, but to a completely new task (e.g., searching for a target letter in the word). The speedup therefore has some generality across targets, but is specific to the practiced process.

The portion of the speedup that is specific to the target trait is theoretically due to the formation during practice of specific procedures that operate efficiently only with the practiced target. This "specialization" (Brooks, 1987) or "proceduralization" (Anderson, 1987) is postulated to occur whenever a skill is practiced with specific contents. For example, consider a general trait-inference production like

IF   the goal is to judge whether ⟨behavior⟩ is ⟨trait⟩ and ⟨trait⟩ implies
         ⟨feature1 and feature2 and . . . ⟩ and ⟨behavior⟩ has ⟨feature1 and feature2
         and . . . ⟩
THEN   respond "yes"

If this general production is executed for the trait *friendly*, it will be strengthened, and in addition, a trait-specific version of the production like the following
will be formed:

IF   the goal is to judge whether ⟨behavior⟩ is friendly and ⟨behavior⟩ has
         ⟨features of friendliness . . . ⟩
THEN   respond "yes"

This production will execute more quickly for friendliness judgments than the
general production can, for it involves a less complex pattern match and less
information has to be retrieved from long-term memory (because the features that
define friendly behaviors are directly incorporated into the production's pattern).
The process of proceduralization can operate at several levels. When this production in turn is executed with a specific behavior like *hugging*, it will be strengthened, and in addition a behavior-specific production like the following will be
formed:

IF   the goal is to judge whether hugging is friendly
THEN   respond "yes"

This production can execute more quickly still if the specific behavior is encountered again, for the same reasons as above (Anderson, 1987). Proceduralization
therefore makes practice effects more evident on practiced content than on new
content, though the latter will also benefit to some extent. Similarly, when one
practices playing a particular Mozart piano sonata, one's ability to perform that
piece benefits most, but one's overall skill (as measured by the ability to play a
new piece) will also improve.

Just as the efficiency of nonsocial cognitive procedures is increased by practice (Newell & Rosenbloom, 1981), the same holds for social judgment and
inference processes. The increase in efficiency can be observed with nonpracticed content, so it is not content specific. For example, judging the friendliness
of the 200th behavior is faster than judging the first, even though that specific
behavior has not been seen earlier in the study. And judging the intelligence of
the 201st behavior benefits to a great extent from judging the friendliness of the
previous 200 behaviors (see Fig. 1.2). However, the increased efficiency is
limited to the practiced procedures: it is process specific (Smith, in press). This
pattern of process specificity without content specificity implies that the effect is
mediated by procedural strengthening rather than some alternative like increased
accessibility of declarative knowledge structures (whose effects would be content

specific but not process specific). Increases in procedural efficiency have implications that go far beyond the speed with which the process can be performed, and I turn next to research that displays some of those implications.

Practice Effects on Category Accessibility.   As already noted, priming (earlier exposure to trait-related materials) can influence people's perceptions of ambiguous behaviors they encounter later. Generally, after such priming people rate ambiguous behaviors higher on the target trait, compared to ratings by control, unprimed subjects. The effect is of particular interest because at least in some versions (Srull & Wyer, 1979) it can last over a 24-day delay between priming and test. It does not depend on subjects' ability to recall the priming materials (Higgins et al., 1985) or even on their ability to report the identity of the primes, as when they are presented in brief flashes followed by a pattern mask (Bargh & Pietromonaco, 1982).

Category accessibility effects have generally been attributed to the activation of general trait schemata or constructs in the subject's memory (Higgins et al., 1985) or, equivalently, to the trait schema's position in a Storage Bin in memory (Wyer & Srull, 1986). Smith and Branscombe (1987) argued that the effects in the Srull and Wyer version of the paradigm could be due to the strengthening of cognitive procedures for inferring traits from behaviors. The priming manipulation could strengthen the subjects' procedures if the priming materials constituted behavior descriptions (as they do in Srull and Wyer's studies). Subjects who read those materials might repeatedly categorize them using the target trait. These categorization judgments, which might or might not be consciously reportable by the subjects, would constitute practice that would strengthen a behavior-to-trait inference procedure for the target trait. Therefore, when the ambiguous behavior is later presented in the category accessibility test, subjects would be more likely to categorize it into the target trait category.

This mediational hypothesis implies particular patterns of specificity. Notably, the effects should be process specific. Priming manipulations that involve behavior-to-trait inference procedures (which are tested by the category accessibility measure) will be more effective than those that do not. This should be true even if other priming manipulations include instances of the target trait word itself or its synonyms, thereby *more directly* activating the target trait schema in memory. Results from several experiments reported in Smith and Branscombe (1987, 1988) supported this hypothesis of process specificity, and one is described here.

In the experiment of Smith and Branscombe (1988), conceptually patterned on Jacoby (1983), subjects studied trait words either by reading them (e.g., reading the word *religious*) or by generating them from a list of related behaviors plus the initial letter of the trait word. For example, subjects in the generate condition saw "read from the Bible to his children daily; followed the Ten Commandments reverently; attended church three times a week R————." Generating the trait should strengthen behavior-to-trait inference procedures and therefore affect a category-accessibility dependent variable by making the inference of the target trait from an ambiguous behavior more probable. On the other hand, reading the trait word should not do this but should strengthen letter-to-word procedures involved in reading.

After a 1-minute delay filled with an unrelated arithmetic task, subjects were given one of three types of test. They were free recall for the trait words, a category accessibility test, where an ambiguously trait-related behavior was given and subjects were instructed to write a trait that it implied, and a word-fragment completion test, where the trait word appeared in fragmented form (−el−giou−) and subjects were to write an English word that fit the fragment. In all, 24 trait words were used in the experiment. Each subject read 8 trait words, generated another 8, and did not see anything related to the remaining 8 traits to provide an unprimed control condition.

The results (Table 1.3) showed process specificity. Generating the trait word increased performance more than reading on the free recall and category accessibility tests, since these tests rely on "conceptually driven" (Roediger & Blaxton, 1987) processes that resemble those involved in the generation priming task. That is, the category accessibility test requires the generation of a trait from a conceptually related behavior, the same process that is strengthened by the generation study task. Recall is also known to depend on elaborative processing that links the to-be-recalled item to other conceptually related information in memory; generation strengthens such links more than does simply reading the word (Roediger & Blaxton, 1987). On the other hand, word-fragment completion requires "data-driven" processes. The target word must be accessed from visual information about its letters rather than from conceptual cues, and practice in reading the word was in fact more effective in strengthening fragment completion performance than was trait generation.

Therefore, it is not the case that simply encountering trait-related information increases the accessibility of the trait construct independent of the process that is performed on the information. Instead, long-lasting effects are evident only when

TABLE 1.3
Results for Category Accessibility, Word Fragment Completion,
and Free Recall Tests Following Three Study Conditions

	Study Condition		
Test	Generate	Read	Control
Category Accessibility	4.18	3.43	2.71
Word Fragment Completion	3.45	4.97	3.31
Free Recall	4.87	3.57	—

Note. All means are out of a possible 8. From Smith and Branscombe (1988).

the test uses the same process (inferring a trait from behaviors) that was strengthened by the priming manipulation. The results of this study, as of Smith and Branscombe (1987), Jacoby (1983), Roediger and Blaxton (1987), and others, underline the fact that it is *what one does* during a particular episode—the procedures that are used in the earlier encounter—that makes the difference in later test performance. In contrast, activation theories propose that any processing of an item will automatically activate its representation in memory and leave it more accessible for future use by any type of test, contrary to the results obtained in all of these studies. Process specificity points to the mediation of an effect by cognitive procedures, rather than by a change (including activation) in declarative knowledge structures.

These studies and others lend support to a theoretical explanation of dissociations between effects of prior experiences (primes) on later *performance* and explicitly reportable *memory* for the prior experiences. That is, priming effects are often detectable (e.g., on word-fragment completion or category accessibility dependent variables) even when the perceiver is unable to recall or recognize the exposure to the priming information. For this reason, such priming effects have been termed "implicit memory" (cf. Schacter, 1987). Various explanations for dissociations between implicit and explicit memory have been proposed, including separate "semantic" and "episodic" memory systems (e.g., Tulving, 1983) that are postulated to mediate implicit and explicit memory effects, respectively. However this separate-systems hypothesis faces severe empirical problems (Anderson & Ross, 1980; Roediger & Blaxton, 1987), including the observation of dissociations among implicit memory measures (Roediger & Blaxton, 1987; Smith & Branscombe, 1988).

The explanation for dissociations that seems to command the most support involves process specificity. Explicit memory measures, such as recall or recognition, depend on a particular kind of processing, termed conceptually driven by Roediger and Blaxton (1987) and Jacoby (1983), which is produced by elaboration, imagery, and other familiar mnemonic strategies. On the other hand, other types of performance, such as the ability to efficiently make an inference about a stimulus item or to read it when presented in fragmented form, make use of other processes. *The conditions under which the prime is encountered encourage specific types of processing, which in turn determine what later performances will be affected. Performances benefit from prior experiences to the extent that they involve processes that overlap with those that were used on the prior occasion.* In other words, simply reading a word (meeting a person, etc.) has effects that depend not only on the content of the word (the person's attributes, etc.) but also on what processing the perceiver carried out on that occasion. Conscious memory is only one type of later performance that may be affected by the prior experience, though its familiarity leads to the impression that effects on performance that are independent of conscious recollection are somehow paradoxical. They are not. They simply illustrate the general principle that performances will often be affected by prior experiences independently of explicit memory if they do not make use of the same processes that underlie explicit memory.

Effects on the Content of Social Judgment. The research just described shows that changes in procedural efficiency can alter people's trait judgments concerning ambiguous behaviors in a category accessibility paradigm. Of course, this process might influence real-life person perception or social behavior if a perceiver witnessed a target person performing such a behavior (e.g., Carver et al., 1983). There is another way in which the content of judgments can be influenced by procedural efficiency, and it involves relatively unambiguous behaviors. Consider a behavior that has implications for more than one trait—after all, most behaviors do. Which of these traits a perceiver is likely to infer may depend on the relative efficiency of the perceiver's procedures of drawing inferences about the implied traits. Recent practice making inferences about one trait, say intelligence, may tip the balance, making inferences from the target behavior concerning intelligence relatively more probable than inferences concerning other traits, such as friendliness or honesty.

To test this hypothesis, I used (for experimental convenience) behaviors that had evaluatively opposite implications on two different traits. In an earlier study (Smith, in press) people in some conditions made 400 judgments over two sessions concerning whether behaviors were intelligent or friendly. They were asked to complete a questionnaire at the end of the experiment in which they rated their overall liking for a hypothetical person who performed each of 20 different behaviors. This questionnaire was presented to subjects as a pilot, intended to secure ratings of materials for a study that was unrelated to the one in which they had just finished participating. Included among a number of evaluatively mixed filler behaviors were 4 unfriendly but intelligent behaviors (e.g., "won the political argument with his roommate," "refused to help his classmate with the homework even though he had understood it all perfectly") and 4 friendly but unintelligent behaviors (e.g., "tried to fix his friend's refrigerator but ended up making it worse," "stopped on the street and picked up the hitchhiker"). Practice judging intelligence should cause perceivers to infer that the target behaviors were intelligent (or the reverse) more fluently, and thus to base their overall liking ratings relatively more on intelligence than on friendliness. Practice judging friendliness should have the opposite effects.

A significant interaction supported this prediction (see Smith, in press). Intelligent/unfriendly behaviors were rated more positively by people who had practiced judging intelligence than by those who had judged friendliness (with means of 4.07 and 3.25 respectively, on a 7-point scale; subjects who did not practice trait judgments had M = 3.80). The reverse was true for unintelligent/friendly behaviors (M = 4.75 and 5.15, with 4.88 for unpracticed subjects).

This effect differs from the category accessibility effects discussed earlier because here the manipulation does not (necessarily) change the perceiver's judgment of a particular behavior on a target trait, as occurs with category accessibility measures. Instead, the practice-induced increase in efficiency of making a particular type of judgment makes that trait inference *more likely to occur spontaneously* when people evaluate the questionnaire behaviors in an unconstrained way, and therefore gives that trait increased weight in an overall evaluative judgment. It is tempting to speculate that a similar process could affect judgments in real social interaction. For example, if I repeatedly judge people's clothes for fit and stylishness (perhaps because of my occupation), the processes involved in that judgment will become quite efficient and likely to be used whenever I encounter and observe someone. My liking and other reactions and interaction with a person are likely to be more heavily influenced by their clothing (and hence less responsive to other attributes of the person) than those of a perceiver who lacks this type of practice.

In general, then, practice can increase the efficiency of a particular judgment process and therefore the likelihood of a particular inference being made, and therefore increase the weight of the target attribute in social judgments (including affective judgments). This resembles an effect discussed theoretically by Medin and Schaffer (1978) and Nosofsky (1987), that attention to a given dimension increases perceptions of differences among stimuli on that dimension, and hence its weight in categorization and other decisions. These researchers emphasize that the current stimulus context influences attention and therefore dimension weighting, and I am pointing out that past practice in making judgments may have similar effects.

Theoretical Implications. The effects described in this section can be summarized in terms of their specificity. At lease some of the effects are *not* content specific. For instance, the increased efficiency of judgment due to practice (a) is evident when new, unrepeated stimulus items (e.g., behaviors) are judged, and (b) transfers in major part to a new target (e.g., a trait; Smith et al., 1988). They are, however, process specific; that is, practicing one task does not influence performance on a different task. This was illustrated by results of Smith (in press) in the practice paradigm and Smith and Branscombe (1987, 1988) in the category accessibility paradigm. Thus, it is not the case that simply encountering information related to a target construct changes the perceivers' later responses to construct-related information. Instead, transfer depends on the *processes* that are applied in the practice (study, priming) context and in the target performance. The prior experience facilitates later performance to the extent that overlapping processes are involved in the two (Roediger & Blaxton, 1987).

These results have a number of implications for mediation. First, the fact that judgments speed up with practice in a way that is process-specific but not target-specific demonstrates that the effect is due to the strengthening of procedures. One theoretical alternative is increased accessibility of information in memory about the target trait, but this would generate a target-specific speedup. The speedup also cannot be due to changes in general, peripheral processes (such as the person's getting faster at reading words on the screen or at pushing response keys), for it does not generalize to a new task that shares such peripheral elements (Smith, in press). Instead, what is changed by practice is the efficiency of task-specific cognitive procedures, the productions that actually perform the task (e.g., derive trait judgments concerning behaviors), which exist in both relatively general and target-trait-specific forms. As noted earlier on p. 3, people are expected to possess procedures at different levels of generality due to proceduralization (Anderson, 1987), so it is not surprising that we find some speedup that is process-specific but general across targets and some that is both process- and target-specific.

Efficiency of cognitive processes has notable practical and social implications that are not, perhaps, clear when one simply asks what is the significance of a few hundred millisecond reduction in the time taken to make a particular judgment. First, Fazio (1986) has demonstrated that practice at accessing one's attitude to a particular object causes the access to occur more quickly and even spontaneously. This can influence both attitude stability (Fazio & Williams, 1986) and attitude-behavior consistency (Fazio, 1986). As Fazio argues, the more efficient the attitude-access process, the more likely the attitude will become activated when the object is encountered, shaping and biasing perceptions of the object and behavioral decisions.

Second, both the category accessibility studies discussed earlier and the questionnaire study with multiple-implication behaviors demonstrate that the *content* of social judgments can be influenced by the relative efficiency of judgmental procedures. In live social interaction, if a particular judgment process is efficient because it has been practiced, the chance that it will actually occur (triggering a particular inference) is enhanced. This notion may have significant implications for issues in personality and individual differences, where perceivers may chronically differ in their sensitivity to particular configurations of information from which they derive inferences about other people, or about situational affordances for particular behaviors (Cantor & Kihlstrom, 1985). So authoritarians may be particularly likely to make inferences concerning others' dominance or submissiveness rather than other traits, and individuals who are high on achievement motivation may be particularly likely to note situational possibilities for appraising their performances against standards of excellence.

Content Specificity of Practice Effects

Prevailing Theory. As noted earlier, current theories in social cognition either pay little attention to procedural knowledge or cite the potential applicability of production systems in an unelaborated way (e.g., Wyer & Srull, 1986). These theories often use the accessibility of declarative knowledge, and its increase with use, to explain changes in efficiency with practice. Therefore, they have difficulty accounting for the types of observations already described, where process-specific but not content-specific increases in efficiency are observed. Effects of increased accessibility of declarative knowledge would be content-specific but not process-specific.

The picture changes somewhat when we consider stimulus-specific effects of practice; that is, the effects of repeatedly judging a particular object. Accessibility theories might predict facilitation from repetition, on the grounds that the first presentation would leave the memory representation of the item in a relatively accessible state and thereby speed up processing on the second presentation. Though plausible on its face, this explanation faces several difficulties. If the effect is both specific and long-lasting we have to question the basic assumption. Extreme specificity of the effect (e.g., an effect for repeating a particular word but not a synonym) would tend to rule out semantic schemata as mediators, for they are said to represent *meaning* rather than surface information, and the same schema should be accessed by synonymous words. Also, if the effect is long-lasting (hours or days), it would be difficult to maintain that a single exposure to schema-related information, on one among hundreds of trials of a task, should activate a schema with such long-lasting effects. Most important, if the effect is process specific, this explanation is in trouble. The accessibility of a schema makes it more readily usable by all processes, not just those that were previously used. That is, the fact that the schema is activated does not carry any information about what processes were applied to it earlier.

Nonsocial Examples.   Some studies of the effects of practice have examined the content specificity of the performance improvement that results. Kolers (1976) had subjects practice the skill of reading text in novel orientations (right to left, backwards, etc.). He observed that (a) they improved with practice, cutting the time taken to read a page from over 15 to about 2 min. (b) One year later, his subjects were still significantly faster than unpracticed people; different measures showed from 60–80% savings over the year. Thus, as is generally known the effects of practice are long-lasting. Most important here, (c) some of the effect was specific to *particular practiced pages of text*. That is, subjects were slightly but significantly faster to read pages that they had practiced a year earlier than comparable new pages in the same typographical orientation. This effect was not related to their ability to recognize the pages as having been seen before. Thus, the practice effect has a specific component that is amazingly long-lasting and that does not depend on conscious recognition of the target information.

Anderson (1987) describes several experiments that make the same point. McKendree and Anderson (cited in Anderson, 1987) had subjects practice programming skills, studying particular combinations of LISP functions. Subjects in different conditions practiced specific combinations different numbers of times per day (2 times for one combination and 6 for another). The study was counterbalanced so that the elementary pieces of information involved (the basic functions) were studied equally often in all conditions. After 4 days of practice, subjects were both faster and more accurate in performance on combinations they had practiced more often than on less-practiced combinations. The effects were somewhat specific to practiced combinations.

These studies demonstrate that practice has effects that are—at least in part—highly specific to both process and content. People become better in general when they practice a task, in that they can perform better even on nonpracticed content. However, the improvement is not uniform. Instead, practiced information shows greater gains than comparable new information (e.g., previously read pages can be read more quickly than new pages in the same textual orientation). In the domains of nonsocial skills and problem solving, then, these results show a high degree of specificity in the effects of practice. Will social judgments show comparable effects?

Social Examples.   The studies on practice effects mentioned above (Smith, in press; Smith et al., 1988) examined the content specificity of the increased efficiency due to making a judgment concerning a particular stimulus behavior. Some behaviors among a subject's hundreds of trials were repeated, at various lags. Lags ranged from 1 (an immediate repetition) to 16 (15 unrelated behaviors intervening) within a block of 50 trials; other behaviors were repeated from one block to the next (with an average lag of 50) and, in Smith (in press), between sessions with 24 hr in between. One can examine, therefore, the extent to which repeated behaviors are judged more quickly than new ones. Not surprisingly, the effect is quite large for immediate repetitions. What may be surprising is that the benefit of repetition beyond lag 4 does not diminish further within a session, being constant up to lag 50; see Fig. 1.3. A long-lasting trace of the word must be established by just a single presentation, which enables people to respond more quickly when the word is repeated.

In Smith (in press) repeated judgments were still significantly facilitated 24 hr after the first presentation of the behavior, though the size of the effect had declined somewhat. Further, the effect of repetition was almost exactly as large when the subject did not even recognize that the word had been presented earlier as when the word was recognized. Thus, like other types of implicit memory performance (Schacter, 1987; Smith & Branscombe, 1988) the facilitation of social judgments from repetition can be dissociated from explicit memory (i.e., recognition).

Conditions were included in this experiment to test the limits of the repetition effect, allowing inferences about its mediation based on the methodological principle of specificity. Some words were repeated from one block to the next across a change in subjects' judgment target (e.g., they changed from making judgments about the friendliness of the behaviors to judging their intelligence). Other subjects had words repeated across a task change, for example from trait judgments to sound judgments (indicating whether or not a particular target

RT Facilitation for Repeated Behaviors

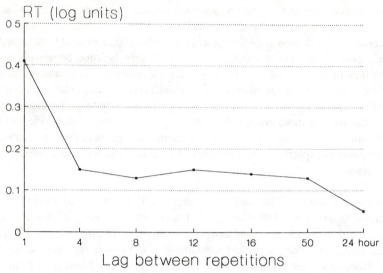

FIG. 1.3.   Amount of facilitation in judgment response time (log units) from repetition of behaviors at varying lags. Data from Smith (in press).

sound was included in the word's pronunciation). One possible mediator of the faster response to repeated items is an increase in the speed with which subjects can *read* the word after they have already read it once, or (empirically indistinguishable from that) an increase in the accessibility of the word's meaning, pronunciation, and other features in memory. Another possible mediator is the formation of item-specific productions as illustrated on p. 31. If a subject uses general productions to judge that *kissing* is friendly, the process of proceduralization should form an item-specific production like

> IF   the goal is to judge that kissing is friendly
> THEN   respond "yes"

which will allow a faster response on the second presentation of the same word.

These two potential mediators predict different patterns of specificity of the effect. The first, facilitation of reading or lexical access, would produce faster responses on the second presentation of a word even if the judgment target or task had changed since the initial presentation. The second, content-specific productions, would not allow faster responses if the judgment target was changed, for the production is target-specific and would not match or apply when the processing goal involves a different judgment target. The item-specific production would not generally be expected to facilitate performance if the task had changed, because different tasks will generally involve different sets of productions. However, it might facilitate later performance if the second task was a subprocess of the first one, because in that case the initial trial with the specific stimulus item would have executed and therefore practiced the productions involved in the second task.

The results were quite clear-cut. As noted earlier, there was strong facilitation of processing for a word repeated between blocks of trials when neither task nor target was changed. There was no facilitation for repeated items across a change in target for either the trait or sound-judgment task. This rules out simple facilitation of reading or accessing the word's memory representation as a mediator. There was, however, facilitation across a change in task from trait to sound judgments, consistent with the suggestion (e.g., Van Orden, Johnston, & Hale, 1988) that reading for meaning usually involves processing a word's pronunciation as a subprocess. If subjects generally access the word's pronunciation in performing the trait judgment task, the pronunciation task will be facilitated by this practice when the word is repeated. This pattern strongly suggests that the formation of new productions that are both item- and process-specific, rather than a general facilitation of reading or accessing the word, is responsible for repetition effects.

Theoretical Implications.   Facilitation of processing of repeated stimuli persists for a long time, at least 24 hr for a trait judgment task (Smith, in press) and is independent of the ability to consciously recognize or recall the earlier encounter. It depends, however, on the item's being processed in the same way (e.g., the same type of judgment being made with respect to the same target) on both occasions.

Long-lasting, item-specific effects of practice are not unique to the social judgment tasks that I have investigated. In fact, they appear ubiquitous. As noted before, Kolers (1976) found that specific pages of inverted text that subjects had read a year earlier could still be read faster than new pages, even if subjects did not recognize them as old. Mitchell and Brown (1988) had subjects name objects depicted in simple drawings, and found that previously named pictures could be named faster than new pictures—even 6 weeks after the initial presentation, and even if the picture was not recognized as having been previously seen. And Sloman, Hayman, Ohta, Law, and Tulving (1988) observed that completion of fragmented words was facilitated by earlier practice reading the word, for as long as 16 months after the initial study (at which time subjects spent an average of less than 7 sec studying each word in a long list). Such facilitation has also been found to be independent of subject's ability to consciously recognize the studied words.

Based on the striking diversity of the perceptual, cognitive, and social-judgment tasks that have been found to exhibit long-lasting facilitation when items are repeated, I conjecture that the effect is universal. *Any* type of processing of an item ought to proceed more efficiently when the item has been previously processed in the same way. As noted earlier, the results of Smith (in press) suggest that the facilitation upon repetition is due to the formation of item-specific productions by ACT*'s mechanism of proceduralization (Anderson, 1987). This hypothesized mediator accounts for the fact that the effect depends on the same process being carried out on both occasions—i.e., for the fact that no facilitation is observed when different processes are carried out on the same item (Smith, in press; Ratcliff, Hockley, & McKoon, 1985, Experiment 2). The process-specificity of the effect also neatly accounts for the usual independence of the performance facilitation from conscious memory measures like recognition: different processes underlie the two types of dependent measure (the judgment or perceptual task versus conscious or explicit memory). This is the explanation for dissociations of implicit from explicit memory that is preferred by Roediger and Blaxton (1987) and others.

Extremely specific and long-lasting practice effects that are independent of conscious recognition of the practiced information may have significant implications for social judgment. For instance, imagine that person I meet quotes frequently from literary classics, and that I infer that she is well-educated. Encountering her at a later time, I may be unable to consciously recall her earlier behavior or my conclusion about her. But increased efficiency of specific judgment processes may remain as a trace of the incident, so that if she repeats the behavior I will make a similar inference more rapidly and with greater probability. Judgments and inferences that we have made before are particularly easy for us to make again, even if we have no conscious memory of the earlier occurrence. This constitutes a form of implicit memory (Schacter, 1987) for our impressions or inferences about others that is separate from our conscious recollections (explicit memories). Along with the relatively stable schematic knowledge that has been emphasized by social cognition researchers, it may also serve as a source of stability and continuity in our perceptions and reactions to the word and to other people.

Stimulus-specific processing efficiency induced by prior exposure to the stimulus is probably also responsible for the well-known effect of mere exposure on liking (Zajonc, 1980), which can even influence real social interaction (Bornstein, Leone, & Galley, 1987). Seamon, Brody, and Kauff (1983) as well as Mandler, Nakamura, and Van Zandt (1987) argue for this viewpoint. The subjective ease of perceiving or judging the stimulus results in an affectively positive feeling of familiarity and increases ratings of liking for the stimulus. As Zajonc and these other researchers have observed, the effect of prior exposure on affect is independent of conscious recollection of the prior exposures, as this viewpoint would predict.

In fact, the influence on affect on specific past experiences with a stimulus object is just a special case of a more general phenomenon that Jacoby has discussed under the heading of "misattribution" (Jacoby & Kelley, 1987). The familiarity due to the perceiver's prior exposure to this person or other object is misattributed, seen as an intrinsic property of the stimulus. Thus, if a subject can easily comprehend a sentence heard through noise (because he or she has previously heard the same sentence), the subjective experience is not that the memory of the previous presentation aided perception, but that the noise level is lower for the old sentences than for the new ones (Jacoby, Allan, Collins, & Larwill, 1988). It also appears that plausible general-knowledge statements that are familiar because of prior presentations are subjectively rated as more valid than comparable novel sentences (Begg, Armour, & Kerr, 1985; Hasher, Goldstein, & Toppino, 1977). Presumably subjects misattribute the familiarity, taking it as evidence of the sentence's truth. The same effect might make persuasive arguments that are repeatedly heard appear to be more convincing. If the previously encountered arguments can be easily processed and understood, they are likely to appear more valid—particularly if subjects have forgotten the earlier encounters. Because of the likelihood that perceivers will misattribute processing fluency to properties of the stimulus rather than to their own prior experience (particularly if the prior exposure cannot be recalled), this form of stimulus-specific processing efficiency might influence many types of social judgment or behavior, even beyond affect and argument-persuasiveness ratings.

Process Specificity: Overall Conclusions

Practice makes perfect, or at least increases processing efficiency. The improvement is process specific: It does not apply unless the practiced process is involved in producing the target performance. It is content specific in part: Specialization of procedures results in the greatest improvement for specifically practiced content. Therefore, a person will be ready to process some specific information with particular efficiency and rapidity, depending on his or her particular past experiences. This residue from the past may have effects on present judgments or interactions of which the person is unaware. Fazio's (1986) findings on attitude accessibility (an increase in the efficiency and hence probability of attitude access due to practice) constitute one example: social behaviors are more consistent with the person's attitude toward a particular object when the attitude access is more efficient (due to previous encounters with the object, or practice accessing the attitude). Increased processing efficiency may also lead to liking based on mere familiarity with an object, increased stability in our perceptions and inferences about particular persons (because it will be easier to repeat previously made inferences than to process new ones), and perhaps even increased persuasion by arguments we have heard before (compared to new arguments).

The strengthening of general (non-content-specific) procedures through practice means that unpracticed content will also benefit from practice. And this general practice will also have significant effects on social judgment and social behavior. Practice inferring a particular trait from behaviors may make that trait more likely to be noted when a related behavior is witnessed, even if other traits are also potential inferences (Smith, in press). This mechanism may well underlie the effects of "chronicity" on a trait, identified by Higgins and his coworkers as an individual difference that influences memory, person perception, and even emotional vulnerability (Bargh & Thein, 1985; Higgins & King, 1981; Strauman & Higgins, 1987). That is, if a perceiver is particularly efficient in deriving the implications of behaviors for a target trait like honesty, (a) impressions of honesty/dishonesty will be formed more quickly than impressions along other "non-chronic" dimensions, (b) honesty will be likely to be part of the perceiver's impressions of other people, (c) the perceiver may better remember honesty-related behaviors than others (because they tend to be processed more deeply), and (d) if we assume that the perceiver holds honesty as a self-standard, he or she may be particularly likely to experience affect (e.g., pride or shame) upon performing honest or dishonest behaviors, because the match or mismatch between the standard and the behavior's implications will be readily noted. These effects are exactly those of the "chronicity" of honesty demonstrated by the earlier-cited research by Higgins and others.

Procedural knowledge as represented in the ACT* framework has numerous properties outlined in Anderson (1983, 1987), but even the simplest and most basic property—that cognitive processes and skills improve with practice—has diverse, nonobvious, and significant implications for social cognition.

RELATIONS OF CONTENT AND PROCESS SPECIFICITY

Content and process specificity are closely interrelated, and in this section I review two of their connections: the fact that the effects of particular past experiences (identifiable by their content specificity as argued above) are often process specific, and the fact that the effects of practice (whose signature is process specificity) are often content specific.

Process Specificity of Exemplar Effects

Particular past experiences can influence future performance. Reading a few religious behaviors can influence the later classification of an ambiguous behavior as religious (Smith & Branscombe, 1988); encountering an unfriendly experimenter may make someone avoid a different person who has a similar hair style (Lewicki, 1986). These effects, however, are not evident across the board on all dependent variables, and in particular the past experience may not have effects on measures of conscious (explicit) memory. Far from being paradoxical, this illustrates the process specificity of these effects. Explicit memory depends on a particular type of processing ("conceptually driven"; Roediger & Blaxton, 1987). Study conditions that encourage that type of processing, such as instructions to elaborate or to form images, or generating an item from conceptual cues rather than simply reading it, will generally lead to consciously accessible memories. On the other hand, study conditions that lead to other types of processing (say perceptual encoding without much conceptual elaboration) may leave traces that influence other types of later performance (say word-fragment completion) without being explicitly retrievable at all. Such study conditions could be created by instructions to make perceptual judgments about words (e.g., about the pleasantness of the word shape) or to search for particular letters in them.

The message is that the effects of an "episodic" memory produced by a single past experience depend not only on the content of the experience, but also on the particular processes that were carried out on the occasion. A record of what the person *did* on the prior occasion is implicit in the patterns of effects that experiences have in the present (cf. Jacoby, 1983; Whittlesea, 1987). The content-specific effects of single episodes are also process specific.

Theoretically, it is likely that process specificity also applies to the influence of specific category exemplars on categorization processes. Brooks (1987) has noted this point, observing that much research on exemplar influences on categorization has just tried "to get the item learned" rather than to consider "the way the item was treated during the original learning period" (p. 144). It is a deep and complex but researchable question whether exemplar effects on categorization depend on the simple availability in memory of an exemplar with known category membership, or on a trace (theoretically, an item-specific production) of a past processing episode in which the exemplar was categorized. If the latter, then

(a) the effect of the exemplar would be expected to be process-specific, depending on the match between the subject's current processing goal (i.e., to categorize the current stimulus object) and the process carried out on the old exemplar. Thus, exemplars that are explicitly or implicitly *categorized* during learning should have larger effects than exemplars that are processed in some other way.

(b) The effect of an exemplar on categorization would be expected to be independent of explicit memory measures—by the same logic outlined above with respect to item-specific practice effects. This prediction is consistent with the data.

(c) Finally, this possibility is most attractive in that it brings exemplar-based categorization into a common framework with item-specific repetition effects: items (exemplars) that were processed (categorized) in a particular way are efficiently recategorized when they are encountered again, and the categorization of new items that are similar to old ones should also be facilitated to some extent.

Though this formulation appears simple and elegant, Brooks' insightful discussion (pp. 160–166) emphasizes how much we have yet to understand about the principles determining "similarity" in this context.

Content Specificity of Practice Effects

Turning around 180 degrees, we also just saw that the effects of practice on strengthening cognitive processes are content-specific in part. Information that is specifically practiced benefits more from practice than does new information, thought the latter also benefits from the strengthening of general procedures. The content-specific benefits may last just as long as the general benefits of practice. In Smith (in press) words that were repeated from 24 hr earlier were judged more quickly than new words (and equally quickly whether or not subjects recognized the words as having been seen before) and in Kolers (1976) pages that had been read a year earlier could still be read faster than new pages in a similar typographical orientation. Thus the history of a person's experience in a particular domain can be read in his or her patterns of current performance. Even in a domain in which the perceiver is generally adept, specific stimulus configurations that have been encountered particularly often will be most efficiently processed (Anderson, 1987; Jacoby & Brooks, 1984).

The theoretical connections between exemplar-based judgment and content-specific practice effects are perhaps most clearly displayed by Logan's (1988) instance-based theory of automatization. In Logan's model, the development of automaticity through practice occurs via the storage of ever-increasing numbers of stimulus-response pairs in memory. When a previously encountered stimulus recurs, a quick memory retrieval process may substitute for the more time-consuming judgment process that was carried out originally, leading to a speedup of responding over trials. The same underlying process, the storage of information about past experiences and its quick, effortless retrieval when similar experiences are encountered again, can be shown to account for several observed properties of automaticity developed through practice (Logan, 1988) and for exemplar-based influences on categorization and judgment (Brooks, 1987; Kahneman & Miller, 1986). Our social and nonsocial knowledge is not so much embodied in encyclopedia-like abstract knowledge structures (as schemata, scripts, or prototypes) as distributed across a large number of memory traces of prior processing episodes. These are often not accessible as conscious memories, but can mediate the effects of prior experiences on a range of measurable performances.

The intertwining of content and process specificity—of cognitive content and process more generally—supports the argument that an adequate theory in social cognition (as in psychology in general) requires attention to both components. Descriptions or investigations of what people know, the content of schemata, etc., will not suffice to explain their judgment or behaviors unless they are accompanied by analyses of the particular processes they can and do perform. This is particularly evident, perhaps, in the dissociations discussed earlier: Knowing what stimuli a person studied does not allow predictions of what later tasks will be affected (e.g., word-fragment completion versus recognition memory) unless it is also known what processes the person carried out during study. I believe (as noted on p. 42) that the effects of particular past experiences on perception, categorization, and other judgments as well as on explicit "episodic" memory tasks like recall or recognition may be best modeled as *content specific productions*. These are formed by the process of proceduralization during the past processing episode and reveal their presence by facilitating future processing in a way that is both process- and content-specific.

This point underlines the advantages of approaching social cognition within the framework of a general cognitive theory that encompasses both content and process. Anderson's (1983) ACT* is perhaps the most prominent such theory, though others may also suffice or even improve on it. My argument is not with adherents of different theories, but rather with those who believe that strong inferences can be drawn about the cognitive mediation of judgment and behavior *without* explicitly modeling both content and process.

IMPLICATIONS

Theorizing in Social Cognition

There are three morals implicit in this paper's discussion and data. First is that in order to explain human social judgment and social behavior in terms of cognitive mediators—the long-run goal of social cognition as a discipline—we need to broaden our thinking about types of cognitive mediators. Schemata and other stable, abstract knowledge structures are important but are not alone in influencing social interaction. We need theories that are general enough to incorporate all these types of mediators—along the lines of Wyer and Srull (1986) or Smith (1984). The neurally inspired PDP models (Rumelhart & McClelland, 1986) may be applicable as well if they can be developed further. They offer a theoretically elegant way to model both abstraction of repeated patterns and storage of unique instances within a single memory framework (McClelland & Rumelhart, 1985). However, these models currently lack an adequate account of cognitive processes other than the mapping of representations from one domain into another.

Second, investigating the pattern of specificity of the effects of prior experiences can help distinguish various mediators. This methodological principle implies that it may be more informative to explore the pattern of effects of a particular type of priming manipulation—including its limits—than to replicate effects over and over again within a single paradigm.

Finally, and perhaps most significantly, our field may be due for more emphasis on the specific. Categorization theorists (Medin & Schaffer, 1978; Nosofsky, 1987) in cognitive psychology and researchers interested in stereotyping, person perception, and social comparison in social psychology (Kahneman & Miller, 1986; Lewicki, 1986; Rothbart & John, 1985) are moving in this direction.

Researchers and theorists in social cognition have banished from our own thinking the pernicious idea that "cognition" invariably refers to thought that is conscious, serial, and slow—though erasing this association from our students' minds is one of the enduring problems in teaching social cognition. Yet in a more subtle form we are often still victims of a related idea: that the most important social knowledge, which influences our perceptions and responses to the current situation, is abstract, propositional, schematic knowledge that we can consciously access and verbally report. This assumption shows up in our research methods (e.g., asking people what traits they attribute to various social groups as a way of assessing their stereotype, then attempting to relate it to the inferences they make in perceiving a specific person). It also shows up in the all-but-exclusive focus by many of our most insightful theorists on schemata and other abstract structures in social memory. Yet it is an overly restrictive assumption. Overturning it may lead us to more fruitful investigations of exactly what stays in the head as a residue of our past experiences and how it may influence our ongoing social and nonsocial judgments and behavior. Here are some instances of what particular areas within social psychology might look like with some theoretical rethinking.

Stereotyping

Stereotypes have often been conceptualized as abstract knowledge structures linking social groups (e.g., Blacks) to particular traits or behavioral attributes. These structures function as expectations when we encounter and perceive members of the relevant group. But stereotypes may instead be thought of as largely *exemplar-based*, implicit memories for prior experiences (either live or mediated) with members of a group. What novel empirical implications might flow from this conceptualization?

(a) Current thinking (e.g., Brewer, 1988) emphasizes the level of *subtypes* rather than broad social groups as the level at which much stereotyping operates. That is, we may apply a stereotype of the street-wise Black or the Black athlete rather than the Black person per se. The issue of the operative level is significant, for it determines how much social learning versus individual experience underlies stereotypes. Social learning probably takes place largely at the level of broad categories; that is, people may be told that "Blacks are . . . " or "women are often . . . " But our impressions of subtypes are probably much more experience- and exemplar-based. I particularly stress this point because (in contrast to researchers who have attempted to identify a canonical list of a few widely shared subtypes) I believe that subtypes are indefinite in number. Consider the earlier examples plus Black comedian, Black civil-rights activist, Black policeman, Black Baptist preacher, Black politician, Black-studies major in college, etc. Most of us have more or less clear images of each of these types and the list could be extended indefinitely, not only with occupational or role subtypes like these examples, but also with person-in-context subtypes (Cantor, Mischel, & Schwartz, 1982): Black running back in Big Ten football game, Black politician speaking at a political rally. Social learning probably cannot account for the ease with which we can conceptualize and apply such a large number of potential subtypes, while a process of retrieving and summarizing known exemplars to generate expectations and draw inferences about the present case can. (A similar argument in the categorization literature shows that we can easily make use of ad hoc categories; Barsalou, 1985.)

(b) A process of retrieving exemplars from memory that are similar to the current target, and summarizing their characteristics to derive expectations and make inferences about the target (Kahneman & Miller, 1986), can lead to a profound degree of *flexibility* in stereotypes. Context can influence which exemplars are retrieved, as can the perceiver's momentary goals and interests. Encountering someone in a situation where social interaction and potential friendship are of concern may lead to the retrieval of known exemplars who share similar interpersonal attributes with the target, though physical-appearance and other relatively stable attributes may also be important. Encountering the same person in an occupational context may lead to the retrieval of a very different set of exemplars because dimensions related to occupational skill and competence may be more salient determinants of similarity and hence of retrieval (cf. Medin & Schaffer, 1978; Nosofsky, 1987). Thus, it is not the case that a given stimulus person will always elicit the same set of exemplars and hence the same categorizations, inferences, and social behavior.

(c) Exemplar-based stereotypes will not only be flexible in the sense of context sensitivity, but also may readily change in response to recent experiences, as Rothbart and John (1985) emphasized. Lewicki's (1986) studies demonstrate the effect: A single encounter with a person with a particular physical attribute influences perceivers' later reactions to another individual with the same attribute. Thus, accessible memories of recent experiences (live or via the media) with members of social categories may influence people's beliefs and inferences about individual members of the groups. This is in sharp contrast to the generally assumed stability of stereotypes conceptualized as social schemata.

(d) In assessing stereotypes, researchers have often asked people to characterize social groups using trait labels (e.g., Deaux & Lewis, 1984; Katz & Braly, 1933). This seems to be a reasonable approach to getting at schema content but may not be adequate if stereotypes substantially depend on specific exemplars Information about exemplars may most effectively be retrieved from memory via perceptually similar cues, in an encounter with another individual member of the category. Thus, inferences about individual group members may not be expected to be consistent with the traits that the same perceivers attribute to the group as a whole. We know that past experiences can affect people's behavior and judgment without the person being able to verbally report on the past experience (cf. Schacter, 1987); similarly, assessment of stereotypes via verbal reports may omit components that influence inferences about concrete target individuals.

(e) If stereotyping depends in part on the retrieval of exemplars from memory based on similarity to the current target individual, the set of exemplars that is retrieved, and hence affect and inferences directed toward the target, may not be uniform within a social category. A schematic approach would presume that any Black target would activate the same stereotype and hence would be subject to relatively uniform inferences and other reactions (e.g., affect; Fiske et al., 1987), though the attributes derived from the stereotype might be averaged in with the individual's other salient attributes in overall judgments. In contrast, the exemplar-based model would say that an encounter with a new Black comedian might trigger the retrieval of memories of Eddie Murphy, Whoopi Goldberg, and Bill Cosby, and so very different inferences, compared to an encounter with a new Black secretary. Stereotype-based inferences may not be uniform within the group.

(f) Finally, stereotyping phenomena may have a process-based component as well as an exemplar-based one. Assume that whenever a perceiver encounters a Black person he or she categorizes them that way (rather than in alternative ways such as gender, age, or occupation). This inference process will become particularly practiced and strong, likely to be invoked on future encounters with Blacks. Thus, efficiency in making particular social categorizations or deriving other inferences (such as inferring that a Black is likely to be hostile) may influence stereotyping phenomena.

Zarate and Smith (in press) have tested hypotheses related to this last suggestion, measuring the speed with which perceivers categorized photos as White, Black, male, or female. Categorization speed depended on the photo's attributes; for example, Whites could be categorized by gender faster than Blacks could, and males could be categorized by race faster than females could. It also depended on the perceiver's own attributes, for same-sex photos were classified by sex faster than opposite-sex photos. Most important for the present argument, categorization speed predicted the attribution of stereotype-related traits to the pictured individuals. In particular, the faster subjects classified Black female photos as Black, and the *slower* they classified them as female, the more Black-stereotype traits they attributed to them. This research gives good evidence that (as many theorists have assumed) social categorization mediates stereotyping. It also validates the use of categorization RT as a measure of the categorization process, which we theoretically interpret as an outcome of competing categorization productions for different social categories. If a production that matches Black targets and infers Black-stereotype traits is stronger for a particular perceiver (through past practice) than a production matching female targets and inferring female-stereotype traits, then the perceiver should be able to categorize Blacks as Black faster than the perceiver categorizes females as females. And when the two productions compete to match the same stimulus person (i.e., a Black female) the stronger should win, determining the content of the attributed traits.

Like all practice effects, these will be somewhat content specific. While a hypothetical perceiver may become adept through practice at categorizing all Blacks as Black (and attributing stereotypic traits to them), the effects will be particularly marked with respect to specific individuals that the perceiver has previously categorized. And as Smith (in press) showed, this effect may be independent of the perceiver's conscious memory of any prior encounter. In effect, the perceiver, without awareness, may become "stuck" repeatedly categorizing and reacting to specific target persons in the same way, because the relevant cognitive processes become more and more efficient relative to their competitors. Recent research has provided preliminary evidence consistent with these predictions (Zarate & Smith, 1988).

In sum, other cognitive mediators besides abstract schematic knowledge about social groups may influence stereotyping phenomena. Our reactions to another person (indeed, to any social or nonsocial object) are likely to be shaped not only by our abstract knowledge about the general characteristics of the category to which the person belongs, but also by concrete past encounters with similar individuals and by the relative efficiency and strength of our cognitive processes that may mediate inferences about the individual, including processes that categorize the individual in competing ways. These patterns of efficiency in turn will depend on past experience (i.e., practice) and on the nature of the cognitive processes we have carried out in the past when confronted with this specific target or with similar individuals.

Personality and Individual Differences

Stable individual differences in social behavior may also owe much to exemplar-based and process-based cognitive mediators. The social intelligence model of Cantor and Kihlstrom (1985) exemplifies this line of argument. People have particular configurations of adaptive social skills ("intelligence") shaped by their past experiences (i.e., by practice) which differ from one person to another. The result is patterned behavior that observers interpret as personality differences.

I would add to Cantor and Kihlstrom's conceptualization the idea that individual's expertise due to practice is likely content and process specific, so patterns of social behavior are likely to be domain specific. An individual may consistently behave aggressively in one type of situation because judgments and behaviors that he or she has performed before become easier to perform again, especially when similar stimulus configurations reappear. In a different domain, the content-specific practice effects would not be visible (because the strong productions' conditions would not match). So a person might be aggressive with his subordinates at work but not with his children. Consistent with this, Wright and Mischel (1987) argue that personality dispositions are best characterized as conditional, if-then contingencies between categories of situations and categories of behavior. Empirically they observe a strong relationship between observers' dispositional judgments and the frequency of category-prototypic behaviors *in specific situations,* rather than high cross-situation consistency of category-relevant behaviors (which would be implied by a view of personality dispositions as generalized response tendencies). Research by Cantor and Kihlstrom (1985), Sorrentino and Higgins (1986), Linville and Clark (1989), as well as Wright and Mischel exemplifies the strong theoretical links that are emerging between conceptualizations of motivation and personality, and cognitive models with a production-like skills component.

Other Issues

A variety of phenomena within social psychology might demonstrate content or process specificity if appropriate investigations were undertaken. I suggest a few of them very briefly, to illustrate the range of issues in social judgment and social behavior whose analysis may benefit from consideration of the effects of specific experiences and cognitive processes.

Affect often arises from social comparisons of outcomes. If I receive a particular outcome (say I come out $60 ahead after playing the slot machines in Las Vegas), will my satisfaction depend on a comparison with an abstract average or expectancy (I know that most people lose money on the slots) or with a particular available exemplar (the person next to me just won $1000)?

Is the chronic accessibility of a trait as conceptualized and measured by Higgins and his associates (Higgins & King, 1981) interpretable as the efficiency of cognitive procedures for inferring that particular trait, as Bargh and Thein's results (1985) suggest? As Higgins' research shows, chronicity is related to person perception, self-perception, and even emotional vulnerability due to negative outcomes.

Appraisal of stressors encountered in everyday life, the resulting triggering of affect, and coping strategies that may be applied to deal with stressors, can be modeled as productions (Linville & Clark, 1988). Could practice of these processes be induced in a way that would increase their efficiency and lead to better coping?

Categorization of a person in a particular way can be induced by social context, as when a single Southerner is encountered in a roomful of Yankees. Will the tendency to categorize that person in that specific way carry over (because of the formation of person-specific categorization productions) and influence how the person is perceived on a future encounter, even in an unbiased context, and even if the initial encounter has been forgotten?

Even when it is unrecognized by the perceiver, familiarity or facility in processing a specific stimulus may underlie effects of mere exposure on liking and the judged validity of facts, among other types of judgment (Jacoby & Kelley, 1987; Mandler et al., 1987). Might social judgments or behaviors be influenced by similar processes? For example, would persuasive arguments seem more convincing and lead to greater attitude change if they have been processed before (but forgotten)?

Is the content of a stereotype constant across contexts, as implied by a schematic or prototype representation, or might it vary when considered in different social contexts or situations, due to the availability of somewhat different subsets of exemplars (cf. Kahneman & Miller, 1986)?

Much social behavior can be considered adaptive (Cantor & Kihlstrom, 1985), intelligent problem solving, as when we recognize situations as ones in which particular actions may be appropriate or beneficial. To what extent are these perceptions and resulting behavioral choices based on general rules, categorizing situations and behavioral opportunities by their match to abstract schemata? Alternatively, to what extent do they depend on similarities to *specific* earlier-encountered situations, in the same way as object categorization often depends on specific exemplars?

Conclusion

If the arguments of this paper have any merit, social cognition faces a series of new and exciting research issues, some of which I hope are illustrated by the suggestions just cited. Cognitive mediators with different properties from those we have emphasized in the past may shape social judgment and behavior in novel and interesting ways. Many or most of these influences may be independent of the perceiver's conscious awareness. The methodological principle of specificity may prove to be one of the most powerful tools in our investigations of these new frontiers.

ACKNOWLEDGEMENTS

This research was supported by the Office of Navel Research under contract N00014-84-K-0288 and by the National Science Foundation under grant BNS-8613584. Correspondence regarding this article should be sent to Eliot R. Smith, Department of Psychological Sciences, Purdue University, West Lafayette, Indiana 47907.

REFERENCES

Alba, J., & Hasher, L. (1983). Is memory schematic? *Psychological Bulletin, 93,* 203–231.
Andersen, S. M., & Klatzky, R. L. (1987). Traits and social stereotypes: Levels of categorization in person perception. *Journal of Personality and Social Psychology, 53,* 235–246.

Anderson, J. R. (1976). *Language, memory, and thought.* Hillsdale, NJ: Lawrence Erlbaum Associates.

Anderson, J. R. (1983). *The architecture of cognition.* Cambridge, MA: Harvard University Press.

Anderson, J. R. (1987). Skill acquisition: Compilation of weak-method problem solutions. *Psychological Review, 94,* 192–210.

Anderson, J. R., & Ross, B. H. (1980). Evidence against a semantic-episodic distinction. *Journal of Experimental Psychology: Human Learning and Memory, 6,* 441–465.

Ashmore, R. D., & Del Boca, F. K. (1981). Conceptual approaches to stereotypes and stereotyping. In D. L. Hamilton (Ed.), *Cognitive processes in stereotyping and intergroup behavior.* Hillsdale, NJ: Lawrence Erlbaum Associates.

Bargh, J. A., & Pietromonaco, P. (1982). Automatic information processing and social perception: The influence of trait information presented outside of conscious awareness on impression formation. *Journal of Personality and Social Psychology, 43,* 437–449.

Bargh, J. A., & Thein, R. D. (1985). Individual construct accessibility, person memory, and the recall-judgment link: The case of information overload. *Journal of Personality and Social Psychology, 49,* 1129–1146.

Bargh, J. A., & Tota, M. E. (1988). Context-dependent automatic processing in depression: Accessibility of negative constructs with regard to self but not others. *Journal of Personality and Social Psychology, 54,* 925–939.

Barsalou, L. W. (1985). Ideals, central tendency, and frequency of instantiation. *Journal of Experimental Psychology: Learning, Memory, and Cognition, 11,* 629–654.

Barsalou, L. W. (1987). The instability of graded structure: Implications for the nature of concepts. In U. Neisser (Ed.), *Concepts and conceptual development: ecological and intellectual factors in categorization* (pp. 101–140). New York. Cambridge University Press.

Begg, I., Armour, V., & Kerr, T. (1985). On believing what we remember. *Canadian Journal of Behavioral Science, 17,* 199–214.

Bodenhausen, G. V., & Wyer, R. S. (1985). Effects of stereotypes on decision making and information-processing strategies. *Journal of Personality and Social Psychology, 48,* 267–282.

Bornstein, R. F., Leone, D. R., & Galley, D. J. (1987). The generalizability of subliminal mere exposure effects: Influence of stimuli perceived without awareness on social behavior. *Journal of Personality and Social Psychology, 53,* 1070–1079.

Brewer, M. B. (1988). A dual process model of impression formation. In R. S. Wyer & T. K. Srull (Eds.), *Advances in social cognition* (Vol. 1, pp. 1–36). Hillsdale, NJ: Lawrence Erlbaum Associates.

Brewer, M. B., Dull, V., & Lui, L. (1981). Perceptions of the elderly: Stereotypes as subtypes. *Journal of Personality and Social Psychology, 41,* 656–670.

Brewer, W. F., & Nakamura, G. V. (1984). The nature and functions of schemas. In R. S. Wyer & T. K. Srull (Eds.), *Handbook of social cognition* (Vol. 1. pp. 119–160). Hillsdale, NJ: Lawrence Erlbaum Associates.

Brooks, L. R. (1987). Decentralized control of categorization: The role of prior processing episodes. In U. Neisser (Ed.), *Concepts and conceptual development* (pp. 141–174). Cambridge, England: Cambridge University Press.

Cantor, N., & Kihlstrom, J. (1985). Social intelligence: The cognitive basis of personality. In P. Shaver (Ed.), *Self, situations, and social behavior: Review of personality and social psychology* (Vol. 6, pp. 15–34). Beverly Hills, CA: Sage.

Cantor, N., & Mischel, W. (1979). Prototypes in person perception. In L. Berkowitz (Ed.), *Advances in experimental social psychology* (Vol. 12, pp. 3–52). New York: Academic Press.

Cantor, N., Mischel, W., & Schwartz, J. (1982). A prototype analysis of psychological situations. *Cognitive Psychology, 14,* 45–77.

Carver, C. S., Ganellen, R. J., Froming, W. J., & Chambers, W. (1983). Modeling: An analysis in terms of category accessibility. *Journal of Experimental Social Psychology, 19,* 403–421.

Clark, M. S., & Fiske, S. T. (Eds.). (1982). *Affect and cognition* (pp. 157–183). Hillsdale, NJ: Lawrence Erlbaum Associates.

Deaux, K. K., & Lewis, L. L. (1984). Structure of gender stereotypes: Interrelationships among components and gender label. *Journal of Personality and Social Psychology, 46,* 991–1004.

Fazio, R. H. (1986). How do attitudes guide behavior? In R. M. Sorrentino & E. T. Higgins (Eds.), *Handbook of motivation and cognition* (pp. 204–243). New York: Guilford Press.

Fazio, R. H., & Williams, C. J. (1986). Attitude accessibility as a moderator of the attitude-perception and attitude-behavior relations: An investigation of the 1984 presidential election. *Journal of Personality and Social Psychology, 51,* 505–514.

Fiske, S. T., Kinder, D. R., & Larter, W. M. (1983). The novice and the expert: Knowledge-based strategies in political cognition. *Journal of Experimental Social Psychology, 19,* 381–400.

Fiske, S. T., Neuberg, S. L., Beattie, A. E., & Milberg, S. J. (1987). Category-based and attribute-based reactions to others: Some informational conditions of stereotyping and individuating processes. *Journal of Experimental Social Psychology, 23,* 399–427.

Fiske, S. T., & Pavelchak, M. A. (1986). Category-based versus piecemeal-based affective responses: Developments in schema-triggered affect. In R. M. Sorrentino & E. T. Higgins (Eds.), *Handbook of motivation and cognition* (pp. 167–203.). New York: Guilford Press.

Fong, G. T., & Markus, H. (1982). Self-schemas and judgments about others. *Social Cognition, 1,* 191–204.

Fried, L. S., & Holyoak, K. J. (1984). Induction of category distributions: A framework for classification learning. *Journal of Experimental Psychology: Learning, Memory, and Cognition, 10,* 234–257.

Hamilton, D. L., Katz, L. B., & Leirer, V. O. (1980). Cognitive representation of personality impressions: Organizational processes in first impression formation. *Journal of Personality and Social Psychology, 39,* 1050–1063.

Hasher, L., Goldstein, D., & Toppino, T. (1977). Frequency and the conference of referential validity. *Journal of Verbal Learning and Verbal Behavior, 16,* 107–112.

Hastie, R., & Park, B. (1986). The relationship between memory and judgment depends on whether the judgment task is memory-based or on-line. *Psychological Review, 93,* 258–268.

Higgins, E. T., & King, G. (1981). Accessibility of social constructs: Information-processing consequences of individual and contextual variability. In N. Cantor & J. F. Kihlstrom (Eds.), *Personality, cognition, and social interaction* (pp. 69–121). Hillsdale, NJ: Lawrence Erlbaum Associates.

Higgins, E. T., Bargh, J. A., & Lombardi, W. (1985). The nature of priming effects on categorization. *Journal of Experimental Psychology: Learning, Memory, and Cognition, 11,* 59–69.

Higgins, E. T., Rholes, W. S., & Jones, C. R. (1977). Category accessibility and impression formation. *Journal of Experimental Social Psychology, 13,* 141–154.

Hintzman, D. L. (1984). MINERVA 2: A simulation model of human memory. *Behavior Research Methods and Instrumentation, 16,* 96–101.

Hintzman, D. L. (1986). "Schema abstraction" in a multiple-trace memory model. *Psychological Review, 93,* 411–428.

Hunt, E., & Lansman, M. (1986). Unified model of attention and problem solving. *Psychological Review, 93,* 446–461.

Isen, A., & Hastorf, A. H. (1982). Some perspectives on cognitive social psychology. In A. H. Hastorf & A. Isen (Eds.), *Cognitive social psychology* (pp. 1–31). New York: Elsevier.

Jacoby, L. L. (1983). Remembering the data: Analyzing interactive processes in reading. *Journal of Verbal Learning and Verbal Behavior, 22,* 485–508.

Jacoby, L. L., Allan, L. G., Collins, J. C., & Larwill, L. K. (1988). Memory influences subjective experience: Noise judgments. *Journal of Experimental Psychology: Learning, Memory, and Cognition, 14,* 240–247.

Jacoby, L. L., & Brooks, L. R. (1984). Nonanalytic cognition: Memory, perception and concept learning. In G. Bower (Ed.), *The psychology of learning and motivation: Advances in research and theory, 18*. New York: Academic Press.

Jacoby, L. L., & Kelley, C. M. (1987). Unconscious influences of memory for a prior event. *Personality and Social Psychology Bulletin, 13*, 314–336.

Jacoby, L. L., & Witherspoon, D. (1982). Remembering without awareness. *Canadian Journal of Psychology, 36*, 300–324.

Judd, C. M., & Park, B. (1988). Outgroup homogeneity: Judgments of variability at the individual and group levels. *Journal of Personality and Social Psychology, 54*, 778–788.

Kahneman, D., & Miller, D. T. (1986). Norm theory: Comparing reality to its alternatives. *Psychological Review, 93*, 136–153.

Katz, D., & Braly, K. (1933). Racial stereotypes in one hundred college students. *Journal of Abnormal and Social Psychology, 28*, 280–290.

Kolers, P. A. (1976). Reading a year later. *Journal of Experimental Psychology: Human Learning and Memory, 2*, 554–565.

Kolers, P. A., & Roediger, H. L. (1984). Procedures of mind. *Journal of Verbal Learning and Verbal Behavior, 23*, 425–449.

Lakoff, G. (1987). Cognitive models and prototype theory. In U. Neisser (Ed.), *Concepts and conceptual development: ecological and intellectual factors in categorization* (pp. 63–100). New York. Cambridge University Press.

Lewicki, P. (1986). *Nonconscious social information processing*. Orlando, FL: Academic Press.

Lingle, J. H., Altom, M. W., & Medin, D. L. (1984). Of cabbages and kings: Assessing the extendibility of natural object concept models to social things. In R. S. Wyer & T. K. Srull (Eds.), *Handbook of social cognition* (Vol. 1, pp. 71–118). Hillsdale, NJ: Lawrence Erlbaum Associates.

Linville, P. W., & Clark, L. (1989). Production systems and social problem solving: Specificity, flexibility, and expertise. In R. S. Wyer & T. K. Srull (Eds.), *Advances in social cognition* (Vol. 2). Hillsdale, NJ: Lawrence Erlbaum Associates.

Locksley, A., Stangor, C., Hepburn, C., Grosovsky, E., & Hochstrasser, M. (1984). The ambiguity of recognition memory tests of schema theories. *Cognitive Psychology, 16*, 421–448.

Logan, G. D. (1988). Toward an instance theory of automization. *Psychological Review, 95*, 492–527.

Malt, B. C., & Smith, E. E. (1984). Correlated properties in natural categories. *Journal of Verbal Learning and Verbal Behavior, 23*, 250–269.

Mandler, G., Nakamura, Y., & Van Zandt, B. J. S. (1987). Nonspecific effects of exposure on stimuli that cannot be recognized. *Journal of Experimental Psychology: Learning, Memory, and Cognition, 13*, 646–648.

McClelland, J. L., & Rumelhart, D. E. (1985). Distributed memory and the representation of general and specific information. *Journal of Experimental Psychology: General, 114*, 159–188.

Medin, D. L., Altom, M. W., & Murphy, T. D (1984). Given versus induced category representations: Use of prototype and exemplar information in classification. *Journal of Experimental Psychology: Learning, Memory, and Cognition, 10*, 333–352.

Medin, D. L., & Schaffer, M. M. (1978). Context theory of classification learning. *Psychological Review, 85*, 207–238.

Medin, D. L., & Shaffer, M. M. (1978). Context theory of classification learning. *Psychological Review, 85*, 207–238.

Medin, D. L., & Smith, E. E. (1984). Concepts and concept formation. *Annual Review of Psychology, 35*, 113–138.

Medin, D. L., & Wattenmaker, W. D., (1987). Category cohesiveness, theories, and cognitive archaeology. In U. Neisser (Ed.), *Concepts and conceptual development* (pp. 25–62).Cambridge, England: Cambridge University Press.

Metcalfe, J., & Fisher, R. P. (1986). The relation between recognition memory and classification learning. *Memory and Cognition, 14,* 164–173.

Miller, G. A. (1956). The magical number seven, plus or minus two: Some limits on our capacity for processing information. *Psychological Review, 63,* 81–97.

Miller, G. A., Galanter, E., & Pribram, K. H. (1960). *Plans and the structure of behavior.* New York: Holt, Rinehart, Winston.

Mitchell, D. B., & Brown, A. S. (1988). Persistent repetition priming in picture naming and its dissociation from recognition memory. *Journal of Experimental Psychology: Learning, Memory, and Cognition, 14,* 213–222.

Neely, J. H. (1977). Semantic priming and retrieval from lexical memory: Roles of inhibitionless spreading activation and limited-capacity attention. *Journal of Experimental Psychology: General, 1,* 226–254.

Newell, A., & Rosenbloom, P. S. (1981). Mechanisms of skill acquisition and the law of practice. In J. R. Anderson (Ed.), *Cognitive skills and their acquisition* (pp. 1–56). Hillsdale, NJ: Lawrence Erlbaum Associates.

Newell, A., & Simon, H. A. (1972). *Human problem solving.* Englewood Cliffs, NJ: Prentice-Hall.

Nosofsky, R. M. (1987). Attention and learning processes in the identification and categorization of integral stimuli. *Journal of Experimental Psychology: Learning, Memory, and Cognition, 13,* 87–108.

Osherson, D. N., & Smith, E. E. (1981). On the adequacy of prototype theory as a theory of concepts. *Cognition, 9,* 35–58.

Ostrom, T. M. (1984). The sovereignty of social cognition. In R. S. Wyer & T. K. Srull (Eds.), *Handbook of social cognition* (Vol. 1, pp. 1–38). Hillsdale, NJ: Lawrence Erlbaum Associates.

Ostrom, T. M., Pryor, J. B., & Simpson, D. D. (1981). The organization of social information. In E. T. Higgins, C. P. Herman, & M. P. Zanna (Eds.), *Social cognition: The Ontario Symposium* (Vol. 1, pp. 3–38). Hillsdale, NJ: Lawrence Erlbaum Associates.

Park, B., & Hastie, R. (1987). Perception of variability in category development: Instance versus abstraction-based stereotypes. *Journal of Personality and Social Psychology, 53,* 621–635.

Park, B., & Rothbart, M. (1982). Perception of out-group homogeneity and levels of social categorization: Memory for the subordinate attributes of in-group and out-group members. *Journal of Personality and Social Psychology, 42,* 1051–1068.

Pirolli, P. L., & Anderson, J. R. (1985). The role of practice in fact retrieval. *Journal of Experimental Psychology: Learning, Memory, and Cognition, 11,* 136–153.

Pryor, J. B., & Merluzzi, T. V. (1985). The role of expertise in processing social interaction scripts. *Journal of Experimental Social Psychology, 21,* 362–379.

Ratcliff, R., Hockley, W., & McKoon, G. (1985). Components of activation: Repetition and priming effects in lexical decision and recognition. *Journal of Experimental Psychology: General, 114,* 435–450.

Read, S. J. (1987a). Similarity and causality in the use of social analogies. *Journal of Experimental Social Psychology, 23,* 189–207.

Read, S. J. (1987b). Constructing causal scenarios: A knowledge structure approach to causal reasoning. *Journal of Personality and Social Psychology, 52,* 288–302.

Roediger, H. R., & Blaxton, T. A. (1987). Retrieval modes produce dissociations in memory for surface information. In D. S. Gorfein & R. R. Hoffman (Eds.), *Memory and cognitive processes: The Ebbinghaus Centennial Conference* (pp. 349–379). Hillsdale, NJ: Lawrence Erlbaum Associates.

Roth, E. M., & Shoben, E. J. (1983). The effect of context on the structure of categories. *Cognitive Psychology, 15,* 346–378.

Rothbart, M., & John, O. P. (1985). Social categorization and behavioral episodes: A cognitive analysis of the effects of intergroup contact. *Journal of Social Issues, 41*(3), 81–104.

Rumelhart, D. E. (1984). Schemata and the cognitive system. In R. S. Wyer & T. K. Srull (Eds.), *Handbook of social cognition* (Vol. 1, pp. 161–188). Hillsdale, NJ: Lawrence Erlbaum Associates.

Rumelhart, D. E., & McClelland, J. L. (1986). *Parallel distributed processing: Volume 1: Foundations.* Cambridge, MA: MIT Press.

Schacter, D. (1987). Implicit memory: History and current status. *Journal of Experimental Psychology: Learning, Memory, and Cognition, 13,* 501–518.

Seamon, J. G., Brody, N., & Kauff, D. M. (1983). Affective discrimination of stimuli that are not recognized: Effects of shadowing, masking, and cerebral laterality. *Journal of Experimental Psychology: Learning, Memory, and Cognition, 9,* 544–555.

Sherman, S. J., & Corty, E. (1984). Cognitive heuristics. In R. S. Wyer & T. K. Srull (Eds.), *Handbook of social cognition* (Vol. 1, pp. 189–286). Hillsdale, NJ: Lawrence Erlbaum Associates.

Sloman, S. A., Hayman, C. A. G., Ohta, N., Law, J., & Tulving, E. (1988). Forgetting in primed fragment completion. *Journal of Experimental Psychology: Learning, Memory, and Cognition, 14,* 223–239.

Smith, E. R. (1984). Model of social inference processes. *Psychological Review, 91,* 392–413.

Smith, E. R. (1988a). Category accessibility effects in a simulated exemplar-based memory. *Journal of Experimental Social Psychology, 24,* 448–463.

Smith, E. R. (1988b). Impression formation in a general framework of social and nonsocial cognition. In R. S. Wyer & T. K. Srull (Eds.). *Advances in social cognition* (Vol. 1, pp. 165–176). Hillsdale, NJ: Lawrence Erlbaum Associates.

Smith, E. R. (in press). Procedural efficiency: General and specific components and effects on social judgments. *Journal of Experimental Social Psychology.*

Smith, E. R., & Branscombe, N. R. (1987). Procedurally mediated social inferences: The case of category accessibility effects. *Journal of Experimental Social Psychology, 23,* 361–382.

Smith, E. R., & Branscombe, N. R. (1988). Category accessibility as implicit memory. *Journal of Experimental Social Psychology, 24,* 490–504.

Smith, E. R., Branscombe, N. R., & Bormann, C. (1988). Generality of the effects of practice on social judgment tasks. *Journal of Personality and Social Psychology, 54,* 385–395.

Smith, E. R., & Lerner, M. (1986). Development of automatism of social judgments. *Journal of Personality and Social Psychology, 50,* 246–259.

Smith, E. R., & Zarate, M. A. (in press). Exemplar and prototype use in social categorization. *Social Cognition.*

Sorrentino, R. M., & Higgins, E. T. (1986). Motivation and cognition: Warming up to synergism. In R. Sorrentino & E. T. Higgins (Eds.), *Handbook of motivation and cognition: Foundations of social behavior* (pp. 3–20). New York: Guilford Press.

Srull, T. K., & Wyer, R. S. (1979). The role of category accessibility in the interpretation of information about other people: Some determinants and implications. *Journal of Personality and Social Psychology, 37,* 1660–1672.

Strauman, T. J., & Higgins, E. T. (1987). Automatic activation of self-discrepancies and emotional syndromes: When cognitive structures influence affect. *Journal of Personality and Social Psychology, 53,* 1004–1014.

Thibadeau, R., Just, M. A., & Carpenter, P. A. (1982). A model of the time course and content of reading. *Cognitive Science, 6,* 157–203.

Tulving, E. (1983). *Elements of episodic memory.* Oxford: Clarendon Press.

Turner, J. C. (1987). *Rediscovering the social group: a self-categorization theory.* Oxford: Blackwell.

Van Orden, G. C., Johnston, J. C., & Hale, B. L. (1988). Word identification in reading proceeds from spelling to sound to meaning. *Journal of Experimental Psychology: Learning, Memory, and Cognition, 14,* 371–386.

Wattenmaker, W. D., Dewey, G. I., Murphy, T. D., & Medin, D. L. (1986). Linear separability and concept learning: Context, relational properties, and concept naturalness. *Cognitive Psychology, 18,* 158–194.

Weber, R., & Crocker, J. (1983). Cognitive processes in the revision of stereotypic beliefs. *Journal of Personality and Social Psychology, 45,* 961–977.

White, G. L., & Shapiro, D. (1987). Don't I know you? Antecedents and social consequences of perceived familiarity. *Journal of Experimental Social Psychology, 23,* 75–92.

Whittlesea, B. W. A. (1987). Preservation of specific experiences in the representation of general knowledge. *Journal of Experimental Psychology: Learning, Memory, and Cognition, 13,* 3–17.

Wilder, D. A. (1984). Predictions of belief homogeneity and similarity following social categorization. *British Journal of Social Psychology, 23,* 323–333.

Wright, J. C., & Mischel, W. (1987). A conditional approach to dispositional constructs: The local predictability of social behavior. *Journal of Personality and Social Psychology, 53,* 1159–1177.

Wyer, R. S., & Srull, T. K. (1986). Human cognition in its social context. *Psychological Review, 93,* 322–359.

Zajonc, R. B. (1980). Feeling and thinking: Preferences need no inferences. *American Psychologist, 35,* 151–175.

Zarate, M. A., & Smith, E. R. (in press). Person categorization and stereotyping. *Social Cognition.*

Zarate, M. A., & Smith, E. R. (1988b). *Person-specific effects of categorization.* Unpublished paper, Purdue University.

On the Indistinguishability of Exemplar Memory and Abstraction in Category Representation

2

Lawrence W. Barsalou
Georgia Institute of Technology

In the target article for this volume, Eliot Smith contrasts two kinds of category representation: exemplar memories and abstractions. After reviewing a wide variety of studies, Smith concludes that exemplar memories play a central role in representing social categories. However, numerous complexities surround claims about representation, and identifying the representation that underlies performance on a particular task is a formidable challenge. In this article, I explore the characteristics of exemplar and abstracted representations and assess our ability to distinguish them empirically.

In the first section, I briefly review work on category learning. To some extent, misunderstandings about category representation reflect a failure to appreciate this history. In the second section, I discuss two issues essential to evaluating representation: (1) the necessity of considering processing; (2) the distinction between information and storage. I then present three dimensions of information storage that are useful in formally assessing representation: (1) information duplication, (2) information revision, and (3) information loss. In the third section, I present three fallacies about abstraction. These fallacies are not only present in Smith's article but seem to prevade how readers interpret work on category learning. In the fourth section, I show how exemplar and abstracted representations in principle are informationally equivalent. Because of this equivalence, we can not determine whether people use exemplar or abstracted representations. In the fifth section, I present four general classes of category learning models: permanent trace models, revisable trace models, cumulative abstraction models, and reductive abstraction models, the last of which includes connectionist models. As is shown, once one considers the wide variety of possible representations in these models, it becomes increasingly difficult to draw even formal distinctions between exemplar and abstracted representations, much less behavioral ones. I conclude that trying to determine whether people use exemplar or abstracted representations is futile. Although this is a seductive distinction to draw, it can not be evaluated on the basis of behavioral data.[1]

A BRIEF REVIEW OF WORK ON CATEGORY LEARNING

Early work on category learning assumed that people abstract definitions of categories as they test hypotheses on exemplars and nonexemplars (e.g., Bruner, Goodnow, & Austin, 1956; Bourne, 1966; Trabasso & Bower, 1968). Posner and Keele (1968, 1970) offered a significant alternative, namely, that people abstract prototypes, which contain characteristic rather than defining properties of exemplars. Because many categories do not have defining properties, passive prototype learning appeared more useful than active hypothesis testing. Posner and Keele did not completely dismiss exemplar information from category learning, but such information only played a secondary role. Bransford and Franks (1971) and Franks and Bransford (1971) proposed a similar view. Eleanor Rosch, Edward Smith, and their colleagues later explored abstracted representations in natural categories (e.g., Rosch & Mervis, 1975; E. E. Smith, Shoben, & Rips, 1974). During this time, investigators increasingly observed that people retain exemplar information and utilize it in categorization decisions. As a result, abstraction models added *abstraction* mechanisms that store exemplar characteristics (e.g., Hayes-Roth & Hayes-Roth, 1977; Neumann, 1974; Reitman & Bower, 1973).

After years of exploring abstraction models, theorists discovered that exemplar models could account for the major trends in category learning. Lee Brooks and Douglas Medin showed that very simple learning mechanisms can behave as if they have abstracted central tendency information from exemplars even though they have not. These mechanisms account for the major findings in category learning simply by storing exemplars and utilizing basic retrieval mechanisms (e.g., Brooks, 1978; Medin & Schaffer, 1978). While demonstrating the viability of exemplar models, these theorists rejected those prototype models that discard exemplar information and that combine characteristic properties linearly (e.g., the models of Franks & Bransford, 1971; Posner & Keele, 1968; also see Reed, 1972). However, exemplar theorists (e.g., Medin & Schaffer, 1978) have been careful to note that they have not rejected all abstraction models, especially those that store idiosyncratic information about exemplars (e.g., the models of Hayes-

---

[1]Although I focus on Smith's arguments about exemplar and abstracted representations, his arguments about declarative and procedural representations suffer a similar predicament. Conclusively determining that certain findings support declarative learning and that others support procedural learning is difficult if not impossible (Winograd, 1975).

Roth & Hayes-Roth, 1977; Neumann, 1974; Reitman & Bower, 1973). Instead the primary goal of exemplar theorists has been to show that certain exemplar models are at least as effective as the early abstraction models that dominated thinking in the area—it has not been to reject the entire class of abstraction models.

Readers of the category learning literature often perceive otherwise. In his target article, Eliot Smith concludes, "Research on nonsocial categorization thus supports the generalization that specific category exemplars are stored and used in making category membership judgments" (p. 11). The distinction between exemplar and abstracted representations is sufficiently salient and seductive that it has misguided interpretation of work in the area.[2]

REPRESENTING EXEMPLARS AND ABSTRACTIONS

To assess the role of representation in learning, it is necessary to consider the relation between representation and processing, the distinction between information and storage, and the dimensions that define exemplar and abstracted representations.

Representation and Processing

Cognitive theorists widely agree that any model of human performance must contain assumptions about both representation and processing. Because we cannot observe people's representations of knowledge directly, we cannot test claims about representation in the absence of processing mechanisms. Instead we can only observe the affects of a representation as they occur through processes that operate on it. Whatever behaviors we observe to assess a representation necessarily reflect processing as well.

It is therefore impossible to conclude from behavioral research on category learning that people represent categories with exemplars or abstractions. Instead we can only conclude that particular *models* (i.e., representation-process pairs) are either supported or rejected. For example, data may support a model that assumes a particular exemplar representation and particular processes that operate on it. Other models with exemplar representations may be rejected because their combination of representation and processing assumptions provides incorrect predictions. Analogously, abstraction models may succeed or fail, depending on the joint adequacy of their representation and processing assumptions. Similar arguments about representation and processing have been made by Anderson (1978) and Palmer (1978).

---

[2]This brief review barely begins to cover the large literature on category learning. For more extensive reviews, see Smith and Medin (1981), Mervis and Rosch (1981), Medin and Smith (1984), and Oden (1987).

Information Versus Storage

Although we cannot empirically assess the psychological presence of exemplar or abstracted representations in the absence of processing, we can address their formal and computational properties. For example, we can try to distinguish exemplar and abstracted representations in terms of the information they contain. We might suppose that abstracted representations contain only properties that occur definingly or characteristically across category members; whereas exemplar representations also contain idiosyncratic information that individuates exemplars. Consider Fig. 2.1. Imagine that a person experiences five exemplars from a category (e_1 through e_5), each having three properties (e.g., e_1 has properties *a*, *b*, and *d*). These properties can represent contextual information

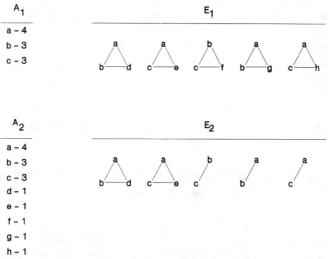

FIG. 2.1. A_1 is an abstracted representation that only contains the characteristic properties of exemplars e_1 through e_5. E_1 is an exemplar representation that contains idiosyncratic information. A_2 is an abstracted representation that contains idiosyncratic information. E_2 is an exemplar representation that only contains the characteristic properties of exemplars e_3, e_4, and e_5.

and operations performed on an exemplar, as well as its physical characteristics. Although only three properties are shown for each exemplar, exemplars may certainly contains more.

As a result of experiencing e_1 through e_5, a person might develop an abstracted representation for the category, such as A_1 in Fig. 2.1. As can be seen, this abstracted representation only contains *characteristic properties*, that is, properties generally true of exemplars (i.e., *a, b,* and *c*), along with their frequency of occurrence (i.e., 4, 3, and 3). Idiosyncratic properties that individuate exemplars have been discarded (e.g., *d* for e_1). In contrast, consider exemplar representation E_1. As can be seen, this exemplar representation contains idiosyncratic properties of exemplars (e.g., *d* for e_1). A_1 and E_1 represent standard assumptions about the information in abstracted and exemplar representations.

But consider representations A_2 and E_2. A_2 is an abstracted representation that maintains idiosyncratic information about exemplars (e.g., *d* from e_1. E_2 is an exemplar representation that loses idiosyncratic information about exemplars, after storing a complete record of the first two. From the third exemplar on, information is only stored in an exemplar memory if it occurs in a previous exemplar. Although the point at which this transition occurs is arbitrary here, it could be well-motivated in an actual model. Consequently, one cannot distinguish between exemplar and abstracted representations in terms of the information they contain. Either type can contain or discard idiosyncratic information.

If information does not distinguish exemplar and abstracted representations, then what does? The distinguishing factor is information storage. In the next section, I present three dimensions that structure how information can be stored as exemplars are experienced. These dimensions serve as the basis for how I define exemplar and abstracted representations.

Dimensions of Information Storage

Three dimensions reflect important differences in how information is stored in exemplar and abstracted representations. They are *information duplication, information revision,* and *information loss.* By no means are these the only dimensions that describe representations.

Information Duplication.   Perhaps the primary distinction between exemplar and abstracted representations concerns information duplication. Exemplar representations exhibit information duplication, whereas abstracted representations do not. As stated by Eliot Smith, "classifying a single category instance leaves a trace in memory" such that "our knowledge of a category . . . is (at least in part) *distributed* in memory across representations of a series of specific instances, rather than embodied in a single prototype representation" (p. 10).

Consider Fig. 2.1 again. As can be seen from exemplar representation E_1, property information is duplicated across exemplar memories. For example, property a occurs four times, once each for the representation of e_1, e_2, e_4, and e_5. Every time a new exemplar containing a is stored, another duplication of a occurs. This allows exemplar information to remain independent. Each exemplar memory contains completely separate information, with information for a given property being distributed across exemplar memories.

In contrast, abstracted representations centralize property information. Each property is only represented once, even if it occurs across many exemplars. As can be seen from representation A_1, a is only represented once, even though it occurs in four exemplars. Every time a given property is encoded, the same memory structure is processed. Abstraction models integrate exemplar information by updating centralized property information.[3]

Information Revision.   Another key difference between exemplar and abstracted representations concerns information revision. In ideal exemplar models, as discussed shortly, an exemplar representation is never revised. Every processing episode produces a new exemplar memory that remains permanently in the system. Previous exemplars may be retrieved, and information from them may control decision making and become part of a new exemplar memory. However, the retrieved exemplar memory must remain unchanged, else information is lost from memory. In general, ideal exemplar models assume that exemplar memories are not revised by subsequent processing (e.g., Bekerian & Bowers, 1983; McCloskey & Zaragoza, 1985).

An exemplar model can certainly allow revision of exemplar memories, and as described later, some do. But such a model may begin to lose its exemplar character and become more like an abstraction model. Consider an exemplar memory that is retrieved on many occasions to help process new members of its category. Across occasions, properties in the memory could be revised, with properties frequently relevant to categorizations being added, and with properties never relevant to categorizations being deleted (e.g., Loftus, 1975). Enough such processing could eventually transform the exemplar memory into a representation of the category's central tendency. Although the exemplar representation once contained idiosyncratic information, it now contains only characteristic information.

Whereas information revision is optional for exemplar representations (depending on the accompanying processes), it is intrinsic to abstracted representations. Consider representation A_2 in Fig. 2.1. Every time a new exemplar is

---

[3]Just because property information is centralized does not mean that representation of the property must be localized neurologically. There is no a priori reason why representation of the property could not be distributed across many processing units. In fact, connectionist models often assume that the representation of a property is distributed.

encoded, all the relevant properties must be revised. If *acf* is encoded, for example, the properties for *a, c,* and *f* are incremented by 1. The essential operation of an abstraction model is to revise centralized category information.

Information Loss.   Typically, theorists assume that exemplar models lose less information than abstraction models, as represented by the contrast between E_1 and A_1 in Fig. 2.1. As we see later, however, this factor does not really distinguish exemplar from abstracted representations. Each type of representation may not lose any information at all, instead containing a complete record of all exemplar information. Or each type of representation may lose substantial amounts of information. Nevertheless, the dimension of information loss is central to distinguishing different representations, as we shall see.

Information may be lost from a representation either through intentional revision or incidental degeneration. In intentional revision, a processor intentionally alters the contents of an exemplar memory or abstraction. In incidental degeneration, the contents of an exemplar memory or abstraction are partially or totally lost due to side effects of other processes (e.g., interference, decay).

In summary, my definitions of *exemplar representation* and *abstracted representation* from hereon reflect the following assumptions about information storage: Exemplar representations exhibit information duplication and may exhibit no information revision, or at least much less revision than occurs for abstracted representations. In contrast, abstracted representations centralize property information and require information revision, because every new exemplar causes centralized property representations to be updated. Information loss does not distinguish these two representations. As we shall see, either may lose no information or may lose information to equivalent extents.

It is important to note that some theorists define exemplar and abstraction models in terms of processing, rather than representation. These theorists adopt an *identical* exemplar representation for *all* models, but then define individual models as "exemplar" or "abstraction" in terms of the decision processes that operate on the exemplar representation (e.g., Estes, 1986; Koh, 1989; Koh & Meyer, 1989). For example, these abstraction models compare the exemplar being classified to an abstraction constructed from existing exemplar representations during classification. In contrast, these exemplar models compare the exemplar being classified to the same exemplar representations individually. Defining "exemplar" and "abstraction" in terms of processing is certainly useful. But because both kinds of processing can operate on either exemplar or abstracted representations, as I define them, this approach is somewhat orthogonal to the representational issue I pursue here. It would be useful if future treatments of the exemplar-abstraction issue assessed its application to representation and processing more systematically.

FALLACIES ABOUT ABSTRACTION

Given these basic assumptions of exemplar and abstracted representations, we can begin to assess claims about them. In this section, I consider three fallacies that reflect false stereotypes about abstraction.

Fallacy 1: Abstractions Do Not Contain Idiosyncratic Information

It is often believed that the knowledge abstracted for a category only contains properties that are defining or generally true of category members. Eliot Smith describes abstractions as representing the typical characteristics of a class of objects or events, rather than the details of a specific experience. According to this view, idiosyncratic properties that distinguish exemplars are discarded at encoding and do not exist in the category representation.

But as we saw earlier in Fig. 2.1, an abstracted representation can contain idiosyncratic information about exemplars (e.g., representation A_2). There is no a priori reason why idiosyncratic information cannot be abstracted from exemplars and integrated into a centralized category representation. An abstracted representation can contain any property occurring in any exemplar, regardless of how often it occurs. Such information might be useful in making later categorizations, assuming that certain idiosyncratic properties occur for one category and not others. The less information discarded, the more optimal categorization is likely to be, generally speaking. No a priori restriction limits the properties in a centralized category representation to those that are defining or generally true.

Reitman and Bower (1973), Neumann (1974), and Hayes-Roth and Hayes-Roth (1977) have all proposed abstraction models that store idiosyncratic information about exemplars in this manner. As discussed later, connectionist models also store idiosyncratic information in the process of abstracting information from exemplars (e.g., McClelland & Rumelhart, 1985).

Fallacy 2: Abstractions Do Not Contain Cooccurrence Information

It is often believed that the knowledge abstracted for a category does not contain information about correlations between properties. Eliot Smith states that "correlated attributes play no special role" when abstracted knowledge is used in categorization decisions. Instead only information about each property's relative frequency of occurrence is stored, independent of how often it cooccurred with other properties. According to this view, if someone experiences exemplars e_6 through e_{10} in Fig. 2.2, only the independent frequencies of properties are abstracted, as exhibited by A_3. Information about how often properties cooccur has been discarded.

e_6	e_7	e_8	e_9	e_{10}
a	a	b	a	a
b	c	c	b	c
d	e	f	d	e

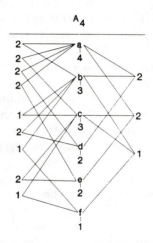

A_3
a – 4
b – 3
c – 3
d – 2
e – 2
f – 1

DYNAMIC EXEMPLAR RETRIEVAL

bfg ⟶ e_6 e_8 e_9

ceh ⟶ e_7 e_8 e_{10}

DYNAMIC N–TUPLE RETRIEVAL

bfg ⟶ b f ab bc bd bf cf abd bcf

ceh ⟶ c e ac ae bc ce ace bcf

FIG. 2.2. A_3 is an abstracted representation of all individual properties occurring in exemplars e_6 through e_{10}. A_4 is an abstracted representation that also contains cooccurrence information for 2-tuples and
3-tuples. The bottom panel demonstrates dynamic retrieval from exemplar and abstracted representations.

However, there is no a priori reason why cooccurrence information cannot be
abstracted as well. As represented by A_4 in Fig. 2.2, the knowledge abstracted to
represent e_6 through e_{10} could contain all the cooccurrence information available
across exemplars. Information about pairwise cooccurrence is represented by the
integers on the left of A_4. For example, the 2-tuple *ab* occurred in 2 exemplars,
and the 2-tuple *cf* occurred in 1 exemplar. Information about property triples is
represented on the right of A_4. For example, the 3-tuple *abd* occurred in 2
exemplars, and the 3-tuple *bcf* occurred in 1 exemplar. Consequently, abstracted

representations can record cooccurrence information by storing the frequency of higher-order n-tuples. A_4 also represents independent property frequencies (1-tuples), as shown by the integers below the properties.

If cooccurrence information is diagnostic for categorization, an abstraction model may utilize this information in categorization decisions. Again, the less information discarded, the more optimal categorization is likely to be, generally speaking. The models of Reitman and Bower (1973), Neumann (1974), Hayes-Roth and Hayes-Roth (1977), and Elio and Anderson (1981) all abstract cooccurrence information from exemplars, as do connectionist models (e.g., McClelland & Rumelhart, 1985).

Abstraction models that store cooccurrence information have sometimes been criticized by exemplar theorists as making unreasonable storage demands (Medin & Schaffer, 1978). As can be seen from A_4 in Fig. 2.2, the number of n-tuples used to represent all possible cooccurrences can quickly become large (i.e., 2^n-1). For example, if an exemplar contains 20 properties, it takes 1,048,575 n-tuples to represent it. However, the following six points *must* be considered in evaluating this problem. First, the number of properties encoded for an exemplar may typically be small, such that a reasonable number of n-tuples is required to store it. For example, if the limited capacity of working memory affects exemplar encoding, then five properties may typically be acquired for each exemplar, thereby requiring 32 n-tuples (cf. Miller, 1956). Second, no one has yet noted a limit on human memory, and the human cognitive system may well have the capacity to store substantial amounts of cooccurrence information. Third, it is essential to compare the relative number of exemplars to properties before concluding that exemplar models are more storage efficient. For example, imagine that a person experiences 1000 exemplars for a category, all of which have 3 properties drawn from a, b, c, d, e, and f (as for e_6 through e_{10} in Fig. 2.2). In this case, the total number of representational units, roughly speaking, is 1000 for an exemplar model (1 unit per exemplar) but only 41 for an abstraction model (6 units for all possible 1-tuples, 15 units for all possible 2-tuples, 20 units for all possible 3-tuples). In some cases, abstraction models that record cooccurrence information require less storage capacity than exemplar models (but not in all cases). Moreover, exemplar models are certainly not storage efficient, relatively speaking, because they often lose little if any information about exemplars. Fourth, it is very unlikely that all possible combinations of properties occur *across* exemplars, especially if properties correlate highly. In A_4, for example, 2-tuples do not exist for *af* and *be,* and 3-tuples do not exist for *abc* and *bce.* If properties form attribute-value structures, this can further reduce the set of possible correlations, because values for the same attribute are often mutually exclusive (i.e., they never cooccur). Even if all perceived cooccurrences are stored, not all possible cooccurrences must be represented. Fifth, abstraction models that extract only a subset of possible n-tuples may often compete favorably with exemplar models, as we shall see at several points later. Sixth, and perhaps most importantly, people may only store combinations of properties that receive focal attention (Trabasso & Bower, 1968), that enter into systematic patterns of correlation (Billman & Heit, 1988), or that are relevant to intuitive theories (Murphy & Medin, 1985). Such mechanisms greatly reduce the n-tuples encoded for exemplars.

Fallacy 3: Abstractions are Static and Unchanging

It is often believed that knowledge abstracted for a category is static and relatively unaffected by exemplars. Eliot Smith states that "the prototype should only change slowly with exposure to new category instances." Although some abstraction models exhibit this characteristic (e.g., Posner & Keele, 1968; Reitman & Bower, 1973), others do not. For example, abstraction models whose learning rules optimize cue predictability can produce large shifts in stable categorization after an unusual event (e.g., Gluck & Bower, 1988; Rescorla & Wagner, 1972). Moreover, some exemplar models become increasingly entrenched after much learning, namely, those that use all previous exemplars in every categorization decision (e.g., Medin & Schaffer, 1978). Each subsequent exemplar has a smaller and smaller impact on categorization, given the increasing number of other exemplars that influence categorization. Analogous to abstraction models, some exemplar models can produce major performance shifts late in learning, namely, those that only use subsets of exemplar memories (e.g., Reed, 1972), or those whose exemplar memories can be activated to different extents (e.g., Hintzman, 1986).

Abstraction models are often construed as representing categories in a static manner. Every time a category is represented, the same abstraction represents the category, regardless of context. But exemplar models sometimes work this way as well, with all exemplar memories affecting every categorization decision (e.g., Estes, 1986; Medin & Schaffer, 1978; Nosofsky, 1988). If one assumes that the entire exemplar set represents the category, then the category representation does not change from trial to trial, except for the addition of new exemplars. In effect, this is no different than updating an abstraction after each new exemplar.

Other exemplar theorists assume that the target stimulus currently being categorized does not retrieve the entire exemplar set. Instead only those exemplars similar to the target are retrieved to control its categorization, with the target being assigned to the category from which the most exemplars were retrieved. Because the exemplars retrieved for a given category can vary widely across categorizations, representation of the category varies. Assume that e_6 through e_{10} in Fig. 2.2 represent the exemplars stored in memory for a category. During the categorization of a target stimulus, imagine that exemplars are retrieved if they share at least one property with the target. Figure 2.2 shows the exemplars that would be retrieved for the targets *bfg* and *ceh*. As can be seen, the exemplars retrieved differ, demonstrating that the category is being represented dynamically during these different categorizations.

However, retrieval from an abstracted representation can also vary in this manner during categorization. Assume that a category is represented by A_4 in Fig. 2.2. During the categorization of a target stimulus, imagine that n-tuples are retrieved if they share at least one property with the target. Figure 2.2 shows the n-tuples that would be retrieved for the targets *bfg* and *ceh*. As can be seen, the n-tuples retrieved differ, demonstrating that the category is being represented dynamically during these different categorizations. Barsalou's (1987, 1989) theory of category representation works in this manner. Connectionist models also exhibit this dynamic quality (McClelland & Rumelhart, 1985).

INFORMATIONAL EQUIVALENCE AND ITS IMPLICATIONS FOR DISTINGUISHABILITY

We have seen that some abstracted representations can support processing often believed to occur only for exemplar representations. But are these two classes of representation completely equivalent? The key issue is assessing their informational equivalence, as I describe next for ideal exemplar and abstraction models. By *ideal*, I do not mean that these models are typical, nor that they are ideal for all purposes. I simply mean that they are ideal in not exhibiting information loss.

Ideal Exemplar Models

Consider an idealized case in which all exemplar representations remain accessible in memory. Under these conditions, every exemplar ever experienced is potentially available for use in processing its category. For example, representation E_3 in Fig. 2.3 maintains all information from the original exemplars, e_6 through e_{10}, in Fig. 2.2. No information is lost.

Because no information is lost, a model with E_3 as its representation can be made equivalent to any abstraction model. Any abstraction model starts with all the information available in exemplars and then integrates it into a category representation. For example, an abstraction model might construct representation A_3 in Fig. 2.2 from e_6 through e_{10}. However, a model with representation E_3 can mimic a model with A_3, if it contains a mechanism that can abstract the independent frequencies of properties at retrieval. Similarly, a model with E_3 can mimic a model with A_4, if it contains a mechanism that can abstract cooccurrence information at retrieval. Any result that an abstraction model explains, an ideal exemplar model can also explain, if it can perform the requisite processes at retrieval.

One might argue that such exemplar models are simply abstraction models that abstract at retrieval instead of encoding. Two points should be noted in this regard. First, it is important to distinguish between models that lose information from models that do not. Exemplar models that abstract at retrieval may never lose information, whereas some abstraction models, such as those with A_3, do. If it can be shown that people do not lose information and are able to abstract, then exemplar models that exhibit both properties should be preferred over abstraction models that do not. Second, such exemplar models should ultimately encode abstractions into memory. Exemplar theorists rarely assume that abstractions constructed at retrieval subsequently become stored in memory. But abstractions should be stored, if they receive sufficient processing. This follows from everything we know about the roles of effort, rehearsal, and depth-of-processing in transferring information from working memory to long-term memory. Because abstractions probably require substantial processing resources to construct and use, their entry into long-term memory may occur often. As a result, exemplar models that abstract at retrieval ultimately encode abstractions into memory, much like abstraction models.

Ideal Abstraction Models

It is easy to construct ideal abstraction models that lose no information about exemplars. In fact, the Reitman and Bower (1973) model, along with certain models in Hayes-Roth and Hayes-Roth (1977) and in Gluck and Bower (1988), are ideal in this sense. Consider A_4 in Fig. 2.3, which represents exemplars e_6 through e_{10} in Fig. 2.2. As can be seen in Fig. 2.3, all the original exemplar information that produced A_4 can be abstracted by decomposing its 3-tuples into the E's shown in A_4'. Once this information is available, an ideal abstraction model can produce any operation possible for an exemplar model, because all the original exemplar information is available.

Decomposition, as shown for A_4 and A_4', works optimally if all exemplars contain the same number of properties. If exemplars contain different numbers of properties, it becomes complicated, using the representation in A_4, to reproduce the original exemplars. Imagine that 2-tuple ax has a frequency of 24 across some set of exemplars. This frequency could have resulted from 6 two-property exemplars that only contain ax and from 18 three-property exemplars that contain ax as a 2-tuple (e.g., abx, acx). Alternatively, ax's frequency of 24 could have resulted from 18 ax exemplars and 6 three-property exemplars that contain ax. To reproduce the original exemplars, an abstraction model could record the frequency of ax as an exemplar, as well as the total frequency of ax. For example, if ax occurs 6 times as an exemplar and 18 times as a 2-tuple in three-property exemplars, then ax-24,6 enables recovery of the original exemplars. This abstracted representation, and others of its form, exhibit no information loss and are informationally equivalent to ideal exemplar models.

It may not be necessary for abstraction models to store the highest-order n-tuples to compete favorably with exemplar models. Nearly every abstraction model that has been rejected by exemplar theorists only stores information about 1-tuples (i.e., prototype models). No information is stored about any level of

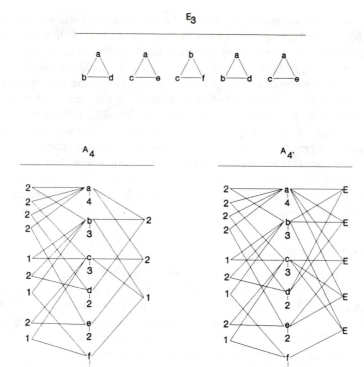

FIG. 2.3. A_4 and A_4' represent how the highest-order n-tuples in an abstraction can be decomposed to recover completely the information for exemplars e_6 through e_{10} in Fig. 2.2.

cooccurrence information (i.e., 2-tuples and higher). But even if only low-order cooccurrence information is represented, it improves prediction substantially. McClelland and Rumelhart (1985) and Gluck and Bower (1988) show that simply storing information about 2-tuples allows abstraction models to represent exemplars to a useful extent. Furthermore, storing information about higher-order n-tuples allows abstraction models to learn non-linearly separable categories (cf. Medin & Schwanenflugel, 1981).

Implications for Distinguishability

One might wonder whether any formal difference exists between storing exemplar memories, as in E_3, and storing the highest-order n-tuples, as in A_4. Why shouldn't we view the 3-tuples in A_4 as exemplar memories? The answer to this question depends on the information-storage distinction described earlier. From an informational perspective, these two representations are indeed equivalent, because they contain the same information. But as we have seen in Figs. 2.1 and 2.2, information content does not distinguish exemplar and abstracted representations. Instead what distinguishes them is information storage. As defined earlier, exemplar memories are distributed data structures that typically receive little if any revision once stored; whereas abstractions are centralized data structures that receive constant revision. Consequently, the 3-tuples in A_4 have different theoretical properties than the exemplar memories in E_3. Although these two representations contain the same information, they store it in fundamentally different manners.

What about empirical distinguishability? Can we determine from behavioral data whether people store category information in exemplar memories or abstractions? First, consider categorization decisions. If we ignore how long a model takes to produce a particular decision, we can always find one exemplar model and one abstraction model that predict the same decisions. Because both models potentially have the same information at their disposal, they can produce identical responses, given appropriate processing assumptions. If data reject a particular abstraction model and support a particular exemplar model, we can always adopt an ideal abstraction model with the processes of the exemplar model to account for the data. We can make a similar move to handle a rejected exemplar model. On the basis of decision data, we can never rule out the entire class of models that uses exemplar representations, nor can we ever rule out the entire class of models that uses abstracted representations.

Can reaction time data distinguish whether people use exemplar or abstracted representations? It is not unreasonable to believe so. For example, exemplar models required to construct abstractions at retrieval might be expected to produce judgments more slowly than models that construct these abstractions at encoding. But consider the wide variety of processing architectures and operations available for use in conjunction with a particular representation. If we assume that an exemplar model has unlimited capacity for computing abstractions in parallel, then distinguishing this model from one that computes abstractions at encoding may be difficult, if not impossible. It would not be at all surprising if exemplar and abstraction models turn out to be indistinguishable with respect to reaction time as well. Without knowing the entire space of processing architectures and operations, this conjecture is impossible to prove deductively. But given previous experience with indistinguishability in other areas of cognitive science, the induction that reaction time will not be diagnostic is reasonable.

Equivalence Following Information Loss

If we discover that humans do lose information in certain ways, exemplar and abstraction models can both represent the loss observed. Because a form of each model can start with all the original information, any information loss in one can be mimicked in the other. For example, imagine that people experience exemplars, each having four properties, and integrate this information into an ideal abstracted representation. Further imagine that, after increasing delays, people lose information about 4-tuples, then 3-tuples, and then 2-tuples, until they are only left with information about 1-tuples. An ideal exemplar model can account for this by decomposing the original exemplars into 3-tuples after some delay, by then decomposing the 3-tuples into 2-tuples after a longer delay, and by then decomposing the 2-tuples into 1-tuples after further delay. Or imagine that properties have a random probability of being deleted from exemplar representations over time. An abstraction model can mimic this by randomly lowering the frequency count of n-tuples by 1 in an appropriate manner. For example, randomly deleting a from an abg exemplar could be mimicked by randomly picking a 3-tuple (which turns out to be abg), randomly picking one of its properties (which turns out to be a), and then lowering the frequencies of the a, ab, ag, bg, and abg n-tuples by 1.

The Role of Process in Revealing Representation

As described earlier, we can never observe a representation directly. Instead we can only observe a representation through processes that operate on it. As stated by Douglas Medin, "There are no free peeks at representation" (personal communication, January 1989). It is useful to reevaluate ideal exemplar and abstraction models in this regard. Even though a model of either type stores all original exemplar information, the information that controls later performance depends on the model's processing assumptions. To see this more concretely, consider six possible processing environments in which an ideal exemplar representation could exist (similar possibilities exist for abstraction).

Unique Access.   An exemplar being categorized retrieves *all* previous memories of that exemplar and *only* memories of that exemplar. This processing environment insures perfect memory of exemplar information and may provide a good "peek" at representation. However, it has major limitations, such as not allowing categorization of novel exemplars (i.e., a novel exemplar retrieves no memories). Furthermore, extensive data on poor exemplar recognition cast much doubt on unique access (cf. Medin, 1986).

Partial Matching.   An exemplar being categorized retrieves, not only previous memories of itself, but also memories of similar exemplars. Similar memories are retrieved because they partially match the exemplar being categorized. Partial matching has benefits, such as enabling the classification of novel exemplars (e.g., a novel exemplar is classified by analogy with the most similar exemplars in memory). But it also has costs, such as making it difficult to determine whether an exemplar is old or new (e.g., a novel exemplar similar to many old exemplars may retrieve many exemplar memories, making it seem old).

Partial Retrieval.   An exemplar being categorized only retrieves fragments of exemplars. The missing parts of exemplars remain in storage but are inaccessible, due to factors that produce retrieval failure (e.g., Crowder, 1976). As a result, we only obtain a partial "peek" at exemplar information.

Reconstruction.   An exemplar being categorized causes exemplar memories to be reconstructed on the basis of other knowledge in memory, such that retrieved memories contain information not originally stored in them (e.g., Bartlett, 1932). Reconstruction thereby produces a distorted "peek" at exemplar information in memory.

Retrieval Failure.   An exemplar being categorized fails to activate previous memories of itself. These memories remain in storage but are inaccessible due to retrieval failure. As a result, the currently encoded exemplar fails to provide a "peek" at memory.

Abstraction at Retrieval.   An exemplar being categorized causes an abstraction of several exemplars to be constructed. Instead of being utilized as individual units, exemplar memories are transformed into a single abstraction that does not correspond completely to any one exemplar (e.g., Hintzman, 1986; Kahneman & Miller, 1986). As a result, our "peeks" at exemplar information produce abstractions.

To the extent that a processing environment exhibits partial matching, partial retrieval, reconstruction, retrieval failure, and abstraction at retrieval, the output of a model increasingly diverges from information in memory. Because most cognitive theorists assume the presence of such mechanisms in humans, we face much difficulty in identifying representations. We can only observe information in a representation if cognitive processes allow us to see it. Moreover, we only observe that information in a form produced by those processes. All category information ever encountered may be stored in memory. But much of it may be unobservable or transformed, given the processing environment.

This state of affairs compounds the difficulty of determining whether people store category knowledge as exemplar memories or as abstractions. Information could be stored in one form, but the processing environment could filter, distort, and transform it so much that identifying the underlying representation is impossible.

GENERAL CLASSES OF EXEMPLAR
AND ABSTRACTION MODELS

The ideal models described in the previous section provide two extreme forms of category learning. However, a wide variety of additional models exist, as defined by the dimensions of information storage described earlier (i.e., information duplication, revision, and loss). Four general classes constitute the most useful parts of this space: permanent trace models, revisable trace models, cumulative abstraction models, and reductive abstraction models. As we shall see, the overlapping characteristics of the representations in these models make it difficult to sharply distinguish exemplar and abstracted representations. Moreover, given the tremendous variety of possible processing assumptions, identifying which representation underlies human performance is indeed difficult if not impossible.[4]

Permanent Trace Models

One class of exemplar models assumes that every processing episode stores a memory trace, which does not necessarily have to be a perfect record of the objective event. These models further assume that once a memory trace is established, it is never revised. Instead each subsequent processing of the trace, or of the exemplar that produced it, results in an additional trace but leaves the original trace intact. Loftus and Loftus (1980) found that 84% of the psychologists they sampled held this view. As discussed by Nosofsky (1988), one possible interpretation of the exemplar representation in Medin and Schaffer's (1978) context model is as permanent traces. All of the models in Estes (1986) assume permanent traces (cf. p. 504). The presence of permanent traces remains the object of much debate and research (e.g., Bekerian & Bowers, 1983; McCloskey & Zaragoza, 1985).

In general, permanent trace models store each exemplar as an independent representation in long-term memory. If the same property occurs in multiple exemplars, duplications of it are distributed across exemplar traces. Although traces are retrieved to support processing, they are not revised and therefore do not suffer intentional information loss. If abstractions are required at some point in processing, exemplar traces can be retrieved to support the necessary computations. In exemplar-only models, these abstractions are not stored. In mixed models, they are stored such that long-term memory contains both exemplars and abstractions. Abstractions in these models may then be treated similarly to exemplars (i.e., they may be duplicated and never revised); or they may be treated as in abstraction models (i.e., they may become centralized and heavily revised).

An important variant of permanent trace models assumes that exemplar traces are subject to incidental information loss. Incidental processes such as interference and decay may cause information about entire exemplars or parts of exemplars to degenerate. Such processes may similarly decrease the accessibility of exemplars or parts of exemplars, even though the information is not completely lost (Hintzman, 1986).

---

[4]By no means is this the only way to taxonomize models of category learning (cf. Estes, 1986; Hayes-Roth & Hayes-Roth, 1977; Reed, 1972; Smith & Medin, 1981).

Revisable Trace Models

In revisable trace models, the contents of an exemplar trace may be intentionally modified by adding and/or deleting properties. Once the trace is returned to memory, information about the original exemplar is lost (e.g., Loftus, 1975; Loftus & Loftus, 1980). Revising a trace in this manner is similar to updating centralized properties in an abstraction: When information is revised, its form prior to revision no longer exists. If both the prior and revised forms are stored, then the model is a permanent trace model.

Like permanent trace models, revisable trace models exhibit information duplication, because a property may be duplicated across traces. But like abstracted representations, revisable traces exhibit intentional information revision. With sufficient processing, a frequently revised trace could become a centralized information structure, much like an abstraction.

Cumulative Abstraction Models

Cumulative abstraction models generally exhibit revision of nonduplicated information: If the same property or combination of properties occurs across exemplars, centralized property information is revised. More specifically, frequencies of n-tuples are revised after each new exemplar, such that frequency information accumulates for properties and/or property combinations. Within this general class of models, many variations are possible. As described earlier, cumulative models are ideal if they store complete information about property cooccurrence (e.g., A_4 in Fig. 2.3). More specifically, ideal cumulative models store the highest-order n-tuples available—what will be referred to as *cardinal n-tuples*. For example, if all exemplars have three properties, then the cardinal n-tuples are 3-tuples. If cardinal n-tuples are stored and distinguishable, all exemplar information is available.[5]

Perhaps the best known model that uses cumulative abstraction is the modal prototype model. This model is the one most often tested and rejected by exemplar theorists (e.g., Medin & Schaffer, 1978). It assumes that an exemplar is represented by a set of attribute values, such as values for *color, shape,* and *size.* For example, an exemplar might be *green, oval,* and *small.* Frequencies of values across exemplars are maintained, at least initially. However, the abstraction (prototype) that is eventually produced and that controls all subsequent processing contains only the modal value for each attribute. Consequently, modal pro-

---

[5]In the literature, cumulative abstraction models are often referred to as "frequency" and "power set" models. Interestingly, some forms of these abstraction models exhibit information duplication, contrary to my definition of abstracted representation (e.g., Hayes-Roth & Hayes-Roth, 1977; Reitman & Bower, 1973). In these cases, a property is often duplicated in different n-tuples (e.g., a in the n-tuples for *ab, abc,* and *ace*). This is one of several cases in this section where the distinction between exemplar and abstracted representations becomes blurred.

totype models initially track frequency information for all 1-tuples but then discard most of it, once the most frequent value for each attribute is identified. In addition, modal prototype models don't record cooccurrence information. The clear rejection of these models in recent studies demonstrates that people do not discard all idiosyncratic and cooccurrence information. As we have seen, however, models that use other abstracted representations, such as A_4, do record these two types of information and are therefore not rejected by these findings.

A wide variety of cumulative abstraction models can be gradually constructed by adding additional assumptions to modal prototype models. First, models can store increasing amounts of information about independent property frequency. The frequencies of all characteristic properties—not just modal properties—could be stored, as could the frequencies of all idiosyncratic properties. Second, models can store increasing amounts of cooccurrence information. Minimally, pairwise cooccurrence could be included, as represented by 2-tuple frequency (e.g., A_5 in Fig. 2.4). Frequencies of higher-order n-tuples could be added gradually to construct models that store greater amounts of cooccurrence information (e.g., A_4 in Fig. 2.4). Once the storage of cardinal n-tuples occurs, the abstraction becomes ideal.

An interesting model—the *cardinal cumulative model*—only stores the frequencies of cardinal n-tuples and not the frequencies of lower-order n-tuples. For example, if all exemplars have three properties, then only information about 3-tuples is stored—not information about 1-tuples or 2-tuples. This model corresponds to the right side of A_4 in Fig. 2.4, after removing the information about 2-tuples and 1-tuples. This model only abstracts at the level of exemplars—abstractions for 1-tuples and 2-tuples are not computed. Of course, one might wish to add a processor that could compute additional abstractions if needed later. Because all information about original exemplars is stored, cardinal cumulative models are ideal. They are also much more storage efficient than other ideal cumulative models, such as A_4.

Cumulative abstraction models, like exemplar models, may also lose information due to incidental degeneration. Incidental processes such as interference and decay may cause entire n-tuples or parts of n-tuples to degenerate. Such processes may similarly decrease the accessibility of n-tuples, or parts of n-tuples, even though the information is not completely lost.

Reductive Abstraction Models

Consider the revision of cumulative abstractions. Revision basically involves adding frequency to n-tuples. As each new exemplar is encoded, every relevant n-tuple being tracked is augmented by 1. Consequently, the revision of n-tuples does not lose information. Because each unit of frequency represents an exemplar, information about that n-tuple in the original exemplars can be reconstructed. Revision of an n-tuple loses none of the original exemplar information about it.

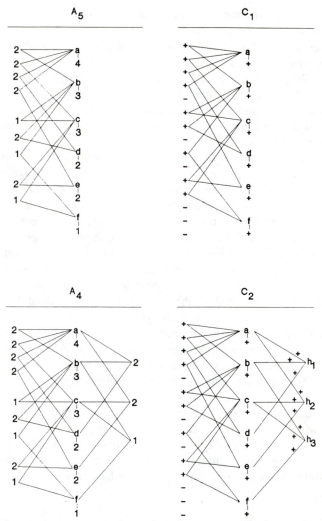

FIG. 2.4. C_1 represents a connectionist representation that captures cooccurrence information between pairs of properties, analogous to abstracted representation A_5. C_2 represents a connectionist representation with hidden units that captures higher-order cooccurrence information for 3-tuples, analogous to abstracted representation a_4.

In contrast, the revision of property information produces information loss in reductive abstraction models. For a given n-tuple, information across exemplars is combined in some way that produces useful category information but that loses information about exemplars. Perhaps the classic case is the average distance model. One way to view this model is in terms of a multidimensional space.

Imagine a category of colored circles varying on the dimensions of *size, bright-ness,* and *hue.* Each exemplar can be viewed as defining a point (vector) in the three-dimensional space defined by these dimensions. According to the average distance model, only the average vector across exemplars represents the catego-ry, namely, the point in the space that represents the average *size, brightness,* and *hue* of the circles. By computing the average vector and discarding exemplar information, this model loses information about the original exemplars. Of course, a model could store every exemplar as a point in the space, but then this would be an ideal exemplar model.

Each value on a dimension can be viewed as a 1-tuple (e.g., *blue* is a 1-tuple for *color*). A prototype can therefore be viewed as those 1-tuples that represent average values across exemplars on relevant dimensions. When a new exemplar is encoded, the revision that takes place on each average 1-tuple is to move it along its dimension toward the exemplar's value for that dimension. In other words, each new exemplar is averaged into the current prototype.

This type of revision differs fundamentally from the revision that occurs in cumulative abstraction models. In cumulative models, the revision of a 1-tuple simultaneously preserves information about individual exemplars while estab-lishing overall information about the category. Information about the number of exemplars containing the 1-tuple is always available, because each unit of fre-quency represents an exemplar. In contrast, averaging 1-tuples loses information about the number of exemplars sharing a given 1-tuple. All that remains is the average. In this regard, average distance models produce reductive abstractions, because revision reduces units of exemplar information to some more distilled form.

Theorists have proposed a wide variety of models that produce reductive abstractions (e.g., Estes, 1986; Hayes-Roth & Hayes-Roth, 1977; Reed, 1972; Smith & Medin, 1981). For the most part, these models either reduce information by transforming frequency information into averages or probabilities (e.g., cue validities). In all cases, information is lost through the transformation of frequen-cy units.

Connectionist Models.   In nearly all previous cases, reductive abstraction models only track 1-tuples, failing to record cooccurrence information. These models typically do not compute averages or probabilities for higher-order *n*-tu-ples. What distinguishes connectionist models from previous reductive models is that connectionist models store cooccurrence information. But in the process of reducing cooccurrence information, connectionist models lose information, which distinguishes them from cumulative models that track cooccurrence.

Figure 2.4 shows how connectionist models store cooccurrence information but reduce it in the process. To see this, first consider A_5, which represents exemplars e_6 through e_{10} in Fig. 2.2. A_5 is a cumulative abstraction that contains information about 1-tuples and 2-tuples. Information about 3-tuples, and there-fore about the original exemplars, has been lost. Now consider representation C_1

in Fig. 2.4, which is a simple connectionist representation. The pluses and minuses to the left represent positive and negative correlations between pairs of properties. The pluses below the properties represent positive correlations between the properties and the category label (not shown).

Like A_5, C_1 tracks information about 1-tuples (correlations between a property and the category) and 2-tuples (correlations between pairs of properties). But whereas A_5 contains complete information about these n-tuples, C_1 has lost information about their absolute frequency. C_1 reduces frequency information to update correlations between pairs of properties, representing these correlations as weights. To the extent that one property is diagnostic of another, their weight becomes positive. To the extent that one property predicts the absence of another, their weight becomes negative.

Next consider representations A_4 and C_2 in Fig. 2.4. A_4 is the ideal cumulative abstraction discussed earlier. Information about every n-tuple has been recorded, and no information has been lost. C_2 is a connectionist representation with hidden units h_1 through h_3.[6] Hidden units allow a connectionist model to store information about complex correlations between properties. Whereas connectionist models without hidden units can only store information about 2-tuples, connectionist models with hidden units can store information about 3-tuples, 4-tuples, etc., depending on the number of initial units that hidden units integrate.

A connectionist model with sufficient hidden units can record correlations for all possible n-tuples across exemplars, analogous to an ideal cumulative model. However, these connectionist models still lose information. Because the weights that represent n-tuples are essentially correlations, it is impossible to reconstruct the original exemplars. Such reconstruction is possible only if absolute frequencies are preserved, as in ideal cumulative models. Connectionist models also lose information through incidental degeneration. Interference and decay typically drive the weights in these models toward zero over time and experience.[7]

Perhaps most unique to connectionist models are the learning rules they use to integrate exemplar information into connection weights (see Gluck & Bower, 1988, for discussion). These rules go far beyond the methods of reduction previously employed in abstraction models. Connectionist models also represent

---

[6]To simplify presentation, inhibitory links between properties and hidden units are not shown in C_2. However, the reader should assume that paths with negative weights connect all properties and hidden units that are not shown connected.

[7]Connectionist models may also lose information in a more severe manner when representing multiple categories. Imagine that the correlation between properties a and b is positive for category X but equally negative for category Y. Across categories, the correlation is therefore 0, assuming equally sized categories and comparable learning sequences. Nonoptimal information about the correlation with respect to each category is stored because the same correlational weight, 0, is used for both categories. This problem can be eliminated by using hidden units that associate particular values of a correlation with particular categories. For example, hidden units that represent a positive correlation between a and b could be associated with category X; whereas hidden units that represent a negative correlation could be associated with category Y. A similar problem exists for cumulative abstraction models, in that a given n-tuple needs to be indexed for each category in which it occurs.

negative correlations between properties explicitly, whereas previous abstraction models have not. However, cumulative abstraction models could probably utilize connectionist learning rules in some form, and they contain the requisite information for producing information about negative correlations.

An interesting limit on connectionist representations may be a difficulty in supporting frequency estimates (e.g., Hasher & Zacks, 1979; Hintzman, 1976). Although connectionist models readily support probability estimates (Gluck & Bower, 1988), it is not clear how they would support estimates of absolute frequency (J. Jonides, personal communication, November, 1988). Moreover, an initial attempt to represent absolute frequency in a connectionist model has met with difficulty (F. T. Durso & T. Dayton, personal communication, November 1988). Because connectionist models reduce frequency information to obtain correlational weights, these models lose information about how often exemplars and n-tuples occur. Traditional reductive representations, such as in the average distance model, also have difficulty producing frequency estimates, given all exemplar information is lost in the process of computing averages or probabilities. In contrast, exemplar representations and cumulative abstractions readily support frequency estimates of how many times a particular exemplar occurred and how many exemplars possessed a particular property.

DEVELOPING THEORIES OF CATEGORY LEARNING

If we cannot determine whether people represent categories with exemplars or abstractions, then what have we learned from years of research on category learning? Clearly we have developed an impressive store of empirical facts about category learning. Some of these are of substantial importance in understanding human knowledge. For example, people use idiosyncratic information about exemplars in categorization decisions; people use cooccurrence information in categorization decisions; people do not represent categories with static representations but instead represent them dynamically. Certainly many other important findings have been established as well (for reviews, see Mervis & Rosch, 1981; Medin & Smith, 1984; Oden, 1987; Smith & Medin, 1981).

As I have argued, we can not say whether category knowledge is distributed in exemplars or centralized in abstractions. But we do know that any account of knowledge that excludes idiosyncratic information, cooccurrence information, or dynamic representation is inadequate. Consequently, the classical theories of knowledge that have dominated philosophy, linguistics, psychology, and computer science for years are probably wrong (Smith & Medin, 1981). Many theorists now believe that the large body of evidence developed from the study of category learning has clearly rejected this position. Similarly, we have rejected large classes of exemplar and abstraction models that are insensitive to idiosyncratic and cooccurrence information (Medin & Schaffer, 1978).

How should we proceed in developing models of category learning? If we can develop models with either exemplar or abstracted representations, which should we chose? One tack is to pursue models that stimulate new research. At one time, prototype models were highly stimulating in this regard, generating numerous lines of productive inquiry. More recently, exemplar models have played this role. We should certainly encourage any model that inspires empirical and theoretical progress.

A second tack is to favor models whose assumptions seem most plausible. As noted by Lee Brooks, "the game is to produce a sufficiently peculiar pattern of data" such that the "opposition is forced into considerable contortions to accommodate it," where "the special assumptions they have to invent do no other useful work . . . in the current research context" (personal communication, January 1989). Because exemplar and abstraction models both have sizable followings, it is not clear that either model has an advantage in this regard. Perhaps future research will produce a greater consensus.

A third tack is to develop the space of category learning models (e.g., Estes, 1986). Formal analyses are often productive in identifying new models of interest and in determining whether models are empirically distinguishable. Much development of learning models remains to be done. Hopefully, such development will direct effort toward issues that are resolvable and away from those that are not.

A fourth tack is to look for guidance outside the category learning literature. One possibility is theory from other areas of cognitive psychology. What assumptions about representation best serve perception, attention, memory, language, problem solving, and reasoning? Findings and theory from these areas may suggest one type of representation over another. A second source of outside constraint is computational efficiency. From implementing different representations on various types of artificial hardware, we may find that one type of representation is computationally more tractable than another. A third source of outside constraint in neuroscience. At some point, we may develop neurological evidence for particular forms of representation.

Clearly, numerous possibilities exist for future research. As I have argued here, however, one must observe caution in making claims about representation. Because exemplar and abstracted representations can potentially represent the same information, and because we can only observe representation through processing, concluding that people use one representation and not another is difficult, if not impossible. Instead our empirical efforts can only support and reject particular models, namely, representation-process pairs.

ACKNOWLEDGEMENTS

Work on this manuscript was supported by National Science Foundation Grant IRI-8609187 and Army Research Institute Contract MD A903-86-C-0172. I am particularly grateful to Douglas Medin for ongoing discussion of this topic and for extensive comments on previous drafts, all of which have had a major impact on this paper. I am also grateful to Brian Ross, Lee Brooks, Mark Gluck, Joel Martin, and David Meyer for helpful comments. None of these colleagues necessarily agrees with any particular point herein. Nor are they responsible for any errors that may remain. Work on this paper was performed while the author was a visitor at the University of Michigan. Address correspondence to Lawrence W. Barsalou, School of Psychology, Georgia Institute of Technology, Atlanta, GA 30332.

REFERENCES

Anderson, J. R. (1978). Arguments concerning representations for mental imagery. *Psychological Review, 85,* 249–277.

Barsalou. L. W. (1987). The instability of graded structure: Implications for the nature of concepts. In U. Neisser (Ed.), *Concepts and conceptual development: Ecological and intellectual factors in categorization* (pp. 101–140). New York: Cambridge University Press.

Barsalou, L. W. (1989). Intra-concept similarity and its implications for inter-concept similarity. In S. Vosniadou & A. Ortony (Eds.), *Similarity and analogical reasoning.* New York: Cambridge University Press.

Bartlett, F. C. (1932). *Remembering: A study in experimental and social psychology.* Cambridge, England: Cambridge University Press.

Bekerian, D. A., & Bowers, J. M. (1983). Eyewitness testimony: Were we misled? *Journal of Experimental Psychology: Learning, Memory, and Cognition, 9,* 139–145.

Billman, D. O., & Heit, E. (1988). Observational learning from internal feedback: A simulation of an adaptive learning method. *Cognitive Science, 12,* 587–626.

Bourne, L. E., Jr. (1966). *Human conceptual behavior.* Boston: Allyn and Bacon.

Bransford, J. D., & Franks, J. J. (1971). The abstraction of linguistic ideas. *Cognitive Psychology, 2,* 331–350.

Brooks, L. (1978). Nonanalytic concept formation and memory for instances. In E. Rosch & B. B. Lloyd (Eds.), *Cognition and categorization.* Hillsdale, NJ: Lawrence Erlbaum Associates.

Bruner, J. S., Goodnow, J., & Austin, G. (1956). *A study of thinking.* New York: Wiley.

Crowder, R. G. (1976). *Principles of learning and memory.* Hillsdale, NJ: Lawrence Erlbaum Associates.

Elio, R., & Anderson, J. R. (1981). Effects of generalizations and instance similarity in schema abstraction. *Journal of Experimental Psychology: Learning, Memory, and Cognition, 7,* 397–417.

Estes, W. K. (1986). Array models for category learning. *Cognitive Psychology, 18,* 500–549.

Franks, J. J., & Bransford, J. D. (1971). Abstraction of visual patterns. *Journal of Experimental Psychology, 90,* 64–74.

Gluck, M. A., & Bower, G. H. (1988). Evaluating an adaptive network model of human learning. *Journal of Memory and Language, 27,* 166–195.

Hasher, L., & Zacks, R. T. (1979). Automatic and effortful processes in memory. *Journal of Experimental Psychology: General, 108,* 356–388.

Hayes-Roth, B., & Hayes-Roth, F. (1977). Concept learning and the recognition and classification of exemplars. *Journal of Verbal Learning and Verbal Behavior, 16,* 321–338.

Hintzman, D. L. (1976). Repetition and memory: In G. H. Bower (Ed.), The psychology of learning and motivation (Vol. 10). New York: Academic Press.

Hintzman, D. L. (1986). "Schema abstraction" in a multiple-trace memory model. *Psychological Review, 93,* 411–428.

Kahneman, D., & Miller, D. T. (1986). Norm theory: Comparing reality to its alternatives. *Psychological Review, 93,* 136–153.

Koh, K. (1989). *Induction of continuous stimulus-response relations.* Unpublished doctoral dissertation. University of Michigan.

Koh, K., & Meyer, D. E. (1989). *Induction of continuous stimulus-response relations. Proceedings of the eleventh annual conference of the Cognitive Science Society.* Hillsdale NJ: Lawrence Erlbaum Associates.

Loftus, E. F. (1975). Leading questions and the eyewitness report. *Cognitive Psychology, 7,* 560–572.

Loftus, E. F., & Loftus, G. R. (1980). On the permanence of stored information in the brain. *American Psychologist, 35,* 409–420.

McClelland, J. L., & Rumelhart, D. E. (1985). Distributed memory and the representation of general and specific information. *Journal of Experimental Psychology: General, 114,* 159–188.

McCloskey, M., & Zaragoza, M. (1985). Misleading postevent information and memory for events: Arguments and evidence against memory impairment hypotheses. *Journal of Experimental Psychology: General, 114,* 1–16.

Medin, D. L. (1986). Comment on "Memory storage and retrieval processes in category learning." *Journal of Experimental Psychology: General, 115,* 373–381.

Medin, D. L., & Schaffer, M. (1978). A context theory of classification learning. *Psychological Review, 85,* 207–238.

Medin, D. L., & Schwanenflugel, P. L. (1981). Linear separability in classification learning. *Journal of Experimental Psychology: Learning, Memory, and Cognition, 7,* 355–368.

Medin, D. L., & Smith, E. E. (1984). Concepts and concept formation. *Annual Review of Psychology, 35,* 113–138.

Mervis, C. B., & Rosch, E. (1981). Categorization of natural object. *Annual Review of Psychology, 32,* 89–115.

Miller, G. A. (1956). The magical number seven plus or minus two: Some limits on our capacity for processing information. *Psychological Review, 63,* 81–97.

Murphy, G. L., & Medin, D. L. (1985). The role of theories in conceptual coherence. *Psychological Review, 92,* 289–316.

Neumann, P. G. (1974). An attribute frequency model for the abstraction of prototypes. *Memory & Cognition, 2,* 241–248.

Nosofsky, R. M. (1988). Similarity, frequency, and category representation. *Journal of Experimental Psychology: Learning, Memory, and Cognition, 14,* 54–65.

Oden, G. C. (1987). Concept, knowledge, thought. *Annual Review of Psychology, 38,* 203–227.

Palmer, S. E. (1978). Fundamental aspects of cognitive representation. In E. Rosch & B. B. Lloyd (Eds.), *Cognition and categorization* (pp. 259–303). Hillsdale, NJ: Lawrence Erlbaum Associates.

Posner, M. I., & Keele, S. W. (1968). On the genesis of abstract ideas. *Journal of Experimental Psychology, 77,* 353–363.

Posner, M. I., & Keele, S. W. (1970). Retention of abstract ideas. *Journal of Experimental Psychology, 83,* 304–308.

Rescorla, R. A., & Wagner, A. R. (1972). A theory of Pavlovian conditioning: Variations in the effectiveness of reinforcement and non-reinforcement. In A. H. Black & W. F. Prokasy (Eds.), *Classical conditioning: II. Current research and theory.* New York: Appleton-Century-Crofts.

Reed, S. K. (1972). Pattern recognition and categorization. *Cognitive Psychology, 3,* 382–407.

Reitman, J. S., & Bower, G. H. (1973). Storage and later recognition of exemplars of concepts. *Cognitive Psychology, 4,* 194–206.

Rosch, E., & Mervis, C. B. (1975). Family resemblance studies in the internal structure of categories. *Cognitive Psychology, 7,* 573–605.

Smith, E. E., & Medin, D. L. (1981). *Categories and concepts.* Cambridge, MA: Harvard University Press.

Smith, E. E., Shoben, E. J., & Rips, L. J. (1974). Structure and process in semantic memory: A featural model for semantic decisions. *Psychological Review, 81,* 214–241.

Trabasso, T., & Bower, G. H. (1968). *Attention in learning: Theory and research.* New York: Wiley.

Winograd, T. (1975). Frame representations and the declarative/procedural controversy. In D. G. Bobrow & A. M. Collins, *Representation and understanding: Studies in cognitive science* (pp. 185–210). New York: Academic Press.

3 Cognitive Signatures and Their Forgery

John N. Bassili
University of Toronto, Scarborough Campus

Smith makes the interesting suggestion that cognitive processes have signatures that can be used for their positive identification. This is a seductive idea, and Smith goes a long way towards demonstrating its validity. Still, going a long way is not the same as going all the way, especially when seduction is at issue. The gist of my commentary is that it is premature to speak of cognitive signatures in social cognition because the results we strive to explain are usually open to several alternative explanations.

At the heart of Smith's paper is the methodological principle of specificity, which focuses on the effects of prior experiences on later performance. The argument is that cognitive mediators can be identified by their pattern of specificity on a number of dimensions (content, process, context and time). Three types of cognitive mediators receive particular attention in the paper, those based on: (a) abstract knowledge structures, (b) exemplars, and (c) procedures. The thrust of Smith's paper is that theorists in social cognition may have paid far too much heed to the power of abstract knowledge structures in explaining social phenomena. Instead, the argument goes, phenomena that have been attributed to abstract knowledge structures in the past can be accommodated by exemplar-based and procedural representations. Moreover, the patterns of specificity revealed by relevant data seem to bear the signatures of these latter mediators rather than that of the former.

My commentary focuses on the parts of Smith's argument having to do with the role of productions in social cognition. Because I have recently been working on a model of the relationship between implicit and explicit memory that is relevant to data collected by Smith and Branscombe (1988), my discussion is organized around the interpretation of these data.

THE EXPLICIT-IMPLICIT MEMORY DISTINCTION

To illustrate the dangers in assuming that patterns of results stand in simple one-to-one relations with cognitive processes as is implied by the notion of "signature," I will focus on the research that Smith and his colleagues have done on category accessibility effects (Smith & Branscombe, 1987, 1988). Recently, Colin MacLeod and I (MacLeod & Bassili, 1989) have proposed an account of the distinction between implicit and explicit memory that provides an interesting alternative to the process view espoused by Smith (see also Roediger & Blaxton, 1987; Roediger, Weldon, & Challis, 1989).

In explicit tests of memory, such as recall or recognition, subjects deliberately attempt to recollect previously learned information. In implicit tests of memory, however, the memory task is not, from the point of the subject, related to a prior episode. For example, one common implicit test of memory requires that subjects complete word fragments without awareness of the fact that many of the fragmented words had previously appeared in a study list.

Some interesting dissociations have appeared in the results of explicit and implicit memory tests. For example, it has typically been found that implicit tests are quite sensitive to the match between study and test modality whereas explicit tests are not (e.g., Bassili, Smith, & MacLeod, 1989; Graf, Shimamura, & Squire, 1985; Kirsner, Milech, & Standen, 1983; Roediger & Blaxton, 1987). At the same time, other variables, such as levels of processing, have been found to have strong effects on explicit test performance but not on implicit test performance (e.g., Graf & Mandler, 1984; Graf, Mandler, & Haden, 1982). Results such as these have prompted efforts to explore differences in the memory mechanisms underlying implicit and explicit test performance.

The Procedural View

A processing view espoused by Roediger and his colleagues (Roediger & Blaxton, 1987; Roediger, Weldon, & Challis, 1989) has enjoyed particular popularity in these deliberations. The basic notion is that information that is encoded via a particular process can be retrieved most effectively by the same or a similar process. This view relies heavily on the distinction between conceptually driven versus data driven processes. According to Roediger and his colleagues, explicit tests involve processes that are primarily conceptually driven whereas implicit tests tend to rely on data driven processes. As a result, manipulations that promote conceptual processing at encoding tend to affect explicit memory tests whereas manipulations that promote data driven processing tend to affect implicit memory tests.

Smith seems to be in general agreement with Roediger's processing view, although his account of implicit and explicit test results is somewhat simpler. For Smith, priming often reflects the strengthening of particular productions. For example, generating traits from behaviors is believed to strengthen behavior-to-trait inference productions whereas reading trait words is believed to strengthen letter-to-word productions. Subjects who have had practice at inferring a trait from behavior, therefore, should be more likely to infer that trait from behavior in the future, while subjects who have had practice at reading a trait word should subsequently have an easier time generating the word from its constituent letters.

It should be noted in passing that Smith's position owes more to Anderson's ACT* theory than to Roediger's process view. This is because the processing view advanced by Roediger and his colleagues relies primarily on the qualitative match between encoding and retrieval operations in memory, whereas Eliot Smith's position is premised on a quantitative notion of procedural strength. It is unfortunate that Smith straddles the two conceptual positions freely because the positions differ in important ways and the memory literature has treated them as distinct. For example, in important reviews of the implicit/explicit memory literature, Schacter (1987) as well as Richardson-Klavehn and Bjork (1988) have assigned the approaches taken by Anderson and by Roediger to different categories of their classification schemes.

Issues of conceptual classification aside, Smith has collected compelling data to support his point of view. The results of the experiment with Branscombe (Smith & Branscombe, 1988) is a case in point. Because these results seem to bear the undeniable signature of procedural strengthening, it would be instructive to explore how they can be accommodated by distinctly different theoretical positions.

Subjects in the Smith and Branscombe (1988) experiment studied trait adjectives either by reading them or by generating them from three behaviors and a letter cue. They were then given three memory tests consisting of the free recall of the traits, a word-fragment completion test involving traits from which letters had been deleted, and a category accessibility test where subjects had to supply a trait implied by an ambiguous sentence. Not surprisingly, words were recalled better when they had initially been generated than when they had been read (cf. Slamecka & Graf, 1978). Also not surprisingly, word-fragment completion performance was superior when words had been read than when they had been generated (cf. Roediger et al., 1989). What is new and interesting in the Smith and Branscombe (1988) study is that performance in the category accessibility test was superior when words had been generated than when they had been read. Smith accounts for these results by pointing out that performance on each test benefitted from the strengthening during study of productions relevant to that test. Before getting into the details of this claim let us consider a different theoretical position that can also account for the results.

A Modified Activation Account

The view Colin MacLeod and I have taken is related to arguments put forth by Graf and Mandler (1984). Specifically, we focus on two elements, one relating to properties of the memory representation that results from encoding operations, and the other relating to the search processes responsible for retrieval. In line with Anderson's (1983) associative model of memory, we assume that information is represented in terms of nodes, representing items of information, and of associations between these nodes. We further assume that two factors are relevant to the retrievability of information represented in nodes. The first factor consists of the level of activation of the node; the second consists of the collective strength of the associations between the node and other nodes with which it is linked. Our account is premised on the notion that these two factors are tapped differentially by test conditions associated with implicit and explicit memory tasks.

To clarify, consider first the nature of node-specific activation. Our account borrows heavily from Morton's logogen model (Jackson & Morton, 1984) where memory for verbal material is made up of logogens (or nodes). For the purpose of the present discussion, logogens will correspond to items of information such as traits. Following Morton's model, it is assumed that each logogen collects evidence that a specific item of information has been encountered. Then, when the evidence exceeds a threshold value, the logogen fires. This feature of the account further implies that logogens can always be characterized by a particular level of activation and that the readiness with which the item of information can be brought to mind depends on this level of activation. Also in line with Morton's model, we assume that logogens comprise modality-specific components that are linked independently to an abstract cognitive component.

The second feature of the representational system consists of associations among logogens. We assume that these associations are formed either as a result of elaborative processing that links studied items with relevant information in memory (e.g., Craik & Tulving, 1975), or as a result of the physical or conceptual structure of the acquisition list (Humphreys 1978; Hunt & Einstein, 1981). In keeping with associative theories of memory, we assume that the network of relations in which a memory item is embedded provides access routes for the retrieval of that item. The richer the network of relations, therefore, the easier it should be to access the relevant node.

The properties of the memory representations, as we have outlined them so far, cannot by themselves account for the findings that have been associated with implicit and explicit tests of memory. In our view, these findings can be accounted for by considering how the properties of the memory representation interact with retrieval mechanisms associated with each of the two types of tests. Specifically, we argue that explicit tests of memory rely primarily on the relational structure within which logogens are embedded whereas implicit tests rely primarily on the level of activation of logogens. There is a good reason for this: Explicit tests involve deliberate retrieval that is guided by a relevant episodic context whereas implicit tests do not.

We assume specifically that in an explicit memory test such as recall or recognition, the subject seeks to reach a particular destination in memory. The search process, therefore, is likely to rely heavily on the associative network containing the relevant item. Implicit memory tests like the word-fragment completion task are, by definition, nondeliberate. Retrieval, therefore, is unlikely to rely on associations developed at study because these associations are not known to be relevant to the task. For this reason, the main feature of the representational network that is useful to the task consists of the level of activation of logogens, most notably the relevant logogen.

The model just outlined can account for the important dissociations that have been observed between explicit and implicit memory test results. For example, the strong impact of the levels-of-processing manipulation on explicit tasks, coupled with its lack of effect on implicit tasks can be accounted for by the relevance of the manipulation to the relational aspect of the memory representation and its lack of impact on the level of activation of logogens. Similarly, the sensitivity of implicit tests to mismatches between study and test modalities and the immunity of explicit tests to such mismatches are also consistent with this account because logogens comprise modality-specific components, whereas associative links are modality-free.

Reconsidering: Category Accessibility as Implicit Memory

Results from the memory literature aside, it is interesting to explore how the present approach can account for the results reported by Smith and Branscombe (1988). There are three elements to these results, each consisting of the effect of the "generate" versus "read" manipulation on a particular type of memory test. Consider first free recall where performance for words that were generated was superior to performance for words that were read. The "strengthening of productions" aspect of Smith's approach does not make specific predictions here because recall is assumed to depend on declarative rather than on procedural knowledge. Our view, on the other hand, readily handles this finding because generating an item of information should result in more elaboration (and a richer set of associative links) than simply reading the item. The deliberate retrieval strategies involved in free recall, therefore, can be executed more effectively in richly interconnected networks.

Consider next the word-fragment completion test where performance for words that were read was superior to that for generated words. Smith argues that this difference results from the strengthening of "letter-to-word" productions that are involved in reading. Our account, instead, focuses on the activation of logogens representing the relevant words. As we saw earlier, logogens collect evidence that an item of information has been encountered and fire when a threshold value is attained. Superior performance for words that are read is thus expected because actual exposure to a word, especially in the same modality as the subsequent word-fragment test, provides a near optimal level of logogen activation in that modality.

The last result relates to the category accessibility test where subjects supplied a trait in response to an ambiguous sentence. The proportion of supplied traits that matched traits that had been implied earlier was higher in the "generate" than in the "read" condition. Smith attributes this result to the strengthening of behavior-to-trait inference productions during the initial trait generation task. Because the initial generation task and the subsequent category accessibility test share so much in common, the procedural interpretation seems obvious. The interpretation, however, hinges to a considerable degree on the assumption that subjects did not rely on deliberate retrieval strategies in the accessibility test. This assumption cannot be accepted uncritically. In particular, it is likely that subjects recognized that the ambiguous sentences shared elements of meaning with the unambiguous sentences seen earlier. In searching for an appropriate trait, therefore, subjects may have relied on the associative network linking the unambiguous sentences with generated traits. This network, of course, would have been more elaborate for generated word than for words that were read. Note that this interpretation does not require that subjects search specifically for previously generated traits. Mere reliance on the relevant associative network would produce the results that were observed.

DISCUSSION

Although the preceding discussion focuses on the data of a single experiment, it makes a broader point. The point is that not much has changed in experimental social psychology and that what may appear to one researcher as the signature of a particular process is likely to appear to another as the signature of a different one. Be that as it may, Smith's procedural approach is so comprehensive in its coverage of theory and data that it will probably win against competing accounts by sheer force of coherence and simplicity. Before conceding this point, however, I would like to elaborate on what I believe to be problems with the criteria that Smith has set out to test the relative merits of schematic and procedural approaches.

Instant Efficiency

Anderson's notion of proceduralization (e.g., Anderson, 1987) has always suggested to me a rather slow, laborious process that occurs over a long series of trials. The vast array of activities that have been shown to benefit from practice (Newell & Rosenbloom, 1981) speaks well for the flexibility of human skills. Unfortunately, these benefits tend to exact a substantial price in toil, manifesting themselves only gradually over long periods of practice. Yet Smith seems willing to accept as evidence of proceduralization results from studies where "practice" consists of very few trials (e.g., Fazio, Powell, & Herr, 1983; Fazio, Sanbonmatsu, Powell, & Kardes, 1986). To illustrate, consider Smith's interpretation of performance in the various conditions of the Smith and Branscombe (1988) study. Are we to assume that reading a word a single time is likely to strengthen noticeably the letter to word productions that are specifically relevant to that word? Similarly, are we to assume that generating a trait from three behaviors a single time is likely to strengthen noticeably the relevant behavior to trait inference productions? I find such assumptions difficult to accept, especially in the case of familiar traits and behaviors such as those used in Smith's research. I think that Smith should clarify his position on this matter and provide reasons for believing that significant procedural strengthening can occur so readily.

On the Specificity of Procedures

The notion of process specificity that Smith invokes to support his procedural view hinges on the identification of the productions that are involved in particular tasks. What are the productions involved in inferring traits from behavior, for example? The answer to this question is never provided in detail.

What is most troublesome is that there is an element of circularity in the logic used by Smith to identify productions. Ideally, Smith's theoretical approach should provide clear means for specifying whether tasks share or do not share productions. Once this has been established, it would be possible to generate predictions about the transfer of acquired efficiency from one task to the other. Unfortunately, Smith bases his predictions about the productions involved in various tasks on intuition rather than on theoretical criteria. Furthermore, instead of using empirical results to test independently derived predictions about the sharing of productions by various tasks, results are often used to determine whether the tasks do indeed share productions (see Smith & Lerner, 1986; Smith, Branscombe, & Bormann, 1988).

A good illustration of the difficulties inherent in the specification of productions comes from the first study reported by Smith et al. (1988). Subjects in this study made a series of judgments of the form "If I ⟨behavior⟩ you, am I ⟨trait⟩?" The nature of the behavior and of the trait was manipulated factorially so that each remained the same or changed across trials. What is interesting about this experiment is that the task in all experimental conditions required the application of productions for inferring traits from behaviors. According to the notion of procedural learning, therefore, there should have been an increase in efficiency (speedup in response time) over trials in all experimental conditions. The results, however, demonstrated that while speedups did occur when either behavior or trait remained constant, there was no speedup when both the behavior and the trait varied across trials. This finding can no doubt be accommodated by invoking concepts that are extraneous to Smith's theoretical position (the distinction between consistent and varied mapping, Shiffrin & Dumais, 1981, is undoubtedly relevant here) but this does not help with the task of evaluating Smith's claims about procedural learning. Instead Smith's position would benefit from still clearer rules for generating hypotheses to test his theoretical claims.

Conclusion

My main point is that there is still a fair bit of looseness in the mapping of empirical results onto conceptual explanations in social cognition. The notion of signature, in particular, may lead us prematurely into claiming to have identified the cognitive mediators of social phenomena without examining alternative mediators sufficiently. In making this point, I have focused particularly on phenomena relating to explicit and implicit memory. This is an area that has received much attention recently in cognitive psychology, and Smith has played a pivotal role in introducing it to social cognition. The fact that one can, as I have, take issue with specific features of Smith's account should not detract from what is globally a very strong theoretical position. I stressed earlier that Smith's position benefits from coherence and simplicity and these qualities may make it preferable to competing accounts. This is probably the strongest feature of the paper. There is also another feature of Smith's recent work that deserves mention and for which social cognition researchers should be grateful. Smith has recently taken a role of leadership in transposing to social psychology the latest developments in cognitive psychology. Exemplar-based representations, productions in Anderson's ACT*, and the notion of implicit memory all constitute important developments in cognitive psychology, and Smith has been masterful in integrating these developments in the context of social cognition. If we are to understand social behavior in terms of cognitive mechanisms, such efforts are crucial to our progress.

ACKNOWLEDGEMENTS

This work was facilitated by Social Sciences and Humanities Research Council of Canada Grant #410-88-0989. I wish to thank Colin MacLeod for his helpful comments.

REFERENCES

Anderson, J. R. (1983). *The architecture of cognition*. Cambridge, MA: Harvard University Press.
Anderson, J. R. (1987). Skill acquisition: Compilation of weak-method problem solutions. *Psychological Review, 94*, 192–210.
Bassili, N. J., Smith, M. C., & MacLeod, C. M. (1989). Auditory and visual word-stem completion: Separating data-driven and conceptually-driven processes. *Quarterly Journal of Experimental Psychology, 41A*, 439–453.
Craik, F. I. M., & Tulving, E. (1975). Depth of processing and the retention of words in episodic memory. *Journal of Experimental Psychology: General, 104*, 268–294.

Fazio, R. H., Powell, M. C., & Herr, P. M. (1983). Toward a process model of the attitude-behavior relation: Accessing one's attitude upon mere observation of the attitude object. *Journal of Personality and Social Psychology, 44,* 723–735.

Fazio, R. H., Sanbonmatsu, D. M., Powell, M. C., & Kardes, F. R. (1986). On the automatic activation of attitudes. *Journal of Personality and Social Psychology, 50,* 229–238.

Graf, P., & Mandler, G. (1984). Activation makes words more accessible but not necessarily more retrievable. *Journal of Verbal Learning and Verbal Behavior, 23,* 553–568.

Graf, P., Mandler, G., & Haden, P. (1982). Simulating amnesic symptoms in normal subjects. *Science, 218,* 1243–1244.

Graf, P., Shimamura, A. P., & Squire, L. R. (1985). Priming across modalities and priming across category levels: Extending the domain of preserved function in amnesia. *Journal of experimental Psychology: Learning, Memory, and Cognition, 11,* 385–395.

Humphreys, M. S. (1978). Item and relational information: A case for context independent retrieval. *Journal of Verbal Learning and Verbal Behavior, 17,* 175–188.

Hunt, R. R., & Einstein, G. O. (1981). Relational and item-specific information in memory. *Journal of Verbal Learning and Verbal Behavior, 20,* 497–514.

Jackson, A., & Morton, J. (1984). Facilitation of auditory word recognition. *Memory and Cognition, 12,* 568–574.

Kirsner, K., Milech, D., & Standen, P. (1983). Common and modality-specific processes in the mental lexicon. *Memory and Cognition, 11,* 621–630.

MacLeod, C. M., & Bassili, J. N. (1989). Are implicit and explicit tests differentially sensitive to item-specific versus relational information, In S. Lewandowsky, J. C. Dunn, & K. Kirsner (Eds.), *Implicit Memory: Theoretical issues* (pp. 159–172). Hillsdale, NJ: Lawrence Erlbaum Associates.

Newell, A., & Rosenbloom, P. S. (1981). Mechanisms of skill acquisition and the law of practice. In J. R. Anderson (Ed.), *Cognitive skills and their acquisition* (pp. 1–56). Hillsdale, NJ: Lawrence Erlbaum Associates.

Richardson-Klavehn, A., & Bjork, R. A. (1988). Measures of memory. *Annual Review of Psychology, 39,* 475–543.

Roediger, H. L., III, & Blaxton, T. A. (1987). Retrieval modes produce dissociations in memory for surface information. In D. S. Gorfein & R. R. Hoffman (Eds.), *Memory and cognitive processes: The Ebbinghaus centennial conference.* Hillsdale, NJ: Lawrence Erlbaum Associates.

Roediger, H. L., III, Weldon, M. S., & Challis, B. H. (1989). Explaining dissociations between implicit and explicit measures of retention: A processing account. In H. L. Roediger, III & F. I. M. Craik (Eds.), *Varieties of memory and consciousness: Essays in honour of Endel Tulving.* (pp. 3–41). Hillsdale, NJ: Lawrence Erlbaum Associates.

Schacter, D. L. (1987). Implicit memory: History and current status. *Journal of Experimental Psychology: Learning, Memory, and Cognition, 13,* 501–518.

Shiffrin, R. M., & Dumais, S. T. (1981). The development of automatism. In J. R. Anderson (Ed.), *Cognitive skills and their acquisition* (pp. 111–140). Hillsdale, NJ: Lawrence Erlbaum Associates.

Slamecka, N. J., & Graf, P. (1978). The generation effect: Delineation of a phenomenon. *Journal of Experimental Psychology: Human Learning and Memory, 4,* 592–604.

Smith, E. R., & Branscombe, N. R. (1987). Procedurally mediated social inferences: The case of category accessibility effects. *Journal of Experimental Social Psychology, 23,* 361–382.

Smith, E. R., & Branscombe, N. R. (1988). Category accessibility as implicit memory. *Journal of Experimental Social Psychology, 24,* 385–395.

Smith, E. R., Branscombe, N. R., & Bormann, C. (1988). Generality of the effects of practice on social judgment tasks. *Journal of Personality and Social Psychology, 54,* 385–395.

Smith, E. R., & Lerner, M. (1986). Development of automatism of social judgments. *Journal of Personality and Social Psychology, 50,* 246–259.

4

Specificity and Generality in the Nature and Use of Stereotypes

David L. Hamilton
Diane M. Mackie
University of California, Santa Barbara

Researchers working in the general area of social cognition have come to expect that papers written by Eliot Smith will be well worth reading, for they typically have several impressive characteristics—they are tightly reasoned, they are well grounded both theoretically and empirically, and yet often are provocative in challenging and/or extending the prevailing viewpoints on a given topic. The target article of the present volume is no exception. We can easily identify several potentially important contributions of this piece, any of which may be of lasting value to the development of social cognition. For example, in drawing our attention to issues of specificity, both of content and of process, Smith has usefully raised a variety of questions about some currently popular emphases in our theorizing and in our interpretations of our data. He is probably correct in asserting that researchers have been too quick to understand their findings as reflecting the role of abstract cognitive structures, without adequately considering alternative explanations in terms of more localized, specific mechanisms. And he has documented this point by posing such alternatives for several topics that have been the focus of research in the recent social cognition literature.

In developing his arguments Smith has drawn on recent theoretical and empirical developments in the cognitive literature, and has pursued their implications for understanding substantive topics in social psychology. He has, for example, shown how social categorization could be based on matching to exemplars rather than to abstract representations; how inferences may be based on procedural rather than declarative knowledge; and how the distinction between explicit and implicit memory can alter our views of the nature of memorial representations. In so doing Smith has broadened the range of conceptual and empirical tools that social cognition researchers can usefully employ to understand their subject matter.

Although we concur with Smith's primary argument that greater attention to specificity effects is warranted, we believe that legitimate questions can be raised regarding the adequacy of the approach he advocates for thoroughly understanding some of the issues he addresses. In commenting on his article our remarks will be focused particularly on the implications of his arguments for understanding the nature of stereotypes and stereotyping (topics to which he devotes considerable attention). We hope to recognize some of the contributions his arguments offer for research on these topics, while at the same time suggesting some of the limitations of his approach to these topics. In particular, we will comment on the implications of Smith's position for the nature of cognitive representations of social groups, how those representations are used in judgment, and the prospects for changing stereotypes.

Traditionally, a stereotype has been viewed as a generalized belief system, abstracted from patterns of specific bits of information one has acquired about the group as well as from more general characterizations of the group one has learned from other sources. This generalized conception of the group as a whole presumably then can influence subsequent processing of information about and judgments of that group and its members (cf. Hamilton & Trolier, 1986). However, we now know that a definition of stereotypes that limits itself to abstract, generalized characterizations of the group as a whole (e.g., a prototype) encounters a number of serious problems. These difficulties include accounting for a perceiver's knowledge about and sensitivity to variability in groups, the context dependency of categorization, the special role of correlated attributes in classification, and conditions under which particular instances have impact in addition to or instead of category-level information.

In emphasizing specificity effects in social categorization, Smith joins a growing number of researchers who have recognized the need to incorporate exemplar information in cognitive representations of social groups (Linville, Fischer, & Salovey, 1989; Park & Hastie, 1987; Rothbart & John, 1985). These exemplar models have in common the notion that, as Smith (p. 20) states, "our knowledge of categories is distributed across multiple exemplars rather than being completely captured in abstract, general, context-free prototypes or rules." In these models judgments about the group or about group members are based primarily on the retrieval of exemplar information rather than by reference to a generalized representation of the group.

Just as pure prototype models cannot incorporate certain phenomena, pure exemplar models have difficulty in providing parsimonious explanations for feature inheritance, exposure to category-level information via social learning, the apparent independence of judgments about a group as a whole and about group members, and the occurrence of on-line judgments about groups. Therefore, Smith (pp. 26) acknowledges the necessity for a mixed model that includes, in some way, both individual instance and group level information in the group representation. Nevertheless, and perhaps to stress the importance of specificity in social cognition, Smith gives predominant emphasis to the role of these exemplar representations. Indeed, much of his discussion implies that such processes as categorization of target persons, retrieval of information about groups, and judgments of group members will be driven primarily by exemplar representations and that group-level conceptions will have relatively lesser impact.

An important point, however, is that the same reasons that make a pure exemplar model untenable may also impose constraints on the role of exemplars relative to category information in a mixed model. If so, then there may be limits on the extent to which our understanding of the nature and functioning of stereotypes will be enhanced by focusing predominantly on the role of these exemplar representations.

THE FUNCTIONAL VALUE OF
GROUP-LEVEL REPRESENTATIONS

In Smith's view the major reason for adopting a mixed model of group representations is the fact that we acquire generalized beliefs about social groups as a part of our social learning experiences, and these become part of our stored "knowledge" about these groups. Therefore our stereotypes include more than an accumulation of exemplars from individual past experiences. While the beliefs we acquire through social learning are clearly important (and their role may be underestimated in Smith's treatment), it seems to us that group level representations, and their potential influence, may derive from other sources as well.

As Smith points out, our category knowledge can sometimes develop from experience with hundreds or even thousands of exemplars. This is certainly the case for the major social groups about whom we all have well-developed stereotypes. Given this continuous processing of exemplars, at what point might it become more cognitively efficient, or even necessary, to abstract group level information rather than rely on keeping track of large numbers of individual group members? Wouldn't the commonalities (real or apparent) of recurring experiences with different group members seem, to the perceiver, to provide a compelling basis for generalization? Limitations of processing capacity and storage would not only influence the way exemplar information becomes represented in memory but would also constrain one's ability to "keep track of" and make effective use of such information. Although Smith wants to avoid assumptions of limited capacity (p. 25), research has shown that constraints on processing, such as time pressure or information overload (e.g., Rothbart, Fulero, Jensen, Howard, & Birrell, 1978), can influence the nature of category representations. These same constraints would seem likely to initiate more abstract, group level processing.

These points also suggest a note of caution regarding the interpretation of some of our experimental data. If, for example, information overload does increase group-level processing, we should be cautious in making generalizations about knowledge representations of large social categories on the basis of experimental studies using only a few, unfamiliar, and perhaps readily distinguishable exemplars.

Exemplar-based models assume that, when a judgment about a category is required, exemplars of the category are retrieved and integrated at the time the judgment is made. Even when category-relevant information is stored in exemplar fashion, however, there are several factors that render making on-line judgments about the category as a whole quite functional.

There is at least some evidence that category-level judgments are spontaneously made on-line as information about group members is processed, at least under some conditions. For example, Park and Hastie (1987) have shown that judgments of variability among group members were not affected by whether some extreme (high and low) behavior items were repeated in the stimulus set. If judgments were based on retrieval of exemplars from memory, such repetitions should increase perceived variability. The absence of this effect suggests that on-line judgments were made. Even phenomena that are based on retrieval of exemplars will, under some conditions, yield to group-level processing. For example, the distinctiveness-based illusory correlation is a bias in group perceptions that has been shown to be memory-based (Hamilton & Sherman, 1989). However, if the perceiver is given a processing goal that would induce on-line integration and group-level judgments, the bias does not occur (Pryor, 1986). Although the findings of these studies are not definitive, they suggest that, at least under some conditions, group judgments may be made spontaneously as exemplar information is encoded. If so, then group-level characterizations are established as part of the category representation at the outset. Obviously we need more empirical work addressing this question before we can comfortably understand the conditions under which on-line judgments of groups are made.

Furthermore, Smith's arguments about the proceduralization of cognitive operations only serve to make these group-level processes all the more important. That is, to the extent that category level implications are abstracted on-line from incoming exemplars, and to the extent that subsequent judgments are based on previously-made group level characterizations, the chances are increased that these inference procedures will become routine.

Regardless of whether a group judgment is made on-line or is memory-based, it presumably would be functional to store that judgment as a part of the group-level representation so that it is available for use in the future. Subsequent judgments then would not require "re-retrieval" of exemplars from memory and recalculation of the judgment, but rather could be made by reference to the representation of the prior judgment. Especially in cases in which such judgments are likely to occur again and again, having a ready-made category level evaluation saves time and processing capacity (Kahneman & Miller, 1986; Linville et al., 1989). Past research has in fact shown that once a decision or judgment is made on the basis of stimulus information, subsequent judgments are often based on the first judgment rather than on reconsideration of the stimulus information for the second judgment (Carlston, 1980; Fazio, Lenn & Effrein, 1984; Lingle, Geva, Ostrom, Leippe, & Baumgardner, 1979; Lingle & Ostrom, 1979). Again, the implication is that the group level representation will influence subsequent judgments.

INTEGRATION OF GROUP AND EXEMPLAR
INFORMATION IN JUDGMENTS

We agree with Smith's position that both pure prototype and pure exemplar models are inadequate and that a mixed model incorporating both group level and exemplar representations is necessary. Here again, though, Smith's discussion focuses heavily on demonstrating that judgments *may* be based only on the more specific, exemplar information retrieved from memory. However, if stereotypes do include both group level and exemplar representations, then either or both can influence judgments of groups and group members. It then becomes important to specify the relative importance of general versus specific representations on judgments and the conditions under which each one adopts greater and lesser influence.

Several attempts have recently been made to address the similar problem of how categorical representations combine with specific items of stimulus information when judgments are made (e.g., Brewer, 1988; Fiske & Neuberg, in press). In these models the categorical representations have typically been treated as generalized group categorizations. Note that if stereotypes include both general and specific levels of information, and if either or both could interact with properties of the stimulus information momentarily available, then the nature of these integration processes becomes more complex. Nevertheless, the approach represented in these models may be a useful strategy toward grappling with this integration process.

THE IMPACT OF CATEGORY LEVEL
INFORMATION ON EXEMPLAR USE

Recognizing that stereotypes include both general and specific knowledge representations has other, more consequential implications as well. Presumably any given stimulus can activate category level information, exemplar information, or both. If so, then a number of important questions arise. Under what conditions will a stimulus activate each of these components of stored knowledge? How does activation of an exemplar, or of the category label, influence activation of the other? At present little is known about these matters, and more research delineating these relations is needed. Nevertheless, some recent conceptual analyses and research findings are germane to these issues and suggest that group-level representations may have profound effects on the recruitment and use of exemplar information.

Perhaps of particular importance for Smith's analysis is the possibility that the activation of some group-level knowledge may actually direct and constrain the range of exemplars that are retrieved. Rothbart and John (1985) have argued persuasively that this is the mechanism that accounts for the relative inertia of social stereotypes. In their view, instances that are typical of the category are much more likely to be stored closely and strongly with it, and therefore they argue that "typical" or category confirming exemplars are the ones most likely to be retrieved when the category label is activated.

In a similar vein, Kahneman and Miller's (1986) norm theory, which emphasizes the role of exemplar retrieval in judgment, suggests that activation of a category label can bias the range of instances evoked by a stimulus in the direction of those most representative on the category. If so, then restriction of the range of exemplars recruited by the category label is a mechanism by which exemplar retrieval can work toward category confirmation.

Although evidence directly substantiating these ideas has not been reported, recent research findings do support some implications of this analysis. For example, Rothbart and Lewis (1988, Experiments 1 and 2) have shown that judgments of a category are more heavily influenced by representative than by atypical exemplars of the category. Their results are consistent with the idea that the instances most likely to come to mind, and therefore available to influence judgments, were those that most closely exemplified category attributes. In addition, exposure to an atypical member of the category has little influence on judgments of a group, whereas a disconfirming feature associated with an otherwise typical exemplar can produce changes in group-level judgments (Rothbart & Lewis, Experiment 3; Weber & Crocker, 1983; Wilder, 1984).

Further support for the impact of category level activation on exemplar recruitment and use comes from an extensive body of work on intergroup judgments (cf. Messick & Mackie, 1989). When category memberships are salient, judgments about groups and group members are both more susceptible to ingroup bias—ingroups are seen positively and out-groups negatively—and more "stereotypic"; the similarities within categories and the differences between categories become pronounced (see Brewer & Kramer, 1985; Turner, 1987; Wilder, 1986, for reviews). Even if such judgments are either partially or even largely based on exemplars recruited from memory, it appears that activation of the category results in exemplars congruent with category attributes having increased impact.

Smith argues that, because judgments are based on exemplar retrieval, and because varying experiences can result in retrieval of different sets of exemplars, category knowledge—and category-relevant judgments—will be characterized by flexibility and change. However, to the extent that any given target activates category level knowledge, the very mechanism by which Smith postulates this flexibility and change—exemplar retrieval—can be constrained in the ways we have indicated. Thus the presence of exemplars in the representation, and their use in judgments, should not be regarded as evidence that group level information is unimportant or inoperative. The activation of a group label may restrict and channel the retrieval of the particular exemplars on which judgments may be based. Such an effect not only represents an important influence of group level information on processing and judgment but also may constitute a confirmatory bias through which stereotypes are self-perpetuating.

JUDGMENT WITHOUT CATEGORY ACTIVATION

Although the preceding analyses indicate how stereotypes can be influential, even when judgments are based on exemplars activated by a target stimulus, Smith raises the additional possibility that judgments can be based on an exemplar without category level information being activated at all (Kahneman & Miller, 1986, make a conceptually similar point regarding the formation of stimulus centered norms). For example, Lewicki's (1986) experiment suggests that the prior experience with the aggressive experimenter with the unusual haircut is all that is used as the basis for inferences about a new target person. Note that if this is the case the reservations indicated in previous sections—for example, category-based constraints on exemplar activation—are irrelevant, as the category label and its associated knowledge are neither activated nor utilized. The issue thus becomes whether a stimulus target can be reacted to purely on the basis of its own unique configuration of attributes, unmediated by category representations.

This question has been the focus of a considerable amount of research investigating the relative impact, under various conditions, of categorical and attribute information on judgments (Brewer, 1988; Fiske & Neuberg, in press; Glick, Zion, & Nelson, 1988; Heilman, 1984; Krueger & Rothbart, 1988; Locksley, Borgida, Brekke, & Hepburn, 1980; Rasinski, Crocker, & Hastie, 1985). In discussing the conditions under which judgments about targets are individuated, rather than category based, most of these approaches have focused on the integration of stimulus attributes without reference to any previously stored information. Smith raises the additional possibility (with which the Lewicki experiment is consistent) that distinctive attributes of the target can provide the basis for judgments by acting as retrieval cues for similar exemplars, but without activating category level knowledge of any type. Given these possibilities, the important questions then concern how frequently and under what conditions subsequent judgments of different stimulus persons are based solely on associations to their features, without categorization of the target occurring.

"PRIMITIVE" CATEGORIES AND SUBTYPING

Smith's argument that judgments about social targets can be made without any level of categorization occurring is in direct conflict with assumptions that "primitive" categories, such as gender, race, and age, are automatically activated when social targets are encountered (Bower & Karlin, 1974; Brewer, 1988; Bruner, 1957; Devine, 1989; Fiske, 1988; Fiske & Neuberg, in press; Taylor, 1981). If certain structures are automatically activated by social stimuli, then the occasions under which judgments are based purely on a match to a single exemplar would seem to be quite limited. Once activated, the content of these structures would be available to guide and restrict subsequent processing and retrieval in a top-down fashion as suggested earlier. Moreover, repeated activation of these primitive categories (and their contents) would increase their likelihood of future activation, either because of their increased accessibility (e.g., Higgins, Bargh, & Lombardi, 1985) or because they would become "proceduralized" through repeated use.

Although many have recognized the potential role of primitive categories, empirical evidence for their operation has been rare. However, the Zarate and Smith study (p. 50) appears to provide impressive evidence of the importance of race and gender as primitive categories. In this study judgments about the race or gender of a target were slower if the target was not a white male. Thus, for example, the gender of whites was judged faster than the gender of blacks due to simultaneous activation of race in the latter case, even though race was irrelevant to the judgment subjects were making. These findings are consistent with the idea that gender and race classification occur automatically.

As Smith points out (pp. 48.), current views of stereotyping have emphasized the progressive differentiation of the major, "primitive" categories into subtypes, presumably as a result of experiences with widely varying members of a superordinate category. In Smith's view such a process of differentiation of major categories would only produce a small number of relatively broad subtypes. The facts that (a) we have images of numerous subtypes of most major stereotyped groups (e.g., blacks), and that (b) these can include some very specific subcategories, persuade Smith that these apparent subtypes are in fact exemplar representations based on specific past experiences.

Smith's challenge to contemporary views of cognitive structures with differentiated subtypes is an interesting one. However, we question whether the two points noted above are, of necessity, problematic for this view. First, why would a subtyping process be limited to producing a small number of subcategories? By adulthood each of us has had probably thousands of encounters with members of the major social categories (through first-hand experiences, anecdotal descriptions from others, media exposures, simple observation, etc.) not all of which can be assimilated into existing structures. Given this rich experience, with each encounter producing new information, it seems quite plausible that initially primitive distinctions might, over a period of years, become highly differentiated, producing numerous subcategories. Second, why would subtyping process be limited to producing fairly broad subcategories? Given the progressively accumulating information conveyed in these experiences, it seems plausible that these structures would become quite refined, producing rather specific representations, especially in any domain where such judgments are either functional or frequent.

These points (as well as the effect of ingroup bias) are humorously illustrated in a monologue by the comedian Emo Phillips, in which he describes a conversation with a man threatening to commit suicide by jumping off a bridge.

> I said, "Are you a Christian or a Jew?" He said, "A Christian." I said, "Me too. Protestant or Catholic?" He said, "Protestant." I said, "Me too. What franchise?" He says, "Baptist." I said, "Me too. Northern Baptist or Southern Baptist?" He says, "Northern Baptist." I said, "Me too. Northern Conservative Baptist or Northern Liberal Baptist?" He says, "Northern Conservative Baptist." I said, "Me too. Northern Conservative Fundamentalist Baptist or Northern Conservative Reformed Baptist?" He says, "Northern Conservative Fundamentalist Baptist." I said, "Me too. Northern Conservative Fundamentalist Baptist, Great Lakes Region or Northern Conservative Fundamentalist Baptist, Eastern Region?" He says, "Northern Conservative Fundamentalist Baptist, Great Lakes Region." I said, "Me too. Northern Conservative Fundamentalist Baptist, Great Lakes Region, Council of 1879 or Northern Conservative Fundamentalist Baptist, Great Lakes Region, Council of 1912?" He says, "Northern Conservative Fundamentalist Baptist, Great Lakes Region, Council of 1912." I said, "Die, heretic!" and I pushed him over.

Thus the fact that we have, over the years, developed well defined, richly articulated conceptions of numerous subtypes of major social categories like blacks and women (and religious groups) does not seem incompatible with a subtyping process.

It is important to note that this subtyping view is not incompatible with the use of exemplar information. Within the framework of a mixed model, subtype representations could also include both generalizations about category members and stored exemplars. An interesting possibility, suggested by Smith and worth pursuing empirically, is that exemplar information will have more impact when a subtype, rather than a broad category, has been activated. More importantly, the central issue, and the challenge for future research, will be to establish criteria for empirically evaluating whether judgments are based only on specific exemplars (in the absence of any category activation) or on narrowly defined subtypes that include category features and stored exemplars.

QUESTIONS OF ACCURACY
IN EXEMPLAR-BASED JUDGMENT

The greater use of exemplar information relative to category level information in judging groups and group members often seems to carry with it the implicit assumption that such processing will result in more accurate perceptions. Somehow there is the sense that exemplar-based judgments are closer to the raw data of social perception.

While this idea may be an appealing one, use of exemplar information may not be a universal remedy for inaccuracies in judgments, for several reasons. First, as noted above, atypical exemplars may be more prone to subclassification in exemplar-based representations. Second, even if appropriately classified, atypical members may be less likely to be retrieved because of the biasing effects of category activation, as discussed earlier. Finally, group judgments based on exemplar recruitment may be particularly subject to retrieval biases (see the logic of Park & Hastie, 1987, Experiment 1; Rothbart et al, 1978). In fact, in some cases, on-line estimates of group characteristics may provide more accurate reflections of the totality of the information presented. To the extent that processing individual exemplar information competes or interferes with the on-line calculation of summary inferences about the group, the accuracy of both on-line group-level judgments and of memory-based judgments would be reduced. Delineating the conditions under which the encoding of on-line group-level compared to exemplar information produces accurate perceptions of groups and group members would seem to be a profitable direction for further research.

CLOSING COMMENTS

In presenting an alternative viewpoint Smith has challenged some of social cognition's conventional ways of thinking about the nature of cognitive representations and the bases of social judgments. He has made the case for specificity quite effectively. Our commentary has focused on the implications of Smith's views for understanding stereotypes. We have tried to highlight the contributions offered by including exemplar knowledge in category representations, while at the same time indicating some of the limits on these specificity effects. We have emphasized the greater explanatory value of conceptual models that include both group level characterizations and knowledge of specific instances. In particular, it is important, we have argued, to recognize how the category level representation can constrain the role and use of exemplar knowledge in such processes as retrieval and judgment. The issues posed by Smith's article have stimulated our thinking and, we trust, will generate new empirical work in this area.

Finally, in addition to these substantive contributions, it seems to us that

Smith's arguments raise provocative questions regarding some of our favorite dependent measures. For example, to what extent do measures that rely on verbal report and conscious thought processes—free recall, judgments, and the like—adequately assess cognitive representations, and to what extent are they useful only for assessing the effects of abstract cognitive structures and declarative knowledge while overlooking the role of specificity effects and procedural knowledge? Similarly, under what conditions do fast response times reflect the accessibility of an abstract construct or proximally-stored representations, and when do they reflect a well-practiced procedure? Such questions will pose additional challenges for the investigation of cognitive representations and their use in social judgment.

ACKNOWLEDGMENTS

Preparation of this paper was supported by NIMH Grant MH 40058 to the first author and NIMH Grant MH 43041 to the second author.

REFERENCES

Bower, G. H., & Karlin, M. B. (1974). Depth of processing pictures of faces and recognition memory. *Journal of Experimental Psychology, 103,* 751–757.

Brewer, M. B. (1988). A dual process model of impression formation. In T. K. Srull & R. S. Wyer, Jr. (Eds.), *Advances in social cognition* (Vol. 1, pp. 1–36). Hillsdale, NJ: Lawrence Erlbaum Associates.

Brewer, M. B., & Kramer, R. M. (1985). The psychology of intergroup attitudes and behaviors. *Annual Review of Psychology, 36,* 219–243.

Bruner, J. S. (1957). On perceptual readiness. *Psychological Review, 64,* 123–152.

Carlston, D. E. (1980). The recall and use of traits and events in social inference processes. *Journal of Experimental Social Psychology, 16,* 303–328.

Devine, P. G. (1989). Stereotypes and prejudice: Their automatic and controlled components. *Journal of Personality and Social Psychology, 56,* 5–18.

Fazio, R. H., Lenn, T. M., & Effrein, E. A. (1984). Spontaneous attitude formation. *Social Cognition, 2,* 217–234.

Fiske, S. T. (1988). Brewer's dual process model and Fiske et al.'s continuum model. In T. K. Srull & R. S. Wyer, Jr. (Eds.), *Advances in social cognition* (Vol. 1, pp. 65–76). Hillsdale, NJ: Lawrence Erlbaum Associates.

Fiske, S. T., & Neuberg, S. (in press). A continuum model of impression formation: From category based to individuating processes as a function of information, motivation, and attention. In M. P. Zanna (Ed.) *Advances in experimental social psychology* (Vol. 23, pp. 1–108). San Diego, CA: Academic Press.

Glick, P., Zion, C., & Nelson, C. (1988). What mediates sex discrimination in hiring decisions? *Journal of Personality and Social Psychology, 55,* 178–186.

Hamilton, D. L., & Sherman, S. J. (1989). Illusory correlations: Implications for stereotype theory and research. In D. Bar-Tal, C. F. Graumann, A. W. Kruglanski, & W. Stroebe (Eds.), *Stereotyping and prejudice: Changing conceptions* (pp. 59–82). New York: Springer-Verlag.

Hamilton, D. L., & Trolier, T. K. (1986). Stereotypes and stereotyping: An overview of the cognitive approach. In J. Dovidio & S. L. Gaertner (Eds.), *Prejudice, discrimination, and racism* (pp. 127–163). New York: Academic Press.

Heilman, M. E. (1984). Information as a deterrent against sex discrimination: The effects of applicant sex and information type on preliminary employment decisions. *Organizational Behavior and Human Performance, 33,* 174–186.

Higgins, E. T., Bargh, J. A., & Lombardi, W. (1985). Nature of priming effects on categorization. *Journal of Experimental Psychology: Learning, Memory, and Cognition, 11,* 59–69.

Kahneman, D., & Miller, D. T. (1986). Norm theory: Comparing reality to its alternatives. *Psychological Review, 93,* 136–153.

Krueger, J., & Rothbart, M. (1988). The use of categorical and individuating information in making inferences about personality. *Journal of Personality and Social Psychology, 55,* 187–195.

Lewicki, P. (1986). *Nonconscious social information processing.* Orlando, FL: Academic Press.

Lingle, J. H., Geva, N., Ostrom, T. M., Leippe, M. R., & Baumgardner, M. H. (1979). Thematic effects of person judgments on impression formation. *Journal of Personality and Social Psychology, 37,* 674–687.

Lingle, J. H., & Ostrom, T. M. (1979). Retrieval selectivity in memory-based impression formation. *Journal of Personality and Social Psychology, 37,* 180–194.

Linville, P. W., Fischer, G. W., & Salovey, P. (1989). Perceived distributions of the characteristics of ingroup and outgroup members. *Journal of Personality and Social Psychology, 57,* 165–188.

Locksley, A., Borgida, E., Brekke, N., & Hepburn, C. (1980). Sex stereotypes and social judgment. *Journal of Personality and Social Psychology, 39,* 821–831.

Messick, D. M., & Mackie, D. M. (1989). Intergroup relations. *Annual Review of Psychology, 40,* 45–81.

Park, B., & Hastie, R. (1987). Perception of variability in category development: Instance- versus abstraction-based stereotypes. *Journal of Personality and Social Psychology, 53,* 621–635.

Pryor, J. B. (1986). The influence of different encoding sets upon the formation of illusory correlations and group impressions. *Personality and Social Psychology Bulletin, 12,* 216–226.

Rasinski, K. A., Crocker, J., & Hastie, R. (1985). Another look at sex stereotypes and social judgments: An analysis of the social perceiver's use of subjective probabilities. *Journal of Personality and Social Psychology, 49,* 317–326.

Rothbart, M., Fulero, S., Jenson, C., Howard, J., & Birrell, P. (1978). From individual to group impressions: Availability heuristics in stereotype formation. *Journal of Experimental Social Psychology, 14,* 237–255.

Rothbart, M., & John, O. P. (1985). Social categorization and behavioral episodes: A cognitive analysis of the effects of intergroup contact. *Journal of Social Issues, 41*(3), 81–104.

Rothbart, M., & Lewis, S. (1989). Inferring category attributes from exemplar attributes: Geometric shapes and social categories. *Journal of Personality and Social Psychology, 55,* 861–872.

Taylor, S. E. (1981). A categorization approach to stereotyping. In D. L. Hamilton (Ed.), *Cognitive processes in stereotyping and intergroup behavior* (pp. 83–114). Hillsdale, NJ: Lawrence Erlbaum Associates.

Turner, J. C. (1987). *Rediscovering the social group: A self-categorization theory.* New York: Basil Blackwell.

Weber, R., & Crocker, J. (1983). Cognitive processes in the revision of stereotypic beliefs. *Journal of Personality and Social Psychology, 45,* 961–977.

Wilder, D. A. (1984). Intergroup contact: The typical member and the exception to the rule. *Journal of Experimental Social Psychology, 20,* 177–194.

Wilder, D. A. (1986). Social categorization: Implications for creation and reduction of intergroup bias. In L. Berkowitz (Ed.), *Advances in experimental social psychology* (Vol. 19, pp. 291–355). Orlando, FL: Academic Press.

5 The Specifics of Memory and Cognition

Larry L. Jacoby
Michael J. Marriott
Jane G. Collins
McMaster University

If periods in the history of psychology were named as are periods in the history of art, the last 20 years or so would be termed the "abstractionist" period. During that period, cognitive psychologists have attempted to invent abstract representations that capture the essence of different classes of events. Those abstract representations are given psychological reality in that they are said to be used in an invariant fashion across a wide range of situations to identify and respond to members of the abstract class or category. For example, it might be claimed that a situation is classified and responded to in terms of some schema that has been abstracted across experience in situations that are similar to a present one (e.g., Hastie, 1981). The abstractionist approach is very well suited to explain stability in performance across situations. Indeed, the focus is on similarities among situations (defined in terms of shared attributes or characteristics) and the use of those similarities to create an abstract representation of some general class or category. The prediction is that performance will be stable across situations that are members of the same general class.

Smith's chapter can be seen as contributing to the demise of the abstractionist period. He argues that schemas and other abstract representations have been given too much importance in theorizing about social cognition. Smith supports his argument by reviewing research to show that the effects of prior experience are often more specific than would be predicted by an abstractionist view. Smith interprets those data as showing that social judgments are often based on the similarity of a current case to a particular remembered exemplar rather than on the use of an abstract representation. Using one of Smith's examples, a person might be classified as being a Republican because his physical appearance reminds me of my Uncle Harry who is a Republican rather than, as an abstractionist view would have it, because he has some characteristics that are shared by most Republicans.

We are very sympathetic toward Smith's view of social cognition. Indeed, his view is similar to our (e.g., Jacoby & Kelley, in press; Jacoby & Brooks, 1984) view of the effects of prior experience on perception and categorization. Our experiments have typically examined effects on word and picture perception, but the issues are the same as for social cognition. Although similar, there are some potentially important differences between our view and that proposed by Smith. We provide comments on some of those differences along with a brief description of our view. Next, we consider differences in research strategies. At issue in that discussion is the choice of goals for future research. We illustrate our research strategy by briefly describing a few lines of research that have grown out of our episodic view of cognition.

AN EPISODIC VIEW OF COGNITION

We have used the specificity of effects of prior experience as evidence that those effects arise from memory for prior episodes rather than from the priming of an abstract representation. The effects of prior experience on social judgment have been described as due to the priming of an abstract representation such as a schema or trait concept (e.g., Higgins, Rholes, & Jones, 1977; Wyer & Srull, 1986). Similarly, the effect of reading a word on its later perceptual identification has been described as produced by the priming of a logogen (e.g., Morton, 1969), a representation of the word that has been abstracted across prior encounters with the word. A priming view predicts that the effects of recent prior experience will be short lived and uniform across members of a primed category. This is because an abstract representation of a category does not preserve any information about the particular event that primed the category, so effects on later perception or interpretation of the earlier presented "prime" should not differ from effects on other members of the category. Counter to a priming view, we have found that presenting a word once in the experimental setting can have a large and long-lasting effect on its later identification. Also, the effect is specific to the details of the earlier processing of the word (e.g., Jacoby, 1983a, 1983b). The pattern of results is the same as used by Smith to argue that social judgments can be based on memory for an earlier-presented exemplar.

Whereas Smith has chosen to talk about memory for exemplars, we have chosen to emphasize the importance of memory for prior episodes. Our episodic view of cognition is generally consistent with the exemplar view of concept learning that Smith adopts. The major difference is that exemplar views have typically described memory for an exemplar as being a veridical copy of the presented stimulus. Contrary to a "copy" theory of memory, most contemporary accounts of episodic memory hold that memory for an item reflects what one did with that item and, consequently, is influenced by task demands, the context in which the item was encountered, etc. This variability in the encoding of a stimulus is important because the encoding of an item constrains its later retrieval. Retrieval depends on the similarity between the retrieval cues and the encoded trace, making it necessary to consider encoding and retrieval jointly rather than in isolation. Transfer is maximal when the earlier processing of an item matches that required by the test of transfer (e.g., Kolers, 1979; Tulving & Thomson, 1973). Our episodic view extends these claims about memory to theorizing about effects of prior experience on performance of perception and categorization tasks. It is the claim that performance reflects differences in the encoding and retrieval of presented exemplars that makes our view an episodic view.

The use of the term "episodic" to name our view is meant to highlight the possibility that many of the factors that are important for performance on tests of episodic memory are also important for showing effects of prior experience on perception and categorization. Much of our research has been aimed at examining the effects of encoding and retrieval factors on performance of perceptual and categorization tasks. For example, by our episodic view, perception and judgment are expected to vary across changes in test context. This is because retrieval factors determine the particular prior episodes that are retrieved from memory to guide perception and interpretation of later events. A disadvantage of using the term *episodic* is that episodic memory has traditionally referred to an aware use of memory as measured by performance on a test of recall or recognition memory. Although we refer to influences of memory for prior episodes, we do not mean to imply that people are always aware of those prior episodes or the effects of memory on their performance. A central theme of our research (e.g., Jacoby & Kelley, 1987; Jacoby, Kelley, & Dywan, 1989) has been that memory for prior episodes often produces unconscious influences on performance.

One point of disagreement with Smith concerns the utility of his distinction between content specificity and processing specificity. By that distinction, the content of stimulus materials and the processing applied to the stimulus materials are separate. We would argue that stimulus materials do not have any content that is separate from the processing of those materials. As stated earlier, we and many others see memory as being for material as processed. Examining content specificity requires presenting stimulus materials in the context of some processing task and the degree of specificity that is found will almost certainly vary with the task that is chosen, showing that it is the interaction between the task and the materials that is important. Kolers and Smythe (1979) discuss other disadvantages of drawing a distinction between processing and content.

A second point of disagreement deals with Smith's claim that the specificity of the effects of prior experience can be treated as a "signature" to identify how those effects were mediated. The specificity of effects can be used to reject some simple abstractionist models of categorization performance. However, more complex abstractionist models can be used to predict that effects of prior experience will be very specific, rendering useless the specificity of effects as a means of rejecting abstractionist models as a class (e.g., Barsalou, this volume; Whittlesea, 1987). Also, exemplar or episodic models do not have to predict that the effects of prior experience will be extremely specific (e.g., Jacoby, Baker, & Brooks, 1989).

FUTURE DIRECTIONS

Is an episodic view useful? Given that the specificity of effects cannot be used to reject abstractionist models, is there any reason to entertain an episodic view of cognition. We believe that the major advantage offered by an episodic view is its heuristic value. Focusing on the theoretical conclusions that can be drawn from a finding of very specific effects of prior experience ignores how one goes about finding such effects. We have found that manipulations taken from experiments on episodic memory are useful for exploring effects on performance of perception and categorization tasks. We illustrate our research strategy by briefly describing three lines of research that have come from our approach. The first line of research examines the effects of an episodic memory variable, test context, on perception and judgments. Next, we describe a line of research that is meant to provide converging evidence for claims based on differences in the specificity of effects. The procedure that we use to investigate differences in social judgments is one that we have previously used in our investigations of memory. Our strategy has typically been to attempt to produce interactions that can be interpreted in terms of a contrast between different bases for perception and judgments. A third line of research explores unconscious influences of memory on subjective experience. We suggest that effects on subjective experience can be used as an indirect test of attitudes and other aspects of social cognition. The nonanalytic judgments revealed by effects on indirect tests contrast with judgments made on a more analytic basis.

Unconscious Retrieval: Effects of Test Context

Reinstating earlier context at the time of test is likely important for showing unconscious influences of memory on social judgments. This possibility can be illustrated with an example of a confusion that is akin to unintentional plagiarism. Coming back from a lecture, a graduate student serving as a teaching assistant for one of my (Jacoby) courses told an anecdote that he suggested could be used to illustrate a point made in the lecture that day. The anecdote was one that I used in exactly the way that the student suggested when teaching the same course a year earlier. Although the student had also been my assistant for the earlier teaching of the course and, so, had likely heard the earlier lecture, he claimed to not remember having heard me tell the story. Rather, he claimed to have heard the anecdote from one of his undergraduate professors. It is unlikely that the student's account was correct because I invented the anecdote and his undergraduate professor, when asked, denied having ever heard the anecdote. The point is that the story came to mind for the student in a context very similar to that in which it was earlier heard although the student did not recollect earlier hearing the story in that context. Reinstating the context of the lecture resulted in retrieval of memory for the story. That effect of context on retrieval was unconscious in that its importance was not realized—the context was not actively used to aid retrieval or else the student would not have failed to recognize the story as earlier heard in the context. We might often show evidence of unconscious retrieval by telling a story to the very person from whom we stole it. Jacoby, Kelley, and Dywan (1989) review evidence of effects of this sort.

As illustrated by the foregoing example, manipulations of retrieval factors can be important for showing unconscious influences of memory for a prior episode. Memory for a prior experience can be unconsciously retrieved and used to guide the perception and interpretation of a later event. We realize that this use of the term *retrieval* is potentially confusing because the word is traditionally used to refer an aware use of memory. However, manipulations of test context (a factor usually considered as influencing retrieval) can have effects that are dissociated from performance on tests of recall and recognition memory.

In our investigations of word perception, we found effects of reinstating context that clearly did not depend on a person's ability to recall or recognize the tested items. We (Allen & Jacoby, in press; Jacoby, 1983b) found that earlier reading a word did more to enhance its later perceptual identification if nearly all, rather than very few, of the words presented for the test of perceptual identification had been earlier read. That is, reinstating study-list context at the time of test increased the effect of reading a word on its later identification. This effect of reinstating context did not result from people consciously using memory for the earlier-read list to aid their later perceptual identification performance. Had that been the case, reinstating list context should have had the largest effect for words that people could recall or recognize as previously presented. However, the opposite was found. The effect was largest for words that people were unlikely to recall or recognize. Although a person was unable to recall or recognize a word as previously presented, reinstating study-list context made unconscious retrieval of memory for the prior presentation of the word more likely as shown by the effects of that memory on word perception.

It is the inconsistency in behavior across situations that is not well captured by a simple abstractionist view. However, the change in judgments across situations is understandable if retrieval factors are important. The effects of retrieval factors that we have obtained are expected given an episodic view but cannot be explained in terms of a simple abstractionist view of perception and judgments. By an abstractionist view, performance should not be influenced by manipulations of context of the sort that we have used. The make-up of a test might also have a large impact on the basis that people employ to make judgments. As described earlier, perceptual performance is most influenced by memory for prior episodes when nearly all the items on the test were previously presented so that study context is reinstated. An analogous effect has been obtained for categorization performance (Allen & Brooks, 1989) and can probably also be found for social judgments.

Abstracting as a Secondary Task

The impossibility of using differences in the specificity of effects to choose among models of categorization performance is less important if one can find sources of converging evidence to support claims that judgments are based on memory for prior episodes. Hastie and Park's (1986) distinction between on-line and memory-based judgments seems to roughly correspond to a claim that judgments are sometimes based on an abstract representation and sometimes based on memory for prior episodes. The evidence that they use to justify their distinction does not rely on differences in the specificity of effects of prior experience. To qualify as a memory-based judgment, Hastie and Park require that a judgment be correlated with memory as assessed by a test of free recall. For example, they conclude that a judgment of a person's suitability for a job is based on memory only if that judgment is correlated with free recall of items of information favoring or opposing the person. The case for the importance of memory for prior episodes would be strengthened if one found that the conditions that are important for producing memory-based judgments are the same as those that are important for producing very specific effects of prior experience on judgments.

From our perspective, one difficulty with Hastie and Park's distinction is that the source of evidence used to support their distinction identifies memory for prior episodes as a basis for judgments exclusively with an aware use of memory. This is true because it is free-recall performance that is used as an index of the basis for judgments. Even if one should choose a test that requires awareness of memory for prior episodes, there is no reason to think that a test of free recall is the best choice. The use of memory for a prior episode as a basis for judgments might sometimes be more similar to performing on a cued-recall or a recognition test than to performing on a test of free recall. Also, as described earlier, unconscious influences of memory for episodes are sometimes observed. This means that judgments could be based on memory for prior episodes although those judgments did not correlate with performance on recognition or recall tests of memory. Other difficulties arise from the use of correlational data by Hastie and Park to support their claim that judgments are sometimes memory-based. Consider the case in which a very high correlation between a judgment and free-recall performance is found. It is tempting to interpret that correlation as showing that the judgment was made by free recalling relevant information and then counting-up evidence for and against a judgment. However, the high correlation could have been produced by other causes.

Considering the interpretation of a high correlation between judgment and free recall, there is a way to reject a claim that the correlation arises because people normally free recall as a means of making judgments. This could be done by comparing judgments from subjects in a condition that only made judgments with those from subjects in a condition that both made judgments and free recalled earlier-presented information. The requirement to free recall might change the judgments that are made. If so, one has evidence that when free recall is not required, judgments are not based on implicit free recall. That is, requiring free recall should have no effect if people only instructed to make judgments implicitly free recall earlier information to make those judgments. The procedure amounts to a comparison of judgments in a dual-task condition (judgment and free recall) to those in a single-task condition (judgment alone). Performing the secondary task is expected to have no effect if the requirements of that task are redundant with the way that the single task is performed. Let us further illustrate this dual-task procedure by describing its use to investigate person perception in a proposed series of experiments. The purpose of those experiments is to uncover the factors that determine whether traits or memory for prior episodes will be used as a basis for social judgments.

By most accounts of person perception, inferences about the general traits of others play an important role in social judgments. For example, people might be said to spontaneously think of a general personality trait of a person and use that trait to judge whether or not the person would engage in some particular act. However, social psychologists have learned to distrust general trait descriptors such as *honesty* because traits can be very situation specific. Knowledge about a general, abstract trait is often a less valuable predictor of future behavior than is knowledge of the person's behavior in earlier situations that are very similar to that in which behavior is to be predicted. Also, arriving at decisions about a person's position on different trait dimensions is not so trivial a task as it should be if general traits were always spontaneously inferred when the behavior of others is observed. When asked to evaluate the suitability of a student for admission to graduate school, for example, many of us feel uncomfortable judging whether or not a student is in the top 20% in "industriousness" of students that we have known. The experience is often closer to one of *creating* an opinion about the person with reference to the trait in question than it is to one of simply expressing an opinion that was held prior to the question being asked. The difficulty of producing trait descriptions and the poor prediction afforded by abstract traits calls into question the claim that predictions concerning specific behaviors are typically mediated by inferred traits. It often would seem easier and more accurate to predict a specific behavior from earlier-observed behavior in similar situations (memory for prior episodes) than to abstract a trait from those earlier observations and then make one's prediction on the basis of that trait.

Phrased in Hastie and Park's (1986) terms, our complaint is that theories emphasizing the importance of traits assume that trait judgments are made on-line (spontaneously inferred), whereas, we suspect that trait judgments are more often memory-based. We plan to use the earlier-described dual-task procedure to determine whether traits are used when predicting specific behaviors. If general traits are spontaneously used, judgments should not change when people are required to engage in the dual task of reporting on a person's general traits as well as judging whether or not the person would engage in a specific behavior. Conversely, if judgments about behavior are typically based largely on memory for prior episodes, then asking subjects to make simultaneous trait judgments should strongly alter the decision process. The goal of our experiments using the dual-task procedure will be to produce interactions involving factors that we think determine the choice between traits and memory for prior episodes as a basis for judgments. The difference between the dual- and single-task conditions should be smallest in conditions that specifically favor making judgments on the basis of traits, rather than on the basis of prior episodes.

We have used the dual-task procedure to ask questions about subjects' monitoring of memory when making judgments (Jacoby, Kelley, Brown, & Jasechko, 1989) and have also used the procedure to separate aware from unaware influences on judgments. When we apply the procedure to investigate the basis for social judgments, we will undoubtedly encounter a number of complexities and difficulties for interpreting the results. A finding of a difference between a dual- and a single-task condition cannot provide conclusive evidence to support claims about mediation. However, evidence of that sort in combination with evidence of differences in the specificity of effects of prior experience can be used to converge toward the conclusion that judgments are based on memory for prior episodes. Also, had we not considered an episodic view, we would not have thought to do the dual-task experiments. Early experiments in that line have returned interesting results that are relevant to issues in addition to that of a choice between theories of categorization.

Effects on Subjective Experience as an Indirect Test

By an abstractionist view of categorization, the making of judgments is a rational, analytic process. One collects pieces of evidence and combines that evidence by some rule to make a judgment. We do sometimes make judgments in that way. However, other times it seems that judgments are based on "first reaction" or "intuition." It is these more nonanalytic bases for judgments that we think are related to memory for prior episodes. After briefly describing evidence to show that memory for prior episodes can produce unconscious influences on subjective experience, we suggest that effects of that sort can be used as an indirect measure of social judgments. Our description of this line of research is brief because it has been discussed elsewhere (e.g., Jacoby & Kelley, in press; Jacoby & Kelley, 1987; Jacoby, Kelley, & Dywan, 1989).

In our studies of unconscious influences of memory, we found that memory sometimes influences subjective experience. In one experiment (Jacoby, Allan, Collins, & Larwill, 1988), previously heard and new sentences were presented against a background of white noise of varying loudness. Subjects judged the background noise as less loud when the sentences were old rather than new. That is, memory for the old sentences produced an advantage in perception and the difference in the ease of perception of old and new sentences was misattributed to a difference in the level of background noise. In future experiments, we plan to use the noise judgment task to gain a measure of nonanalytic social judgments. For example, the background noise accompanying a statement of a belief might be judged as less loud if one agrees rather than disagrees with the stated belief. The rationale underlying the use of noise judgments as an indirect test is the same as that underlying projective tests such as the Rorschach. One advantage of our procedure over the use of standard projective tests is that judgments of a physical dimension can be easily and objectively scored.

We mention our planned research using noise judgments to illustrate the strategy for contrasting effects as evidence of a difference in bases for judgments. One's first reaction or "gut feeling" about an issue is sometimes very different from the attitude that is expressed in response to a direct question. Similarly, we expect that attitudes as revealed by performance on an indirect test will sometimes conflict with those revealed by performance on a direct test of attitudes. Conflicts are expected if the judgments have different bases. It is likely that directly asking for an attitude often results in the use of a basis for responding that is more analytic than that responsible for a first reaction. Our plan is to test our notions about differences in bases for judgments by seeing whether or not they are sufficient to allow us to produce interesting differences between performance on direct and indirect tests of social judgments.

CONCLUDING COMMENTS

Smith ends his chapter by suggesting that if his arguments have any merit, social cognition faces a series of new and exciting research issues. We agree that an exemplar or episodic view serves as a valuable alternative to the abstractionist view that has dominated theorizing about social cognition. However, we do not think much is to be gained by attempting to use specificity as a "methodological principle" to determine how effects are mediated. There is reason to doubt that any single piece of evidence can be used to determine whether a judgment was mediated by an abstract representation or by memory for exemplars. As discussed by Barsalou in his comments on Smith's chapter, exemplar and abstractionist theories can be made to mimic one another in ways that make it impossible to choose between them by traditional methods of theory testing. This does not bother us because we have very little interest in testing formal theories in a traditional way. Rather, we are trying to produce a program of research that will show the advantages of thinking in terms of effects of memory for prior episodes. In part, we start by assuming that an episodic view is correct and then use that view to gain a new look at old issues. An episodic view leads one to ask questions and to seek contrasts that have been ignored because of the dominance of abstractionist views of cognition. Similarly, the merit of Smith's arguments do not rest on the possibility of conclusively choosing between theories of representation. The questions about specificity of effects that he poses are important ones. There is good reason to want to know, for example, how effects of stereotypes differ across situations even if those differences cannot be used to choose among formal theories. Indeed, social cognition does face a series of new and exciting research issues.

REFERENCES

Allen, S.W., & Brooks, L. R. (1989) *Specializing the operation of an explicit rule.* Submitted for publication.

Allen, S. W., & Jacoby, L. L. (in press). Reinstating study context produces unconscious influences of memory. *Memory and Cognition.*

Hastie, R. (1981). Schematic principles in human memory. In E. T. Higgins, C. P. Herman, & M. P. Zanna (Eds.). *Social cognition: The Ontario symposium on personality and social psychology (Vol. 2).* Hillsdale, NJ: Lawrence Erlbaum Associates.

Hastie, R., & Park, B. (1986.) The relationship between memory and judgment depends on whether the judgment task is memory-based or on-line. *Psychological Review, 3,* 258–268.

Higgins, E. T., Rholes, W. S., & Jones, C. R. (1977). Category accessibility and impression formation. *Journal of Experimental Social Psychology, 13,* 141–154.

Jacoby, L. L. (1983a). Remembering the data: Analyzing interactive processes in reading. *Journal of Verbal Learning and Verbal Behavior, 22,* 485–508.

Jacoby, L. L. (1983b). Perceptual enhancement: Persistent effects of an experience. *Journal of Experimental Psychology: Learning, Memory and Cognition, 9,* 21–38.

Jacoby, L. L., Allan, L. G., Collins, J. C., & Larwill, L. K. (1988). Memory influences subjective experience: Noise judgments. *Journal of Experimental Psychology: Learning, Memory and Cognition, 14,* 240–247.

Jacoby, L. L., Baker, J. G., & Brooks, L. R. (1989). Episodic effects on picture identification: Implications for theories of concept learning and theories of memory. *Journal of Experimental Psychology: Learning, Memory and Cognition, 15,* 275–281.

Jacoby, L. L., & Brooks, L.R. (1984). Nonanalytic cognition: Memory, perception and concept learning. In G. H. Bower (Ed.), *The psychology of learning and motivation: Advances in research and theory, Vol. 18.* (pp. 1–47). NY: Academic Press.

Jacoby, L. L., & Kelley, C. M. (1987). Unconscious influences of memory for a prior event. *Personality and Social Psychology Bulletin, 13,* 314–336.

Jacoby, L. L., & Kelley, C. M. (in press). An episodic view of motivation: Unconscious influences of memory. In E. T. Higgins & R. M. Sorrentino (Eds.), *Handbook of Motivation and Cognition: Vol. 2.* New York: Guilford Press.

Jacoby, L. L., Kelley, C. M., Brown, J., & Jasechko, J. (1989). Becoming famous overnight: Limits on the ability to avoid unconscious influences of the past. *Journal of Personality and Social Psychology, 56,* 326–338.

Jacoby, L. L., Kelley, C. M., & Dywan, J. (1989). Memory attributions. In H. L. Roediger & F. I. M. Craik (Eds.), *Varieties of memory and consciousness: Essays in honour of Endel Tulving* (pp. 391–422). Hillsdale, NJ: Lawrence Erlbaum Associates.

Kolers, P. A. (1979). A pattern-analyzing basis of recognition. In L. S. Cermak & F. I. M. Craik (Eds.), *Levels of processing in human memory* (pp. 363–384). Hillsdale, NJ: Lawrence Erlbaum Associates.

Kolers, P. A., & Smythe, W. E. (1979). Images, symbols, and skills. *Canadian Journal of Psychology, 33,* 158–184.

Morton, J. (1969). Interaction of information in word recognition. *Psychological Review, 76,* 165–178.

Tulving, E., & Thomson, D. M. (1973). Encoding specificity and retrieval processes in episodic memory. *Psychological Review, 80,* 352–373.

Whittlesea, B. W. A. (1987). Preservation of specific experiences in the representation of general knowledge. *Journal of Experimental Psychology: Learning, Memory and Cognition, 13,* 3–17.

Wyer, R. S., & Srull, T. K. (1986). Human cognition and its social context. *Psychological Review, 93,* 322–359.

6 Specific Encoding Yet Abstract Retrieval of Social Categories

Charles M. Judd
University of Colorado

As Eliot Smith amply shows, there is abundant literature in social cognition demonstrating that specific prior experiences and social encounters can have profound effects on a person's current perceptions, judgments, and reactions to others. Taken by itself, this generalization from the accumulating empirical literature in social cognition is hardly surprising. It simply amounts to the conclusion that individuals are social learners, that they profit from past experience with other individuals, and that their future social behavior is modified accordingly.

This social learning conclusion is not, however, the primary focus of Dr. Smith's Target Article. Rather than simply demonstrating the effects of prior social experiences on current social judgment and behavior, he wishes to explore the cognitive mediation of those effects. He argues that there exist a variety of potential mediators that have been discussed in the social cognition literature, that each of these mediators should have distinctive patterns or "specificities" of effects, and that therefore we can answer the question about what mediates the effects of prior experiences on current social judgment and behavior by examining these distinctive specificities.

The primary distinction that is made between types of cognitive mediators concerns how abstract or specific they are. On the one hand, there exist rather abstract representations of whole classes or categories of social objects, things that go by labels such as prototypes or schemas or abstract representations. Prior social experiences may exert their influence on current social judgments and behavior in part because they affect these relatively abstract social knowledge representations that come to be relied upon in the current situation. On the other hand, individual past experiences may be retained in memory also in the form of very specific exemplars or traces of those particular experiences and these exemplars may then be relied upon to guide current judgment and social behavior.

123

According to Dr. Smith's argument, exemplars, as relatively specific cognitive mediators, have relatively specific patterns of effects: their effects tend to be content, process, and context specific. Their effects also tend to be relatively long-lasting. On the other hand, relatively abstract cognitive representations, when activated, tend to have short-lived effects that are neither content, process, nor context specific. Since, as Dr. Smith documents, there is much evidence to suggest that the effects of past experiences tend to be content, process, and context specific, he convincingly argues that social cognition researchers have laid too much emphasis upon relatively abstract cognitive representations as mediators of prior experiences. He suggests that the specificity of effects of prior experiences is much more compatible with models in which the cognitive mediators of those prior experiences are relatively discrete individual exemplars or traces that are subsequently activated in ways that are content, process, and context specific.

WHAT IS THE QUESTION THAT IS BEING ASKED?

Given the question that Dr. Smith sets for himself in this article, his thesis and conclusions are measured, exceedingly reasonable, and very well justified. That question concerns, once again, the vehicle by which specific prior social experiences are represented in memory in a manner such that they subsequently influence social behavior and judgment. Since the effects of specific prior experiences are amply demonstrated to be content, process, and context specific, it seems perfectly reasonable to suggest that they exert their influence primarily by being represented as specific exemplars in memory that may underlie subsequent social behavior. Thus, specific prior events and experiences are represented specifically rather than abstractly and the effects of those representations tend to be specific as well.

Phrased in this way, the conclusions of Dr. Smith's article are perhaps not terribly surprising, even though he suggests that the implications of his argument are at odds with much of the traditional work in social cognition concerning the level of abstractness of cognitive representations. As Dr. Smith himself argues on page 7 of the article, if a specific single event or experience has an effect on behavior or judgment on a future occasion, that effect must be produced via a relatively specific memory representation of the prior event or experience. For, if the form of the moderating representation were considerably more abstract, then the impact of that single prior event on the relatively abstract representation or schema must necessarily be relatively small since the abstract representation presumably summarizes a great deal of prior experience and social knowledge.

Given Dr. Smith's question, the conclusions that he reaches are then quite reasonable and even self-evident. For a specific prior experience can obviously have an impact on subsequent behavior and judgment only if it has some impact on the cognitive representation which serves as a mediator. And if abstract representations represent summary information from a large number of prior experiences and events, then one specific event will necessarily have very little impact upon such an abstract representation. Accordingly, the impact of that specific event must necessarily be via a more specific exemplar representation in memory.

Given other questions, however, questions which Dr. Smith implicitly seems to wish to address in addition to the one he explicitly does address, the answers and conclusions he provides seem to me to be a fair amount less compelling and less obviously correct. To illustrate my argument here, let me focus on the area of group representations and stereotypes, an area to which Dr. Smith devotes considerable attention himself. Dr. Smith's explicitly posed question in this domain can be phrased somewhat imprecisely as follows: "Given a previous specific encounter with a member of some social group, what sort of cognitive representation moderates the impact of that specific encounter on subsequent encounters with other members of that social group?" His entirely reasonable answer, of course, is that the earlier encounter affects subsequent ones because it is represented in memory as a specific event or exemplar that may guide subsequent judgments and behaviors in content, process, and context specific manners.

The danger that Dr. Smith falls into, however, is that he tends to confuse the question that he really is posing with the following rather different question: "When one encounters an individual who is a member of a particular social group or category, what is the form of the representation that is retrieved from memory about that individual's social group that affects current behavior and judgment?" The difference in these two questions, the one that Dr. Smith explicitly poses and answers and the one that I believe he implicitly suggests he has answered, are quite marked. Hence, they may call for radically different sorts of answers. Dr. Smith seems to assume that in answering the first question he has also provided at least a partial answer to the second. Such a result need not in fact be the case.

I am entirely willing to agree with Dr. Smith about the likely form of the representation of a past encounter with a specific group member that has an impact upon subsequent encounters with members of that same group. In order to have an impact, the past encounter must be represented in a very specific manner and its effects are likely to be content, process, and context specific. On the other hand, it seems to me to be a rather different argument to suggest that whenever I encounter a group member, the information that comes to mind about that group and the attributes of its members comes in the form of specific exemplar information. It may well be the case that the group relevant information that is accessed when a new group member is encountered tends in fact to be relatively abstract or prototypic information about the group as a whole and its modal or typical characteristics.

Obviously, if previous encounters with group members come to mind as well, they will do so in the form of specific exemplar information. But there is no guarantee upon meeting any particular group member in the present that any particular previous encounters with other group members will in fact come to mind. Instead, it is entirely possible that the only group relevant information that is retrieved from memory comes in the form of relatively abstract information about what the group as a whole is known to be like.

My disagreement with Dr. Smith here is frankly one of emphasis rather than one of substance. He certainly acknowledges that information about social groups may be stored at a relatively abstract level, particularly in the case of stereotypes about social groups that have been learned without any direct contact with individual members of those social groups. Thus, I am sure that he would be willing to grant my argument that relatively abstract information about the group as a whole may come to mind when a specific group member is encountered. Nevertheless, based on his arguments about the use of exemplars as the cognitive mediators of prior specific encounters with group members, he suggests that past social cognition research on stereotypes has probably overemphasized the role of relatively abstract group representations and underemphasized the importance of exemplar representations of prior encounters with specific group members. While I agree with Dr. Smith that past encounters with group members are likely to be represented as individual exemplars, it does not necessarily follow from this that there has been an overemphasis in the literature on abstract representations of groups and their attributes. It may in fact be the case that for the vast majority of social stereotypes, particularly for those involving relatively unfamiliar social groups, the majority of information is stored at the group level and that group-level information is what comes to mind when a new group member is encountered.

CLARIFYING THE DIFFERENCE IN QUESTIONS IN RESEARCH ON THE CONTACT HYPOTHESIS

To clarify the difference in the question that Dr. Smith explicitly asks and answers and the one I believe he suggests he has answered as well, consider research on the Contact Hypothesis conducted by Stuart Cook and others (Cook, 1969, 1971, 1985). Research conducted under the guidance of this hypothesis has examined the extent to which cooperative contact with a member of some negatively evaluated outgroup will lead to a breakdown in prejudice both toward the specific outgroup member with whom interaction occurs and toward the outgroup in general.

In reviewing this work, Cook (1985) suggests that equal-status contact in a cooperative setting has the anticipated positive effects on attitudes and behavior toward the specific outgroup member with whom one has contact. Even if subjects are quite prejudiced against the outgroup as a whole, cooperative contact seems to induce the development of respect and liking for the specific outgroup members with whom one has interacted. However, generalized attitude change and the breakdown of prejudice toward the outgroup as a whole is a much rarer and relatively unpredictable outcome of intergroup contact with specific outgroup members. While it seems that contact can lead to the development of positive attitudes towards specific outgroup members, it is not the case that this necessarily generalizes into positive attitude change toward the outgroup as a category.

The question that Dr. Smith asks and the conclusions he reaches fit quite nicely into this context. The contact of a prejudiced individual with an outgroup member in a cooperative, equal-status setting is a specific encounter that may have effects upon social judgments and behaviors in the future. If it does so, following Dr. Smith's reasoning, then those effects are likely to be relatively long-lasting and they are likely to be content, process, and context specific effects. The specificity of these effects is exactly what researchers on the contact hypothesis have demonstrated. That is, in future encounters with the same individual (content specificity), involving the same sort of tasks (process specificity), and/or in the same context (context specificity), behaviors should show the benefits of the cooperative, equal-status interaction. Accordingly, behavior toward other specific outgroup members may be modified, but only when the other members, the task at hand, and the context are similar enough to the original contact to result in the retrieval of the original encounter from memory. According to this point of view, it would be surprising if the specific encounter with a particular outgroup member in a cooperative context would in fact generalize and modify attitudes toward the outgroup as a whole and toward all outgroup members, regardless of their resemblance with the prior specific encounter. This is because the specific encounter is unlikely to have large effects upon any relatively abstract or prototypic representation about the group as a whole that might be stored in memory. Rather, the specific encounter is likely to be stored in relatively specific exemplar form, having relatively specific effects upon future behavior and judgment.

As this analysis shows, Dr. Smith's conclusions provide a rather nice interpretation for the results of a wealth of work on the contact hypothesis. The specificity of the effects of contact and the failure to find much generalization of contact on attitude change and prejudice reduction toward the outgroup as a whole are quite consistent with his specificity principles. Yet, I believe that it would be quite erroneous from these principles to suggest that relatively abstract and prototypic representations of the outgroup as a whole have relatively little to do in guiding behavior and judgments made about specific outgroup members. While an earlier specific encounter with an outgroup member may have only relatively specific and focused effects upon future interactions, that result does not seem to me to have any necessary implication about the kind of information that is likely to be retrieved from memory on future encounters with outgroup individuals. Future social interactions with outgroup members may well be driven nearly exclusively by relatively abstract characterizations of the outgroup as a whole that are retrieved from memory, even though any one particular prior encounter with an outgroup member is likely to be stored in specific exemplar form.

Thus, in spite of Dr. Smith's forceful and persuasive analysis, it does not seem to me necessarily to be the case that the existent social cognition literature has relatively overemphasized the role of abstract representations in guiding social judgment and social behavior. When dealing with highly prejudiced individuals, as has been the case in some of the research on the contact hypothesis, it seems quite likely that prejudicial behavior is so pervasive, in spite of a possible few cooperative equal-status encounters with outgroup members in the past, precisely because it is relatively abstract characterizations of the group as a whole that come to mind and guide behavior rather than the few exemplars of cooperative contact in the past that might also have been stored. Thus, past cooperative encounters with specific outgroup members have so little effect upon subsequent attitudes toward the group as a whole because they may be swamped by the relatively abstract group-level characterizations that are most likely retrieved whenever outgroup members are encountered or characterized.

CONCLUSION

I hope to have made clear my basic sympathy with Dr. Smith's major arguments and conclusions. I am totally convinced that in fact specific prior experiences are most likely to have effects upon subsequent behavior and judgment, when they do, in forms that are relatively specific. Accordingly, it seems quite appropriate to argue that they are stored in very specific exemplar forms in memory rather than being stored exclusively in relatively abstract characterizations or prototypes of the category as a whole. However, I do believe that Dr. Smith has perhaps been guilty of overgeneralizing this result himself to some small extent, taking his argument a second step by suggesting that it therefore follows that category information tends to be represented by a series of exemplars rather than by a central prototype or abstract representation. I think it is far from clear that research in the social cognition tradition has relatively overemphasized the role of abstract representations of category information. While prior encounters may indeed have their effects in relatively specific forms, it does not necessarily follow from this that when category members in the future are encountered the most likely information to be retrieved from memory about the category is exemplar information or recollections of past specific encounters of individual category members. For many social categories, it may be that the most likely information that comes to mind when a category member is encountered remains relatively abstract, category-level information. We still don't know to what extent this is true. The argument that prior specific experiences are most likely encoded as specific exemplars or memory traces seems to me to be a fine argument, just so long as one doesn't take it to imply that all we have stored and all we retrieve are specific exemplars or memory traces.

REFERENCES

Cook, S. W. (1969). Motives in a conceptual analysis of attitude-related behavior. In W. J. Arnold & D. Levine (Eds.), *Nebraska Symposium on Motivation*. Lincoln: University of Nebraska Press.

Cook, S.W. (1971). *The effect of unintended interracial contact upon racial interaction and attitude change* (Final report, Project No. 5-1320). Washington, D.C.: U.S. Department of Health, Education and Welfare, Office of Education.

Cook. S. W. (1985). Experimenting on social issues: The case of school desegregation. *American Psychologist, 40,* 452–460.

7

The Role of Abstract and Exemplar-Based Knowledge in Self-Judgments: Implications for a Cognitive Model of the Self

Stanley B. Klein
Trinity University

Judith Loftus
University of Texas at San Antonio

Eliot Smith presents some important implications for social cognition of a trend in cognitive psychology away from models that rely primarily on abstract representations toward those that incorporate storage and use of both abstraction and specific instances. A greater emphasis on specific instances as mediators of the social judgment process is long overdue, and the methodological principle Smith outlines should prove useful in developing models that reflect this change.

The focus of our comments will be to relate some of the issues Smith raises to a particular area of modeling in social cognition—models of the representation of information about the self. We will show that in contrast to the overemphasis on mediation by abstract knowledge structures that typifies social judgment models, current self-judgment models tend to attribute too great a role to specific instances as mediators of peoples' judgments about their personality characteristics. Most cognitive models of the self describe a network in which there is direct access both to abstracted trait knowledge and to trait-relevant behaviors to which trait knowledge is linked (for reviews, see Greenwald & Pratkanis, 1984; Kihlstrom & Cantor, 1984; Wyer & Srull, 1989). In these models (see Fig. 7.1) judgments about one's traits may be mediated by either trait concepts or trait-relevant behavioral exemplars.

Unfortunately, empirical tests of those models of the self are scarce. A major reason for this is that experimental paradigms of the sort that have been useful in studying social judgment models are not easily transferable to the self domain. For example, Smith presents an elegant paradigm for assessing the contributions of prototype and exemplar information to social judgments about unknown others that requires that subjects learn either category prototypes and exemplars

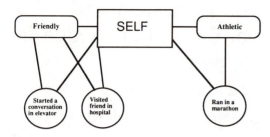

FIG. 7.1. Model of the self in which trait judgments may be mediated either through abstract trait information or by trait-relevant behavioral exemplars.

concurrently, prototypes first and then exemplars, or exemplars only (Smith & Zarate, 1987). By contrast, subjects' abstract trait knowledge and behavioral exemplar knowledge about themselves usually is well-developed, and thus not easily manipulated in an experimental setting.

Within the constraints inherent in studying self-judgments, however, we have found that response latencies for subjects performing self-related tasks can be informative about the roles of abstract and exemplar self-knowledge in the self-judgment process. In the next section we present the findings of several studies that use response latency measures to examine the degree to which behavioral exemplars play a part in judging the self-descriptiveness of traits.

INVESTIGATIONS OF THE SELF-JUDGMENT PROCESS

A feature common to self-representation models like that shown in Fig. 7.1 is that trait concepts are linked to trait-relevant behaviors in an associative network. If we assume that excitation spreads along links from an activated node to connected nodes, which in turn become activated (e.g., Anderson, 1983; Collins & Loftus, 1975), these models imply the prediction that making a trait judgment about the self will lead to the activation of behaviors to which that trait concept is linked. For example, a subject's judgment of whether or not she is friendly would begin at the "self" node, with activation spreading to the trait node for "friendly" and to trait-relevant behaviors. If she is asked next to retrieve a behavior in which she was friendly, she should be able to do so relatively quickly since such behaviors already are activated in memory. It follows that one way to test whether trait-relevant behaviors become activated during trait judgments is to assess the degree to which judging a trait for self-descriptiveness leads to a decrease in the time required to then retrieve a behavior exemplifying the trait from memory. This reasoning underlies the approach we have taken in studying this question (Klein, Loftus, & Burton, 1989; Klein, Loftus, & Trafton, 1989).

Our studies used three tasks: A *descriptive* task required subjects to judge a stimulus trait word for self-descriptiveness, an *autobiographical* task required subjects to retrieve from memory a specific behavioral incident in which they manifested the stimulus trait, and a *semantic* task required subjects to generate a definition of the stimulus trait. The semantic task was assumed to access information about the word's meaning without activating self-related trait and behavioral information (evidence presented in Klein, Loftus, & Trafton, 1989, strongly supports this assumption). A trial consisted of performing two tasks in succession, an initial task and a target task, on the same trait word. The initial and target tasks both were selected from the three task types (descriptive, autobiographical, and semantic). The assignment of trait words to the initial task-target task pairs (15 words per pair) and the order in which the task pairs were presented were randomized across subjects (a fuller presentation of our procedure can be found in Klein, Loftus, & Burton, 1989).

We predicted that if self-descriptiveness judgments result in the activation of relevant behavioral exemplars, then compared to a semantic task, a descriptive task should be more facilitating to the performance of an immediately following autobiographical task. This is because trait-relevant behaviors that have already been activated should be more readily retrieved in the autobiographical task than trait-relevant behaviors that have not already been activated. Initial performance of a descriptive task, but not of a semantic task, is assumed to promote such activation. By contrast, if trait-relevant behaviors are not activated by a descriptive task, then the time required to perform an autobiographical task should be unaffected by whether the initial task is descriptive or semantic. In both cases, the trait-relevant behaviors retrieved will not have been activated previously.[1]

We conducted several tests of these predictions (Klein, Loftus, & Burton, 1989; Klein, Loftus & Trafton, 1989), and our results consistently offered no support for the proposal that the descriptive task involves the activation of trait-relevant behaviors in memory. The results of Klein, Loftus, and Trafton (1989, Experiment 1) are typical of our findings: Response latencies for the autobiographical task were no faster when it followed a descriptive ($M = 6,145$ ms) than when it followed a semantic ($M = 6,156$ ms) task ($t < 1$).

---

[1]Although a spreading activation model seems to predict that the initial performance of an autobiographical task should facilitate the subsequent performance of a descriptive task, we have chosen to restrict the analyses presented in this paper to those examining the effects of an initial descriptive task on a subsequent autobiographical task. Our reason for doing so is that performing an initial autobiographical task does not ensure that the behavior retrieved is part of network that forms one's self-representation. We clearly know a great deal about ourselves, and it does not seem reasonable to argue that every behavioral memory with trait implications is linked to the self: Some behaviors are more central in defining the self than are others. By contrast, if in the process of performing an initial descriptive task, behaviors linked to the self are activated, these behaviors will be most likely to be retrieved during performance of an autobiographical task due to their enhanced availability. It should be noted, however, that for all the studies presented in this paper, an initial autobiographical task was no more facilitating than an initial semantic task on a subsequent descriptive task.

Given these results, it was tempting to conclude that people make trait judgments about themselves without activating representative behaviors. However, a potential limitation of our paradigm merits consideration. Our expectation that autobiographical task facilitation would be found if a preceding descriptive task had activated trait-relevant behaviors is based on the assumption that the set of trait-relevant behaviors activated by a self-descriptiveness judgment for a particular trait will be the same set of behaviors retrieved for that trait in the autobiographical task. For self-descriptive traits this seems reasonable, but for traits that are inconsistent with one's self-concept another possibility seems equally likely. Inconsistent traits may not be represented explicitly in one's self-representation. Subjects decide that inconsistent traits are not self-descriptive by the ready availability of trait knowledge or behaviors that imply the opposite of these traits (e.g., an unselfish subject, deciding whether the trait "selfish" describes her, either readily accesses her trait knowledge or herself as unselfish or readily thinks of an incident in which she was unselfish, and decides that the trait "selfish" does not describe her). The same subject performing the autobiographical task would retrieve an incident in which she was selfish. Thus, the descriptive and autobiographical tasks activate two different sets of behaviors for this trait, and there would be no reason to expect that the descriptive task would result in facilitation of the autobiographical task. It could be argued then, that the lack of facilitation effects in our studies should be interpreted not as evidence against behavioral activation, but rather as a result of our failure to distinguish between responses for traits that are consistent and inconsistent with the self. In light of this possibility, it seems more prudent to predict that, relative to a semantic task, a descriptive task should facilitate performance of an autobiographical task for traits that are consistent with the self, but not necessarily for traits that are inconsistent with the self.

We tested this hypothesis (Klein, Loftus, & Burton, 1989, Experiment 2) in an experiment identical to the one just described, except that after subjects completed the response latency part of the experiment they saw each trait word again and indicated whether or not it was self-descriptive. We then analyzed target task response latency, excluding traits rated as non-self-descriptive. The results were straightforward: again, no facilitation effects were found. The time required to perform an autobiographical task was not differentially influenced by the previous performance of a descriptive ($M = 4,826$ ms) task or a semantic ($M = 4,608$ ms) task ($t < 1$).

In their failure to find evidence that trait-relevant behaviors are activated during trait self-judgments, the foregoing experiments argue against links between trait knowledge and trait-relevant behaviors. However, before accepting this conclusion we decided to look at one other possibility. It seemed to us that the situation in which behavioral exemplars are most likely to mediate trait judgments is when the trait being judged is irrelevant to one's self-concept. Because a subject may not have abstract self-knowledge about an irrelevant trait, self-descriptiveness judgments would have to be inferred from the retrieval of trait-relevant behaviors in memory. Consider, for example, Fig. 7.2, which shows a small portion of a hypothetical subject's mental representation of her personality. There is a direct link between the self and the trait "friendly," but not between the self and the trait "generous." In other words, the trait "friendly" is part of the individual's characterization of herself and she can readily retrieve that information about her friendliness. By contrast, the trait "generous" is not one in terms of which she typically characterizes herself. When asked to judge herself along that dimension she must do so by generating an inference after first retrieving relevant behavioral evidence (e.g., I remember giving money to a beggar. I must therefore be generous). Thus, facilitation effects should be evident only when judgments are made about traits that are not relevant to one's characterization of oneself.

To explore this possibility, Klein, Loftus, and Trafton (1989) repeated the task facilitation procedure, and then asked subjects to rate the stimulus traits on a 9-point scale marked "extremely unlike me" (1), "irrelevant" (5), and "extremely like me (9). These ratings allowed us to sort subjects' response latencies into three degrees of self-descriptiveness (High, Medium, and Low). For each initial task-target task pair (15 words per pair), the five traits receiving the highest ratings were placed in the High category, the five traits receiving the next highest ratings were placed in the Medium category, and the remaining five traits were placed in the Low category. In case of ties where the trait could be assigned to adjacent categories, random assignment was employed.

To ensure that subject's variability in their use of the full range of the rating scale did not invalidate our assignment of traits to the three categories, we first computed the mean ratings for traits in our High, Medium, and Low self-descriptiveness categories. These means did indeed reflect scale values consistent with the category headings (Ms = 8.2, 6.1, and 4.1, for high, medium, and low, respectively). Further corroboration of our groupings was found when we examined initial task response latencies for the descriptive task. Previous

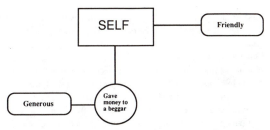

FIG. 7.2. Model of the self in which self-judgments activate behavioral exemplars only when the trait being judged is irrelevant to one's self-concept.

research has shown that when response latencies for self-descriptiveness judgments are segregated on the basis of trait self-descriptiveness, subjects are fastest to judge traits very much like them and very much unlike them, and slowest to judge traits that are not integral to their self-concept (e.g., Kuiper, 1981). Consistent with these findings, descriptive task response latencies produced the anticipated inverted "U", with latencies from the Medium self-descriptiveness category significantly greater than latencies from either the High or Low categories.

If mediation of self-judgments by trait-relevant behaviors occurs primarily when the traits being judged are those that are not relevant to a subject's self-concept, then facilitation effects should be evident for those traits rated near "irrelevant" in self-descriptiveness. When we examined target task response latencies for traits in the Medium self-descriptiveness category, however, we again found no facilitation effects: The time required to perform an autobiographical task was not differentially affected by previous performance of a descriptive ($M = 6,203$ ms) or semantic ($M = 6,129$ ms) task ($t < 1$) (response latencies for traits in the High and Low categories also showed no facilitation effects).[2]

IMPLICATIONS FOR A COGNITIVE
MODEL OF SELF-KNOWLEDGE

The experiments we have described offer evidence that the role of trait-relevant behavioral exemplars in the self-judgment process has been overemphasized by current models of the mental representation of self. The absence of facilitating effects of trait judgments on the retrieval of behavioral incidents argues against models of self-representation in which abstracted trait knowledge about oneself is linked to relevant behavioral exemplars. Such representations imply that priming abstract trait knowledge by performing a descriptive task should activate

---

[2]These findings also argue against a criticism that our failures to find facilitation effects may be related to the "fan" effect described by Anderson (e.g., Anderson, 1983). According to this interpretation, the greater the number of behaviors linked to a trait node, the less the excitation available to activate any particular behavior. The failure of a descriptive task to facilitate the retrieval of specific behaviors thus may reflect the fact that subjects' trait concept nodes may have a great number of behavioral instances linked to them. Work by Markus (1977), however, suggests that this interpretation is limited to traits judged to be very self-descriptive. Markus found that a person's ability to generate trait-relevant behaviors is directly related to the applicability of the trait to the self, with few behaviors produced for traits judged to be uncharacteristic of the self. Consequently, a "fan" effect explanation is less compelling for our failure to find facilitation effects with traits rated as Medium in self-descriptiveness.

relevant behavioral information in memory, thereby facilitating its retrieval in a subsequent autobiographical task. The present studies found no evidence of this kind of facilitation.

However, Smith's arguments related to the notion of process specificity could raise some question about our conclusions. Smith cites research in which the effects of a single past experience are evident only to the extent that the priming manipulation and the subsequent test involve overlapping processes. This view raises the possibility that making trait judgments about the self does activate relevant behavioral exemplars, but that the processes involved in activating behavioral exemplars during self-descriptiveness judgments and those involved in explicitly retrieving the behaviors from memory differ sufficiently that the effects of one would not be evident in the performance of the other.

Other evidence presented by Smith, however, suggests that the applicability of this argument to the present data is limited. Smith and Branscombe (1987, Experiment 2), for example, report priming effects that are not process-specific; the effects were limited, however, to a relatively short duration (e.g., 15 s). The delay between our initial and target tasks was only 1 s; thus regardless of the processes involved in the descriptive and autobiographical tasks, if they activate the same underlying cognitive structure, then priming by the descriptive task should facilitate the immediate performance of the autobiographical task. We believe that our failure to find that facilitation is good evidence that abstracted trait knowledge and behavioral exemplar knowledge about the self are not part of the same cognitive structure. Rather, they are stored and accessed independently.[3]

This is not to say that subjects' descriptions of themselves cannot be influenced by the retrieval of relevant past behaviors. Salancik and his colleagues (e.g., Salancik, 1974; Salancik & Conway, 1975), for example, showed that manipulations that induced the recall of either proreligious or antireligious behaviors differentially influenced subsequent self-judgments of religiousness. When subjects were induced to recall behaviors that implied a positive attitude toward religion, they judged themselves to be more religious than when they were induced to recall behaviors that implied a negative attitude toward religion. Clearly, people *can* retrieve and utilize behavioral information when making trait judgments about themselves. We suggest, however, that in general they do not.

A model of the self that assumes the independent storage and retrieval of trait and behavioral information offers a new perspective from which to understand a variety of puzzling psychological phenomena. For instance, it can help explain the often observed contrast between individuals' beliefs about themselves and

---

[3]We are not suggesting that behavioral information plays no role in the initial establishment of abstract trait representations. Clearly it must. We are arguing that once a trait representation has been established, it typically is addressed independently of the behavioral record.

contradictory behavioral evidence. It might seem that maintaining a judgment about oneself that is at odds with one's behavior would require some sort of effortful self-deception, but the model of self that we propose would allow such contradiction as a natural consequence of a system in which behavioral episodes normally are not activated when judging one's personal characteristics.

CONCLUSION

Eliot Smith makes a strong case for the importance of both abstract knowledge structures and a record of unique experiences as mediators of social judgments. His demonstration of the inadequacies of pure abstraction models is compelling and should stimulate a good deal of interesting and fruitful research. The work we discuss in this chapter addresses inadequacies in models of self-judgments. Our findings complement Smith's by showing that models of self-judgments have placed and undue emphasis on the role of exemplars (e.g., behavioral instances) in the self-judgment process. Our results suggest that both behavioral exemplars and abstract trait knowledge about the self are available in memory, but that exemplar information ordinarily does not play a part in judging the self-descriptiveness of personality traits.

ACKNOWLEDGEMENTS

We would like to thank Greg Trafton and Dan Wegner for their insightful comments on an earlier version of this paper. Correspondence concerning this paper should be addressed to Stanley B. Klein, Department of Psychology, Trinity University, 715 Stadium Drive, San Antonio, Texas, 78284.

REFERENCES

Anderson, J. R. (1983). A spreading activation theory of memory. *Journal of Verbal Learning and Verbal Behavior, 22,* 261–295.

Collins, A. M., & Loftus, E. F. (1975). A spreading-activation theory of semantic processing. *Psychological Review, 82,* 407–428.

Greenwald, A. G., & Pratkanis, A. R. (1984). The self. In R. S. Wyer & T. K. Srull (Eds.), *Handbook of social cognition: Vol. 3* (pp. 129–178). Hillsdale, NJ: Lawrence Erlbaum Associates.

Kihlstrom, J. F., & Cantor, N. (1984). Mental representations of the self. In L. Berkowitz (Ed.), *Advances in experimental social psychology* (Vol. 17, pp. 1–47). New York: Academic Press.

Klein, S. B., Loftus, J., & Burton, H. A. (1989). Two self-reference effects: The importance of distinguishing between self-descriptiveness judgments and autobiographical retrieval in self-referent encoding. *Journal of Personality and Social Psychology, 56,* 853–865.

Klein, S. B., Loftus, J., & Trafton, J. G. (1989). [*The mental representation of self*]. Unpublished raw data.

Kuiper, N. A. (1981). Convergent evidence for the self as prototype: The "inverted-U RT" effect for self and other judgments. *Personality and Social Psychology Bulletin, 7*, 438–443.

Markus, H. (1977). Self-schemata and processing information about the self. *Journal of Personality and Social Psychology, 35*, 63–78.

Salancik, G. R. (1974). Inference of one's attitude from behavior recalled under linguistically manipulated cognitive sets. *Journal or Experimental Social Psychology, 10*, 415–427.

Salancik, G. R., & Conway, M. (1975). Attitude inferences from salient and relevant cognitive content about behavior. *Journal of Personality and Social Psychology, 32*, 829–840.

Smith, E. R., & Branscombe, N. R. (1987). Procedurally mediated social inferences: The case of category accessibility effects. *Journal of Experimental Social Psychology, 23*, 361–382.

Smith, E. R., & Zarate, M. A. (1987). *Exemplar models of person memory and categorization.* Unpublished manuscript.

Wyer, R. S., & Srull, T. K. (1989). *Memory and cognition in its social context.* Hillsdale, NJ: Lawrence Erlbaum Associates.

8

Social Cognition Gets Specific

Gordon D. Logan
University of Illinois

Eliot Smith's article, "Content and process specificity in the effects of prior experiences," is timely and important. It is another in a series of landmark reviews documenting the importance of specific prior experiences. Earlier reviews established the importance of specific experience in episodic memory (Hintzman, 1976), semantic memory (Landauer, 1975), explicit and implicit memory (Jacoby & Brooks, 1984), categorization and category learning (Brooks, 1978; Jacoby & Brooks, 1984; Medin & Smith, 1984), problem solving (Ross, 1984), judgments of normalcy (Kahneman & Miller, 1986), and automatization (Logan, 1988). Smith's article adds significantly to the series, introducing new paradigms and new theoretical issues in which specific experiences have influence, and providing ways to integrate them with existing theory and data. Smith is a theorist of broad vision, aiming to create a cognitive psychology that covers social phenomena as well as the nonsocial, using his extension of Anderson's (1983) ACT* theory to capture the important effects (see Smith, 1984).

I have strong sympathy for Smith's position on specificity and I appreciate the value of the coherent theoretical perspective he takes. However, his focus on ACT* mechanisms for certain effects (content specificity and skill acquisition) leads him to focus on some phenomena and inadvertently ignore others. I suspect he may have missed some important demonstrations of the priority of specific experience in doing so. My commentary begins with a discussion of content specificity and skill acquisition, sketching a framework within which to complete the picture begun by Smith's review. I illustrate my points with recent experiments from *nonsocial* cognition and leave it to experts like Smith and the reader to come up with examples from social cognition. My commentary ends with more general remarks on the priority of the specific. First, I ask why one should

141

have to argue for the priority of the specific in the first place (we live life in the particular; the real question is, where do generalizations come from?). Then, given that we must argue, I have some suggestions about how one should carry out the argument.

SPECIFICITY OF CONTENT

Smith distinguishes between *content* and *process* in dealing with specificity. Content is essentially the stimulus presented to the subject and process is what the subject does with the stimulus. This separation follows naturally from the ACT* production system approach Smith follows: Content is the symbol structures in working memory and process is the productions that operate on them. However, it may not be so easy to separate content and process in other approaches to modeling, such as exemplar models like Hintzman's (1986, 1988) or connectionist, parallel-distributed-processing models like McClelland and Rumelhart's (1985). In those models, content reflects the interaction of many specific traces of past experience, filtered through a retrieval process (in the case of Hintzman) or a learning process (in the case of McClelland and Rumelhart). In radical connectionist models, content is process.

Smith's sharp distinction between content and process invites the reader to equate content with the stimulus, and that may be misleading. I believe the content that is relevant to the issues at hand is *mental content*. Mental content is not the stimulus as presented but rather the stimulus as interpreted by the subject. Mental content is produced by running a stimulus through a process, so it is bound to be both stimulus specific and process specific, at least to some degree.

Smith must endorse this position. He can avoid making it explicitly in his experiments on social judgments because he uses words to represent the social phenomena his subjects are to judge. Thus they decide whether "kiss" is "friendly." In the real world, social judgments are made about actual people interacting dynamically. To decide whether a kiss is friendly in that context, one must first interpret a person's action toward another as a kiss (vs. mouth-to-mouth recussitation). Smith does the interpretation for them by providing the word "kiss." It is an interpreted symbol to begin with, and should be treated as such theoretically, not as a "raw stimulus."

Smith's review looked for evidence of content specificity in experiments in which the same process was transferred to novel stimuli. Subjects would be trained to do one kind of judgment (e.g., friendliness) on one set of stimuli and then transferred to a new set of stimuli. Content specificity would be evident as poor transfer to the new stimuli. His definition is consistent with the idea of content as the stimulus-as-presented and with content as the stimulus-as-interpreted. It doesn't distinguish between them, and it invites the reader to confuse them. However, content specificity can be defined in other ways that allow the two senses of content to be separated and contrasted. One way is to use a design in which the same stimuli are transferred to a new process. Subjects could be trained to do one kind of judgment on one set of stimuli and transferred to another kind of judgment on the same set of stimuli. If content is the stimulus-as-presented, there should be strong positive transfer here because the stimulus-as-presented remains the same. But if content is the stimulus-as-interpreted, there should be poor transfer because the interpretation changes.

Some recent experiments of mine used these designs to test whether mental content is the stimulus-as-presented or the stimulus-as-interpreted. One set of experiments used the latter design and demonstrates that transfer occurs when a stimulus is interpreted in the same way at study and test but not when it is interpreted differently. Another set used Smith's design to show that changes in properties of the stimulus that are irrelevant to its interpretation have little effect on transfer.

In the first set of experiments, subjects were shown words (e.g., brat), pronouncible nonwords (e.g., blat), and unpronouncible nonwords (e.g., bjlt) under two task sets. In the *lexical decision task,* they discriminated between words and nonwords, grouping the pronouncible nonwords together with the unpronouncible ones, but in the *pronunciation task,* they discriminated between pronouncible and unpronouncible strings, grouping pronouncible nonwords together with the words. Transfer was assessed in a variety of ways, but the basic design involved comparing groups who were trained and tested on the same task with subjects who were trained on one task and transferred to the other. In general, there was good transfer (i.e., faster reaction times on repeated presentations) if the task remained the same at study and test but poor transfer (i.e., no benefit from repetition) if the task changed from study to test. Note that in all cases, the same stimuli were presented at study and test; the effects of prior experience depended on whether the interpretation of the stimuli changed or stayed the same (see Logan, 1988, 1990a).[1]

In the second set of experiments, subjects performed lexical decisions on red and green words that appeared in one of three positions in a display. The other two positions were occupied by white consonant strings the same length as the words. These experiments again used the transfer design, varying whether color and position were the same at study and test. The results showed a small advantage for words in the same color at test, though there was substantial transfer

---

[1]It is interesting to note that other experiments in this series showed near perfect transfer to other stimulus-response mappings (e.g., pressing a different key to indicate "yes, it's a word"; see Logan, 1990a). This reinforces the point that what is learned is the stimulus-as-interpreted. The fact that the same data were well fit by Logan's (1988) instance theory points out a misconception in Smith's interpretation of the instance theory: He claims that instances are memorized stimulus-response pairs. These data suggest they are stimulus-interpretation pairs. The theory itself could be consistent with either alternative; it assumes that the knowledge contained in instances is associative, though it does not prescribe what should be associated with what.

(compared to new words) for words in a different color. Varying position from study to test had negligible effects. In these cases, different stimuli were presented at study and at test, but the interpretation remained the same so transfer was observed (see Logan, 1990b).

These results are hard to accommodate with the view that content is the stimulus-as-presented, suggested by Smith's sharp distinction between content and process. They are easy to accommodate with the view that content is the stimulus-as-interpreted. Indeed, much of the evidence for content specificity in Smith's review can be reinterpreted with content as the stimulus-as-interpreted. Such a view may lead to broader interpretations of the results than Smith's ACT* perspective affords, which may suggest new experiments and new lines of research to test alternatives to Smith's perspective.

SPECIFICITY IN SKILL ACQUISITION

Smith's model of skill acquisition is essentially Anderson's (1982, 1983) ACT* learning theory. He distinguishes sharply between *declarative* and *procedural* knowledge, and interprets skill acquisition (as Anderson does) primarily in terms of acquiring and strengthening procedural knowledge. Anderson's theory is powerful, and Smith adroitly extends it to social judgment phenomena, but there are other ways to construe skill acquisition. In some of them, skill acquisition may depend on the acquisition and strengthening of declarative knowledge.

My instance theory of automatization (Logan, 1988) is a case in point. In that theory, skill acquisition depends on the acquisition of a large domain-specific knowledge base, and skilled (or automatic) performance depends on single-step, direct-access retrieval of the required information from the knowledge base, rather than on some algorithmic computation. There is no reason why the knowledge base cannot be declarative. With practice, as memory grows stronger, information will be retrieved more rapidly, mimicking the growth in speed associated with strengthening procedural knowledge.

The mimicry is very close quantitatively. Anderson shows that his assumptions about strengthening productions produce learning curves that follow the power law of practice (see Newell & Rosenbloom, 1981). Similarly, one can prove that the instance theory predicts power law learning. The proof emerges from the basic assumptions of the theory: The theory assumes (a) that attention to an object or event is sufficient to encode it into memory, (b) that attention to an object or event is sufficient to retrieve whatever was associated with it in the past from memory, and (c) that the each encounter with an object or event is encoded, stored, and retrieved separately (for a discussion of these assumptions, see Logan, 1988). The first assumption causes a domain-specific knowledge base to be built up with experience. The second assumption causes relevant information to be retrieved when identical or similar objects or events (mental contents) are encountered again. Together, the first and second assumptions imply that the more experience a person has with specific objects or events, the more will be retrieved about them. This and the third assumption, the assumption of *instance representation*, lead to the power law prediction.

One can model the retrieval process as a race between the various traces in memory. As soon as one of them finishes (i.e., is retrieved), the person can respond (i.e., memory will have provided sufficient information to choose a response). If we assume that each trace has the same distribution of retrieval times, then the problem is equivalent to a well-studied problem in the statistics of extreme values: How does the minimum of n samples from the same distribution decrease as n increases? It is possible to prove for a large class of distributions, that the minimum decreases as a power function of n (for formal and informal discussion of the proofs, see Logan, 1988). Not only will the expected value of the minimum decrease, but the whole distribution of minima will decrease as a power function of n. Since reaction time equals the minimum of n samples plus some residual time, the entire distribution of reaction times should decrease as a power function of n. This is a very strong prediction not made by other models.[2] It can be tested simply by comparing power-function fits and parameter values for means and standard deviations. Both should decrease as power functions of n and, since they are functions of the same distribution, both power functions should have the same exponent. Logan (1988) tested and confirmed this prediction in several data sets.

Thus the instance theory, which assumes a build-up in declarative knowledge with practice, predicts the same power law as Anderson's and Smith's ACT* theory, which assumes strengthening of procedural knowledge with practice. More generally, the instance theory suggests that skill acquisition may be an example of content specificity rather than process specificity, whereas Smith's and Anderson's perspective suggests the opposite. There is probably a little truth in both perspectives. The instance theory cannot deal with the ready transfer to new items that Smith observes in his social judgment tasks and the Smith–Anderson theory cannot deal with the poor transfer to new stimuli in lexical decision (Logan, 1988, 1989a) and alphabet arithmetic (Logan & Klapp, 1989). The point for the reader is that skill acquisition may increase both procedural and declarative knowledge. One may wish to go beyond Smith and look for further evidence of skill based on declarative knowledge.

---

[2]For example, a model in which performance was a probabilistic mixture of skilled and unskilled processing (e.g., ''automatic'' vs. ''controlled'' processing) could predict a power-function reduction in mean reaction time, but it could not predict a power-function reduction in the standard deviation. In mixture models, the standard deviation is an inverted U-shaped function of the probability mixture. It is smallest when one process or the other dominates and largest when their contributions are roughly equal. For a mixture model to predict a power-function reduction in reaction time, the mixture probability would have to change monotonically over practice from 0 to 1.0 (or vice versa). Consequently, the standard deviation would first increase and then decrease with practice. Such patterns are not observed in real data (see e.g., Logan, 1988).

Stuart Klapp and I have conducted a series of experiments on *alphabet arithmetic* that show evidence of skill based on declarative knowledge. We had subjects verify alphabet arithmetic equations such as $A + 2 = C$ and $B + 3 = F$, asking them whether C was 2 letters down the alphabet from A (it is), whether F was 3 letters down the alphabet from B (it isn't). Subjects initially report performing this task by counting serially through the alphabet, one count for each unit of the digit addend, and comparing the last letter counted with the presented answer (e.g., $B + 3 = F$ would be counted as $C, D, E,$ and E would be compared with F, leading to a "false" response). Analysis of reaction times confirms introspection: Reaction time increases linearly with the magnitude of the digit addend (i.e., the number of counts) with a slope of 400–500 ms/count.

As subject practice the task, their introspections suggest they learn specific responses to specific problems. The need to count through the alphabet diminishes and is eventually replaced by memory retrieval. Their reaction time data confirm their introspections: The slope of the function relating reaction time to the digit addend decreases over practice, asymptoting near zero. (At asymptote, performance is based on direct-access memory retrieval, which does not depend on the magnitude of the digit addend, hence retrieval time is the same for all addends; the slope is zero.) The mean and standard deviation of reaction time decrease as power functions of the number of trials per item, and the power functions have the same exponent, as the instance theory predicts. Moreover, there is very little transfer to new problems: learning is content-specific. But is it declarative knowledge that is retrieved from memory?

Stuart Klapp and I sought an answer to this question in experiments that compared learning alphabet arithmetic by doing it (i.e., performing the verification task) with learning it by rote memory for the facts. Learning-by-doing subjects performed the verification task for several blocks of trials, just as previous subjects had. Rote-learning subjects were not trained on the verification task. Instead, they were shown the facts and instructed to memorize them. We tried a number of different learning methods, from subject-paced free learning to experimenter-paced learning that was yoked to learning-by-doing subjects. After a period of rote learning, subjects were transferred to the verification task and their performance was compared to that of learning-by-doing subjects. In each case, rote learning flattened the slope just as learning-by-doing did. Rote learning was quantitatively equivalent to learning-by-doing when the two were yoked. Performance depended on the number of exposures to each alphabet arithmetic fact but not on the method of exposure. The slope flattened at the same rate for rote learning as for learning-by-doing.

These results are strongly suggestive of a declarative knowledge base underlying alphabet arithmetic. It is easy to imagine that rote learning would produce declarative knowledge, and the equivalence of rote learning and learning-by-doing is perfectly consistent with the idea they both rely on the same declarative knowledge base. Most likely, the results are not definitive. How definitive they prove to be will depend on the cleverness and tenacity of theorists like Anderson and Smith in coming up with alternatives based on procedural knowledge. The point for the reader is that skill in alphabet arithmetic and domains like it (e.g., "real" arithmetic, like adding, subtracting, and multiplying; some mathematical knowledge) may be based on declarative knowledge. There is at least one precedent for going beyond Smith's claim that precedural knowledge underlies skill.

WHY SHOULDN'T THE SPECIFIC HAVE PRIORITY?

My initial reaction to Smith's article was enthusiastic: Here was a person advocating a position I agreed with, providing many supportive examples that were new and interesting to me. Upon reflection, my enthusiasm remains, though it is tempered by some puzzling thoughts about the reasons for my enthusiasm in the first place. I suppose I read some missionary zeal into Smith's prose. I find myself arguing the priority of the specific with my colleagues and apparently I have found an ally in Smith. But why should we need to argue so zealously? The priority of the specific should be obvious. We live life in the particular. I am writing this on a particular afternoon on my very own computer in my very own office. You are reading it in a particular context, sitting in a specific position, thinking about specific other concerns. Moreover, we remember the particular. Our memories are filled with details of particular experiences with particular people in particular settings with particular purposes and cross-purposes. The question should be not whether specific experience is important but rather, how anything other than specific experience is possible. Where to generalizations come from? How do concepts, schemas, and scripts result from specific experience?

Of course, these questions are not new. They have been asked in one form or another throughout the history of psychology. Theoretical and empirical attacks have been both vigorous and successful in the last 20 years. Now, there are several theories to choose from and many powerful empirical phenomena that demonstrate the importance of abstract data structures like concepts, schemas, and scripts. As a result, the prevailing view is that cognition is largely controlled by abstract data structures. The belief has become so entrenched in modern thought that it is hard for many to see that anything else is possible. People see no room for the effects of specific experience. That is why Smith's review appears so revolutionary, as did the reviews that preceded it (e.g., Hintzman, 1976; Jacoby & Brooks, 1984; Medin & Smith, 1984). The priority of the specific may be obvious in everyday life, but it runs against the grain of the current academic zeitgeist.

RECONCILING THE SPECIFIC AND THE GENERAL

How are we to reconcile the priority of the general with the priority of the specific? One approach would be to change one's ideas about cognition to accommodate both the general and the specific, to assert cognition depends on both general and specific knowledge structures.[3] The question then would be, which does what? In which domains is specific knowledge especially influential, and in which does general knowledge predominate? Researchers could map out the cognitive terrain, defining the dominions of the general and the specific. The interesting cases would be those in which both general and specific knowledge are important. The question there would be, how do they interact?

Smith's approach to the priority of the specific has this flavor. His ACT* mechanisms capture knowledge at several different levels, from the specific to the general. For example, Smith's version of content specificity can be captured in productions whose conditions are tokens rather than types, and his version of process specificity can be captured in productions whose conditions are types rather than tokens. And so on down (up) the line.

Smith's formalism is attractive because it seems to capture the essence specificity effects and reconcile the general and the specific. However, there may be enough flexibility in the formalism to model specificity in different ways. For example, one could model content specificity by assuming that the productions that make a particular judgment leave a propositional trace that is retrieved when the same judgment is made again on the same item. Smith's judgment productions could be supplemented by another production that said "IF the goal is to judge whether X if friendly and X retrieves a trace that says X is friendly, THEN say 'yes'." This production would fire only if specific items are repeated in the context of the same judgment, which is the essence of content specificity.

This approach is different from Smith's in that the productions themselves need not strengthen for experience to have an effect, yet it is expressed in (roughly) the same ACT* language that Smith uses. For me, this diminishes the impact of Smith's modeling somewhat. His views on specificity can be described very clearly in ACT* mechanisms, but so can contrary views. There is nothing in the formalism or the model as developed so far to compel Smith to describe specificity the way he does. So he uses ACT* more as a descriptive language than as a deductive tool. Nevertheless, he provides a coherent way to reconcile the general with the specific (by admitting that both are important and by describing both in a common theoretical language), and that is an important accomplishment.

A more radical approach to reconciling the general with the specific is to try to assimilate one into the other. This is the strategy taken by radical instance or exemplar theorists who try to explain apparently general phenomena with only specific knowledge. These theorists would want the entire cognitive terrain to be the dominion of specific knowledge. Parts of the terrain, like episodic memory, should be easy to capture. They are primarily specific to begin with. The difficult (and interesting) parts are those in which general knowledge seems most firmly

---

[3]Note that models that assume only general knowledge can be ruled out a priori. They cannot account for the effects of specific knowledge reviewed by Smith and his predecessors. Thus, the alternatives are general plus specific knowledge or specific knowledge alone.

entrenched: concepts, rules, schemas, and scripts. There have been some preliminary successes in these domains (e.g., Hintzman, 1986; Medin & Schaffer, 1978) but there is some suggestion that specific knowledge by itself may not always be sufficient. For example, instance theories have provided very good models of categorization, explaining most of the major phenomena without recourse to abstract, general or *prototypic* representations (see e.g., Hintzman, 1986; Medin & Schaffer, 1978). They argue that a thing is categorized by comparing it against similar instances in memory and assigning it to the category whose instances it is most similar to. Effects that others attributed to prototypes emerge out of the similarity structure as it interacts with the memory retrieval process. However, Murphy and Medin (1985) argued that pure instance models (and other similarity-based models) cannot explain why categories are coherent. They argue that categories are based on *theories* that provide *explanations* of category membership, and the coherence of a category depends on the adequacy with which category membership can be explained by the theory. For example, photographs, children, pets, and computers appear to have little in common, yet they form a coherent category of "things to take out of your house in a fire" (Barsalou, 1985).

The approach one takes to reconciling the general and the specific—accommodation or assimilation—has important implications for falsifiability. It is easy to see how an assimilative approach might be falsified: One could propose that all so-called general effects could be produced and accounted for by an exemplar model, for example. That theory would be falsified by its first failure to describe and account for a phenomenon (provided the phenomenon could be accounted for coherently by theories based on general knowledge structures). By contrast, an accommodative approach would be very hard to falsify: The approach assumes a priori that any given phenomenon could depend on either specific or general knowledge. Finding that it depended on specific knowledge would not falsify the model, nor would finding that it depended on general knowledge. Either result could be perfectly consistent. Thus, the assimilative approach seems more testable than the accommodative approach.

These are extreme cases, however; things may be different in practice. For example, dedicated instance theorists may take failure to account for a phenomenon not as falsification of instance theory but rather as the failure of a particular formulation of the general idea. They may be convinced that instance theory is false only when they have exhausted all possible formulations, and that process may never end. It may be possible to falsify particular instance models, but instance theory in general may prove hard to falsify.

Similarly, no single experiment could falsify the accommodative perspective (e.g., Smith's and Anderson's ACT*), but experiments could falsify particular formulations of the general theory. One could use experiments to revise and refine an accommodative theory even if they could not falsify the theory as a whole. Thus, researchers of both persuasions may be prone to the same errors.

I would recommend attempting to account for all general effects with models based on specific knowledge. The attempt is bound to be provocative because it runs against one's intuitions about general, abstract knowledge (developed in the 1970s and 1980s). It calls into question fundamental, often implicit assumptions that are often illuminating when articulated clearly. Faced with sometimes hostile criticism, it requires more careful deduction from first principles. It inspires creativity, suggesting unforeseen relations between apparently diverse phenomena, and providing new empirical distinctions and suggesting new experiments. Even if it is wrong, the exercise of proving it wrong should improve the fitness of the field.

I would also recommend developing and challenging Smith's approach to specificity. The breadth of the theory, in Smith's hands and Anderson's, makes it a worthy opponent, a "man" much more substantial than straw to challenge and attack. One might also wish to build on Smith's accomplishments. At the very least, they provide high standards of clarity, coherence, and rigor that future theories must match or better.

REFERENCES

Anderson, J. R. (1982). Acquisition of cognitive skill. *Psychological Review, 89,* 369–406.

Anderson, J. R. (1983). *The architecture of cognition.* Cambridge MA: Harvard University Press.

Barsalou, L. W. (1983). Ad hoc categories. *Memory and Cognition, 11,* 211–227.

Brooks, L. R. (1978). Nonanalytic concept formation and memory for instances. In E. Rosch & B. B. Lloyd (Eds.), *Cognition and categorization* (pp. 169–216). Hillsdale NJ: Lawrence Erlbaum Associates.

Hintzman, D. L. (1976). Repetition and memory. In G. H. Bower (Ed.), *The psychology of learning and motivation* (pp. 47–91). New York: Academic Press.

Hintzman, D. L. (1986). "Schema abstraction" in a multiple-trace model. *Psychological Review, 93,* 411–428.

Hintzman, D. L. (1988). Judgments of frequency and recognition memory in a multiple-trace model. *Psychological Review, 95,* 528–551.

Jacoby, L. L., & Brooks, L. R. (1984). Nonanalytic cognition: Memory, perception, and concept formation. In G. H. Bower (Ed.), *The psychology of learning and motivation* (pp. 1–47). New York: Academic Press.

Kahneman, D., & Miller, D. T. (1986). Norm theory: Comparing reality to its alternatives. *Psychological Review, 93,* 136–153.

Landauer, T. K. (1975). Memory without organization: Properties of a model with random storage and undirected retrieval. *Cognitive Psychology, 7,* 495–531.

Logan, G. D. (1988). Toward an instance theory of automatization. *Psychological Review, 95,* 492–527.

Logan, G. D. (1990a). Repetition priming and automaticity: Common underlying mechanisms? *Cognitive Psychology,*

Logan, G. D. (1990b). *The retention of irrelevant properties in the development of automaticity.* Submitted.

Logan, G. D., & Klapp, S. T. (1989). *Automatizing alphabet arithmetic: Is extended practice necessary to produce automaticity?* Submitted.

McClelland, J. L., & Rumelhart, D. E. (1985). Distributed memory and the representation of general and specific information. *Journal of Experimental Psychology: General, 114,* 159–188.

Medin, D. L., & Schaffer, M. M. (1978). Context theory of classification learning. *Psychological Review, 85,* 207–238.

Medin, D. L., & Smith, E. E. (1984). Concepts and concept formation. *Annual Review of Psychology, 35,* 113–138.

Murphy, G. L., & Medin, D. L. (1985). The role of theories in conceptual coherence. *Psychological Review, 92,* 289–316.

Newell, A., & Rosenbloom, P. S. (1981). Mechanisms of skill acquisition and the law of practice. In J. R. Anderson (Ed.), *Cognitive skills and their acquisition* (pp. 1–55). Hillsdale, NJ: Lawrence Erlbaum Associates.

Ross, B. H. (1984). Remindings and their effects in learning a cognitive skill. *Cognitive Psychology, 16,* 371–416.

Smith, E. R. (1984). Model of social inference processes. *Psychological Review, 91,* 392–413.

9 The Maturing of Social Cognition

Thomas M. Ostrom
Ohio State University

All seemed tranquil in the garden of social cognition. In surveying contemporary research, it was clear that nearly every social psychological domain could be better understood by applying principles of categorization and schematic structure from cognitive psychology. The relevance of these principles was established for areas like person perception, stereotypes, attitudes, aggression, judgments, and attributions. Social categories and social schema dominated the cognitive explanations that were offered in comprehensive reviews of the field like those of Fiske and Taylor (1984), Markus and Zajonc (1985), and the *Handbook of Social Cognition* by Wyer and Srull (1984). With the publication of each new study, confidence grew that these principles provided the right nutrient for improved conceptual understanding within all areas of social behavior.

Theoretical inspiration for much of this work had been drawn from a small handful of sources in cognitive psychology. Readings on categorization by Rosch (1978) and on schema by Alba and Hasher (1983) seemed obligatory for social psychologists who were entering the field of social cognition. Beyond a few basic sources such as these, little additional reading seemed necessary. At best, the researcher might look into some specific studies in the cognitive literature to see if those sources presented data congruent with the researcher's current empirical work.

The basic ideas of categorization and schematic processing were rich enough to enable productive and insightful advances in social cognition. One needn't know much more from cognitive psychology to uncover interesting and important social psychological phenomena. The garden was peaceful.

Eliot Smith's treatise disrupts this tranquility. It blows through the garden like a turbulent springtime thunderstorm. In doing so, it has uprooted some of the field's most favored plants. It provides a critical reexamination of our dependence on principles of categorization and schematic processing. And even more importantly, it brings with it the seeds of new constructs that have properly belonged in the garden all along.

The treatise makes a persuasive case for the role of episodic traces and condition-action production units as important processes underlying social behavior. For me, this is the key contribution of the present volume. These processes are conceptually independent of categorical and schematic structures, and highlight the deficiencies that resulted from our past reliance on social categories and schemas. There is no question that the constructs of episodic knowledge and production systems have been ignored in the past. Smith's treatise insures that they will not be ignored in the future.

The treatise provides a major transition in the maturing of social cognition. It unequivocally establishes how important it is for researchers in social cognition to be closely acquainted with advances in the cognitive literature. Surface knowledge of a few cognitive principles will no longer suffice. This is now starting to be recognized at the level of graduate training. More and more, graduate programs in social cognition are requiring their students to minor in cognitive psychology and to read widely the primary journals of cognitive psychology. The important contributions to social cognition in the future will be made by persons well steeped in the cognitive literature.

The remainder of my commentary addresses three other areas in which the treatise moves the field of social cognition forward. It furthers our understanding of how the information processing approach goes beyond the dimensional theories of the past. It raises questions regarding the parallels between social and nonsocial cognition. And it offers an analysis of specificity as a methodological principle.

DIMENSIONAL VERSUS INFORMATION PROCESSING CONCEPTIONS OF COGNITION

Social psychology has always been cognitive. The area of social cognition was not the first to discover the importance of cognitive activity for understanding social behavior. Indeed, social psychology proudly carried the cognitive banner throughout the dark years of behaviorism (e.g., Krech & Crutchfield, 1948).

So if we accept the premise that social psychology has always been cognitive, the question arises as to how the new area of social cognition differs from the previous approaches to cognition in social psychology. This is a problem that I have been puzzling over for the last several years (Devine & Ostrom, 1988; Ostrom, 1987, 1988a). One major difference is in the metatheoretical assumptions made about the properties of cognition. Earlier theory in social psychology was dimensional, whereas social cognition theory adopts the more qualitative, non-linear categorical and structural constructs of the information processing approach.

Theory construction under the dimensional approach involved three steps. A prototypic example is the area of attitudes. The first step was to propose that attitudes fall on a unidimensional evaluative continuum ranging from extremely positive to extremely negative. The next theoretical step was to devise a model that explained how a person's attitude came to be located at a particular point (or to move from one point to another) on that continuum. The final theoretical step was to explain how overt responses were influenced by the location of the attitude on the continuum.

This dimensional reasoning had been applied to nearly every problem area in social psychology. For example, attribution research posits a dimension ranging from dispositional to situational causes, impression formation research posits a dimension ranging from likeable to dislikeable, and aggression research posits a dimension ranging from low to high aggressiveness. Analogous reasoning also applies to areas like social influence, interpersonal attraction, altruism, cooperation/competition, and prejudice.

In most of these topic areas there have been robust theoretical disputes. Different theorists highlight the importance of different forces operating on the person. Studies are conducted to differentiate between the alternative explanations. But all these disputes have been in regard to the last two theoretical steps. That is, theoretical combat has been restricted to how a person becomes located on the continuum (Step 2) and on how that location affects overt responses (Step 3).

Social cognition differs from the earlier, dimensional cognitive theory in that it contests the first step. It abandons the assumption that all theory should start with positing a continuum. It insists on tackling all the traditional problem areas in social psychology, along with their accumulated empirical phenomena, from a different theoretical starting point.

Smith's treatise offers an excellent illustration of how the information processing perspective goes beyond the dimensional approach. It highlights several of the inadequacies inherent in the dimensional approach and shows how they can be overcome. The maturing of social cognition is facilitated by papers like this one that help differentiate the field from the earlier style of cognitive theorizing.

Multiple Dependent Variables

Dimensional theories are theories of dependent variables. The focus of the theory is always a latent variable, which in turn is regarded as something to be measured. This is well illustrated by the preceding list of problem areas that are studied in social psychology. It is further illustrated by glancing through a list of chapter titles in any textbook on introductory social psychology. All refer to dependent variables.

The present treatise has just the opposite orientation. It focuses, as the title indicates, on the "effects of prior experience." The focus is on an independent variable rather than a dependent variable. Prior experience refers to a broad class of more specific independent variables. For example, in the section on "Practice Effects on Social Judgments," the specific independent variables are amount of practice, length of time between practice and test, the specificity of the test trait to the practice trait, and whether practice involved reading or generating the traits.

The dimensional approach would obligate the theorist to funnel the effects of these independent variables through a single latent variable, one that would typically be measured with a single instrument. The information processing mechanism that Smith used, a production system analysis, does not suffer from this limitation.

A good example of this freedom from a single latent variable is the experiment of Smith and Branscombe (1988). The independent variable was whether persons read or generated words. Three dependent variables were used: free recall, a category accessibility test, and a word-fragment completion test. The production system approach successfully predicted that word generation would lead to superior performance on the recall and category accessibility tests, whereas reading would lead to better performance on the word-fragment completion test. Dimensional theories would have to posit the existence of separate dimensions to accommodate such findings.

Which Dimension is Involved?

Dimensional theories are silent on the questions of when any particular dimension will be affected by incoming information and when that dimension will contribute to current social behavior. A behavior like "refused to help his room mate write a term paper" has implications for honesty, helpfulness, likeability, and friendliness. Will the behavioral information affect just one of these trait inferences, or will more than one be affected? If only one is affected, which one will it be? Could there be circumstances under which it would affect no trait judgments? These questions are outside the conceptual capacity of dimensional theories.

Smith's treatise reports a study (Smith, 1988a) that shows how this problem can be solved using a production system analysis. If through frequent or recent practice, productions linking a behavior to one trait (e.g., intelligent) are strengthened more than productions linking it to another trait (e.g., friendliness), then the ambiguous behavior is predicted to activate the stronger production. This should occur even though the a priori relevance of the behavior to the two traits is equivalent. Smith's (1988b) results were consistent with this analysis.

Another problem for the dimensional approach is its reliance on the concept of information weight. Dimensional theorists such as Anderson (1981) explicitly incorporate a weight paramenter in their model to account for the finding that some information items have more impact than others on the resulting judgment. But these theories offer no explanations of how items acquire their weight. Why do some items carry more weight for a particular dimension than other items? An equivalent question, but one that evokes little interest within the dimensional approach, is why an item has more weight on one dimension than on another dimension.

A production system analysis would suggest that a particular behavior may match the condition side of more than one condition-action (e.g., behavior-trait) production unit. Only the strongest production would be activated in the context of a particular dimensional judgment. If the action side of that production matches the focal dimension, then the behavior would be relevant and so have an impact on the judgment (i.e., appear to have been given a high weight).

SOCIAL VERSUS NONSOCIAL
DOMAINS OF COGNITION

Labeling a field "Social Cognition" invites the question of how this kind of cognition differs from nonsocial cognition. The question is even more strongly highlighted by the present treatise. At several points Smith emphasizes parallels between studies from the two domains, even to the extent of emphasizing the distinction through the use of subheadings. However, he does not discuss how (or whether) the two domains differ. Nor does he discuss whether a rapprochement is near.

I have written elsewhere (Ostrom, 1984) on the distinction between social and nonsocial cognition. Two issues must be addressed in asking whether the field is maturing in its analysis of this distinction. One pertains to the nature of social knowledge and the other to the nature of cognitive processes. I address each separately, and then turn to a third issue of whether current research in social cognition is merely derivative of work in cognitive psychology.

The Nature of Social Knowledge

The earlier paper (Ostrom, 1984) offered an extended discussion on the nature of social knowledge, identifying four different bases of differentiation between social and nonsocial knowledge. They are (1) characteristics of the object, (2) characteristics of the perceiver, (3) contingencies in human action, and (4) the perceiver as an interaction participant.

The most primitive difference has to do with the properties of the stimulus object. Nonsocial objects (like cups or chairs) tend to be static and the forces that induce change are external to the object. Social objects (like persons and their actions) tend to be labile, and the forces that produce change can be internal to the object. This appears to be the main basis on which Smith differentiated between social and nonsocial cognition. Nonsocial categorization research uses stimuli like cups and saucers, whereas the reported Smith and Zarate (1988) study involved classifying persons according to group membership. In discussing work on judgment efficiency, a nonsocial example involved the practice of computer programming skills (i.e., evaluating LISP functions) and the social example had subjects make trait inferences from behaviors.

The research reported by Smith really did not involve any of the more complex components that characterize social knowledge. In its richest form, social knowledge must incorporate all the complexities of the perceiver immersed in interaction with one or more others. The cognitive demands in such interpersonal contexts extend way beyond those experienced by subject in any of the studies reported in this treatise, regardless of whether they were labeled social or nonsocial.

Face-to-face interaction is cognitively demanding. The perceiver must compress into a very short space of time (say, the period between the end of a partner's utterance and the onset of one's own) multiple cognitive acts. They include encoding and interpreting the preceding utterance, and they include formulating, selecting, and articulating the ideas that make up a reply. One would expect that the cognitive activities that take place in this interval would involve at least some of the kinds of categorization processes (of persons into groups) and judgment processes (of traits from behaviors) that were reviewed in Smith's treatise.

But if this is true, we encounter a real-time problem. Smith's data (see Fig. 1.2 on p. 30) show that it takes over 2 sec to make an unpracticed trait inference. And this is true despite the fact that the inference is made in a low demand setting where none of the obligations of speech production and coherence monitoring are present for the subject. All the subject needs to do is to make a single inference, pure and simple. No doubt the response time would be longer if the studies imposed concurrent task demands on the subject.

How many of these inferences would it be possible to make during the pause between comment and reply in a typical conversation? Probably not more than two or three, given that each takes about 2 sec. Yet given all the processing that must occur during that interval, it is likely that dozens and dozens of such cognitive acts are involved. This leads me to question whether the kind of categorization and judgment mechanisms invoked by subjects in these studies (whether they used social or nonsocial objects) are the same as those that occur in the richer interaction settings.

It would appear at this point in time that very little maturing has yet occurred in terms of the field's ability to evaluate the role of information processing concepts as they apply to truly complex domains of social knowledge.

The Nature of Cognitive Processes

The term "process" is used in a variety of ways in psychology. I will retain the referent argued for in my earlier paper (Ostrom, 1984), using it to refer to the set of conceptual features and dynamics that make up a theoretical account. I generally use the term *processes* (as in production system processes or the processes by which we access episodic information) to designate the set of principles by which production systems and episodic stores are formed and are accessed.

Smith appears to use the term in a very different (and to me, somewhat confusing) way. He uses it to convey his concerns over "process specificity." Here process seems to refer to the task demands or response goals adopted by the subject. When introducing the term at the beginning of his treatise, he offered several illustrations of the meaning of "processes." They were the tasks of reading a word, counting syllables in a word, and making a trait inference. No mention was made of the specificity of the theoretical mechanisms engaged by these tasks. His later use of the term suggests that this theoretical referent may have been intended, but the ambiguity is left unresolved.

The treatise does offer an advance on the question of whether the same processes are involved in social and nonsocial cognition, but only at the most primitive level of social knowledge. Smith shows that parallel findings were obtained across both social and nonsocial objects. This result cannot yet be regarded as a generalizable, well-established conclusion. It is true that such parallels were reported in my earlier review (Ostrom, 1984), but there was not a great deal of available literature on the topic. It was especially useful for Smith to show that parallelism obtains when studying constructs other than categories and schemas. Models based on episodic and production unit codes are shown to be as relevant to social behavior as to nonsocial behavior.

Smith seems content to accept the fundamentalist position on the relation between social and nonsocial cognitive processes. This position favors the notion that there are no intrinsic differences between the two sets of processes. The person has a fundamental set of processes that developed from birth on and are used to respond to all stimulus events, regardless of whether those events were social or nonsocial in nature. (See Ostrom, 1984, for a full discussion of the building-block view, the fundamentalist view, and the realist view of this distinction.)

I personally favor the realist view. It argues that persons are born into a world that is characterized by the highest, most complex level of social experience. We are interaction participants from the very start. It is plausible, then, that the first processes to develop are the ones that enable coping with that social reality. Responding to nonsocial stimuli requires subsequent learning that not all objects are social. Some data exist that support the primacy of social processes over nonsocial processes (Ostrom, 1984).

Unfortunately, this is an area where the field has shown very little movement toward maturity. At our present stage of methodological sophistication, it appears to be quite difficult to empirically trace the role of categories, scripts, episodic stores, and production systems as they are engaged during interpersonal interaction. Perhaps it is time to seriously examine alternatives to button pushing and recall protocols as indices of these processes. These traditional indices are designed to be used when subjects are socially isolated. Alternative methods need to be explored. Eye movements, punctuating gestures, question-reply intervals, and chunking in oral speech patterns may provide on-line indices of these processes as they operate in interaction settings.

Is Social Cognition Derivative?

Social cognition has sometimes been criticized as being derivative. Some view it as copy-cat research, involving little or no creative contribution to social psychology. Social cognition studies merely replicate published studies in cognitive psychology. This criticism has been voiced by persons in both social and cognitive psychology, and often in a snide and demeaning fashion. Many past contributors to social cognition have encountered this reaction, myself included.

These critics could point to Smith's treatise as support for their invidious attitude. Smith goes to some length to point out the parallels between studies with social and nonsocial tasks. In all cases the nonsocial studies provided the springboard for the social studies. The social studies, then, would be viewed as "mere replications" by the critics.

This criticism is most disturbing when advanced by cognitive psychologists. They should know better. Cognitive psychologists study a wide variety of tasks, including recall, recognition, text comprehension, audition, classification, reasoning, vision, and inference processes. What is common to the cognitive perspective is a concern with core issues such as representation, informational codes, attention, and encoding and retrieval.

Researchers in one of these content areas (e.g., classification) may find some of the constructs and methods from another area (e.g., recall) of some use in understanding the phenomena in their area. However, no one views work in classification as derivative of work on recall. The fact that they share a common theoretical perspective is viewed by cognitive psychologists as being a source of strength rather than a basis for belittlement.

The content areas of social psychology include topics such as impression formation, attributions, attitudes, trait inferences, stereotypes, and prejudice. In all these areas, the social cognition theorist is concerned about the fundamental issues of representation, informational codes, attention, and encoding and retrieval. These are the very same issues that absorb cognitive psychologists. The study of these issues is even more difficult for social information that involves a combination of visual, auditory, and semantic components. Social cognition is not derivative; rather, it offers new domains of phenomena in which the nature of cognitive processes must be explored.

Smith's treatise provides an excellent example of the benefits of this approach. In doing so, it advances the maturing process of social cognition to a point where the critics can be more effectively answered.

THE SPECIFICITY PRINCIPLE
AND CONSTRUCT VALIDITY

Smith strongly emphasized the idea of specificity as a methodological principle. It is the focus of the first major section of his treatise, and provides its dominant organizational structure. I have no disagreement with any of the points he makes regarding this issue. Indeed, it allows him to persuasively display the advantages of his alternative conceptual approaches.

I do question whether this methodological principle constitutes a novel perspective in social cognition. I believe it does not. It articulates a strategy of theory testing that is already well known in social cognition, as well as in social and cognitive psychology generally. Basically, it raises the familiar issue of construct validity.

The logic behind the specificity principle coincides with Garner, Hake, and Eriksen's (1956) advocacy of converging operations. And predicting that an independent variable will have different effects on different dependent variables is our old friend discriminant validity (Campbell & Fiske, 1959) applied to randomized experiments. Theory testing research generally seeks to devise circumstances under which different theories make different predictions, and this appears to be the basic message of Smith's advocacy of specificity as a methodological principle.

Smith's presentation does go beyond current approaches to construct validity in one important way. He delineates four bases of specificity (content, process, context, and time) that offer useful guides to the researcher. These are all plausible empirical arenas in which different theories may make different predictions. Smith's four bases of specificity may not be exhaustive, but they do provide a nice array of starting points for the theorist.

CONCLUDING COMMENTS

The maturity of a scientific field is always difficult to gauge, especially when it is one's own field that is being evaluated. To know where you are now requires knowing where you have been and knowing how much further you have to go. We are naturally better at looking back than looking forward, and it is this looking back that was the focus of my commentary. Unquestionably, Smith's treatise has provided a major advance in the maturing of social cognition.

Looking forward is a much more speculative enterprise. Two guesses can be ventured. First, there is a rich array of cognitive codes that can be used to represent sensory and motoric experience, such as those used in imagery, audition, speech production, and task performance. Social behavior operates at the intersection of these multifarious representations. Ultimately the field of social cognition will need to explicitly address them, both singly and in combination.

Second, Smith's treatise provides a glimpse of another part of the field's future. He described a computer simulation (Smith, 1988b) that established the plausibility of explaining categorical priming effects without positing the existence of categories. The effects were explained solely on the basis of accessing an episodic store. As we come to recognize the existence of multiple codes and multiple processing systems, computer simulations like this will come to be adopted more and more as a symbol system for formally expressing theory (Ostrom, 1988b).

On these two grounds alone, we can see that the field of social cognition still has a long way to go before it even reaches middle age. We must continue to hope for future treatises like Smith's that dispel any tendency to view the garden complacently.

ACKNOWLEDGMENTS

Correspondence regarding this chapter should be sent to Thomas M. Ostrom, Department of Psychology, Ohio State University, Columbus, OH, 43210. I am grateful to Mary Brickner for her comments on an earlier version.

REFERENCES

Alba, J. W., & Hasher, L. (1983). Is memory schematic? *Psychological Bulletin, 93,* 203–231.

Anderson, N. H. (1981). *Foundations of information integration theory.* New York: Academic Press.

Campbell, D. T., & Fiske, D. W. (1959). Convergent and discriminant validation by the multitrait-multimethod matrix. *Psychological Bulletin, 56,* 81–105.

Devine, P. G., & Ostrom, T. M. (1988). Dimensional versus information-processing approaches to social knowledge: The case of inconsistency management. In D. Bar-Tal & A. W. Kruglanski (Eds.), *The social psychology of knowledge* (pp. 231–261). Cambridge, England: Cambridge University Press.

Fiske, S. T., & Taylor, S. E. (1984). *Social cognition.* Reading, MA: Addison-Wesley.

Garner, W. R., Hake, H. W., & Eriksen, C. W. (1956). Operationism and the concept of perception. *Psychological Review, 63,* 149–159.

Krech, D., & Crutchfield, R. S. (1948). *Theory and problems of social psychology.* New York: McGraw-Hill.

Markus, H., & Zajonc, R. B. (1985). The cognitive perspective in social psychology. In G. Lindzey & E. Aronson (Eds.), *Handbook of social psychology* (Vol. 1, pp. 137–230). New York: Random House.

Ostrom, T. M. (1984). The sovereignty of social cognition. In R. Wyer & T. Srull (Eds.), *Handbook of social cognition* (Vol. 1, pp. 1–38). Hillsdale, NJ: Lawrence Erlbaum Associates.

Ostrom, T. M. (1987). Bipolar survey items: An information processing perspective. In H-J. Hippler, N. Schwarz, & S. Sudman (Eds.), *Social information processing and survey methodology* (pp. 71–85). New York: Springer-Verlag.

Ostrom, T. M. (1988a). Dimensional versus information processing conceptions of social judgment. *Wissenschaftliche Zeitschrift der Friedrich-Schiller-Universitaet* (Special issue on social judgment), *6*, 629–638.

Ostrom, T. M. (1988b). Computer simulation: The third symbol system. *Journal of Experimental Social Psychology, 24*, 381–392.

Rosch, E. (1978). Principles of categorization. In E. Rosch & B. B. Lloyd (Eds.), *Cognition and categorization*. Hillsdale, NJ: Lawrence Erlbaum Associates.

Smith, E. R. (1988a). *Procedural efficiency: General and specific components and effects on social judgments*. Unpublished paper, Purdue University.

Smith, E. R. (1988b). Category accessibility effects in a simulated exemplar-based memory. *Journal of Experimental Social Psychology, 24*, 448–463.

Smith, E. R., & Branscombe, N. R. (1988). Category accessibility as implicit memory. *Journal of Experimental Social Psychology, 24*, 490–504.

Smith, E. R., & Zarate, M. A. (1988). *Exemplar- and prototype-based social categorization*. Unpublished paper, Purdue University.

Wyer, R. S., & Srull, T. K. (Eds.), (1984). *Handbook of social cognition*. Hillsdale, NJ: Lawrence Erlbaum Associates.

10 Content and Process Specificity: Where do we go from here?

Thomas K. Srull
Robert S. Wyer, Jr.
University of Illinois at Urbana-Champaign

It is clear from the target article that Eliot Smith is one of those whose theoretical reach exceeds his empirical grasp. While many people will interpret that as a rather lefthanded compliment, we sincerely do not. In fact, we think it's one of the highest compliments a theorist can receive. Our impression is that most theorists, in social cognition as well as in social psychology more generally, only reach as far as they can grasp. The result is a grab-bag of miniature, carefully circumscribed theories of specific phenomena, each stated in a different language, and rarely generalized or applied to more than one or two research reports.

In contrast to the myopia that is so often manifested, Smith thinks big. And, because of this, he develops theories whose "range of convenience" is truly impressive. The downside, of course, is that he leaves loose ends—unaccounted for phenomena here, unaddressed questions there, and occasional exaggerations that are used to make a point. This is inevitable at such an early stage. But even when his reach exceeds his grasp, his thinking is heuristic and exceptionally important. To give just two examples, Smith points to directions in which it is *important* to reach, and sometimes even shows us *how* to reach. These are indeed rare and important accomplishments. And, because the level of theorizing is broader than we usually see, we at least have the potential of tying together areas that heretofore have been considered separate and distinct—to find order and consistency among the chaos. For this reason alone, Smith's work needs to be considered very carefully.

In the present commentary we try to evaluate Smith's work critically but constructively. We rarely take issue with, or even question, his specific claims. But we do think a number of important issues have escaped his attention, and he has finessed a number of others in ways that could prove dangerous as the theory becomes more articulated. Rather than reinforce the many important insights he has provided, we orient the rest of our discussion around these loose ends.

THE SPECIFIC AND THE GENERAL: A PARADOX

Smith alludes to, but does not pursue, something of a paradox. It may be easiest to convey through the use of an example. One of us teaches a course in Cognitive Psychology and is consistently struck by how undergraduates—laypeople, if you will—think about memory. The concept of *episodic memory* is easily understood. And is it really any surprise why? All of us live in the particular. We see specific people do specific things in specific contexts. Moreover, all of us remember such episodes, often in surprising detail. In contrast, *semantic memory* is a little less obvious. And even undergraduates understand that the truly interesting question is how we ever come to represent abstractions from the particular world in which we live—to develop categories and impressions of *types* of people, *types* of situations, and so on.

It is ironic that existing theories of social cognition have manifested exactly the opposite approach. Smith is surely correct when he suggests that social cognition theorists invariably emphasize categories, prototypes, schemata, and various other types of abstractions. And he is correct that we sometimes appear to ignore entirely the representation of specific, concrete episodes that have occurred to us. Although Smith takes this as a given and quickly moves on, it is instructive to pause for a moment and consider how we ever got to such a backward position.

Information Processing Models in Social Cognition

Although there are doubtlessly many reasons for the current state of affairs, we suggest the primary one is that most work in social cognition has not been guided by detailed information-processing models. Because of this we often fail to appreciate the marvelous capabilities and flexibilities of the human cognitive system. Most of the time people are able to perform a large number of exceedingly complicated activities, and they often accomplish these acts very quickly and with a minimum of effort. To take just one example, we are able to converse with friends, encode their words and phrases, extract out the larger meaning, integrate the new information we acquire with what we already know about the person, create a "problem space" and search for various solutions, and think about alternative responses and how to phrase them according to certain rules. And we do it all *without missing a beat*. There is very little in the social cognition literature that helps to explain such commonplace social acts (cf. Ostrom, 1984).

What we do have in our literature are repeated references to people being cognitive misers, subject to various heuristics and biases, and general caricatures of people making consistent errors and mistakes. We do not quarrel with such phenomena; they are important and need to be studied. It is important to remember two things however. First, and most important, all of this work stems from very simple input–output models. Whenever there is a mismatch or some inconsistency between what is input and what is output, a bias or mistake is said to occur; people are said to be lazy or inefficient, or maybe even incapable of processing information logically. And there is often the unarticulated suggestion that *these* are the interesting phenomena to study. The second thing to remember is that these are not the only interesting phenomena. And by concentrating on them, we may indeed be missing the forest for the trees.

Consider as an alternative model the past two decades of research on reading. Although this literature is rarely cited in social cognition, the issues are actually very similar: Readers must integrate individual facts into coherent wholes, draw inferences about unstated events, form impressions of the individual characters, engage in causal reasoning, and so on. Many of the phenomena studied are also similar: the use of stereotypes, the making of inferences that are logically unwarranted, memory biases, heuristic reasoning, and so on. In addition to studying these shortcomings, however, there is a strong and persistent theoretical commitment to understanding what people do *well*, and not only what they do poorly; after all, unique patterns of light rays somehow get transformed into new learning, which is integrated with old knowledge, and important and creative ideas become represented in the brain and are often carried around for decades, sometimes actually becoming part of the reader's *self*. One doesn't have to be a psychologist or bibliophile to recognize what a wonderful and awe-inspiring process that is. The important point, however, is that social cognition researchers have concentrated much more on what people do poorly than on what they do well. Smith's chapter is important because it reminds us of what a complicated, efficient, and delicate piece of machinery we are dealing with. In order to analyze it theoretically, however, we need precise, detailed, and process-level models of cognition in all of its forms.

Developing (New) Versus Applying (Old) Theories

If one accepts these premises, and we believe that Smith does, the question becomes one of what to do next. The most obvious and tempting thing is to go to existing theory in cognitive psychology, to look for some theory that is broad enough and stated at the right level of abstraction and then apply it to various social psychological phenomena. This is more or less what Smith does. Moreover, he applies it to a large number of tasks and phenomena and it is only a minor exaggeration to say that, each time, the theory works perfectly. One problem, however, is that in borrowing the ACT* theory, Smith takes along with it the rather constrained research paradigm that has traditionally been used to evaluate its implications. At best, he ends up with a theoretical analysis that is deeper than we in social cognition usually see, but also one that is far less broad than he would lead us to believe. At worst, he ends up with an elegant theory of a small set of experimental tasks.

To see the strengths and weaknesses of Smith's approach, it is useful to consider a general model of the research process outlined by David Brinberg and Joseph McGrath. They argue that any scientific investigation has three sets of components: the conceptual, methodological, and substantive. The conceptual is the world of concepts and hypotheses, the methodological is the world of measurement, sampling, and other related issues, and the substantive is the domain in which phenomena are observed. The Brinberg and McGrath framework is very intricate and developed but, for our purposes, there are only two points to remember. First, any scientific investigation must engage all three components. Second, the order in which these components are considered is very important because, as each additional decision is made, more and more constraints are placed on any subsequent ones.

Most cognitive psychologists begin with the conceptual and then move to the methodological. Finally, they find a substantive domain in which the theory can be tested with a particular method. Smith follows exactly the same sequence but, in so doing, the weakness of his approach becomes apparent. Because he begins with a particular theory (usually ACT*) and a particular method (usually some type of reaction time paradigm that requires a binary response), there are severe constraints placed on the type of substantive questions he can ask.

This is a problem that cognitive psychologists rarely confront. To the degree one is interested in coding processes, learning rates, the development of new productions, cuing or reminding phenomena, problem-solving strategies, and so on, the substantive domain is simply not important. But in social cognition it is important and this fact alone presents us with unique challenges.

Smith's approach is adequate, and maybe even ideal, to the extent one wants to develop a complete theory of how the mind works. Its strength—and we believe it is a very important one—is that it will lead to a much broader cognitive psychology, one that includes many of the concerns and processes that social psychologists have identified and emphasized over the years. As others have pointed out, however, a cognitive psychology of the social is not quite the same as a social psychology of the cognitive (cf. Higgins, Kuiper, & Olson, 1981). They are related, and share a common core of concerns, but each embraces a unique set of issues as well.

Starting With the Substantive

To illustrate the tradeoff involved, imagine Smith had started with the substantive and *then* moved to the conceptual and methodological. He almost certainly would have asked a very different set of questions, for example:

1. Social stimuli, and the conditions that surround them, change. Because of this, people are forced to make *current decisions* based on anticipated or *imagined futures*. Friends imagine what it would be like to be married, students try to imagine what it would be like to be a lawyer rather than an engineer, supervisors try to imagine how an employee will react if criticized in one way or another, and so on. In fact, much of our social life is based on constructing mental models of what will happen *if* we do one thing or another. When constructing such mental models, do we rely on specific episodes from the past, or on more abstract representations?

2. Smith places considerable emphasis on attributes concerning group membership, categorization processes, the development of subtypes, and so on. These things are undoubtedly important, but are they overemphasized because of the restrictive paradigms in which they are studied? For example, Brewer (1988) has recently argued that people will engage in much more individuated processing when the other person is personally relevant.

3. People often "see" the same thing differently. This is just another way of saying that the link between the perceptual aspects of behavior and the mental coding or categorization of it is very important. Because Smith uses words to represent behaviors, he essentially performs this first step for his subjects and he is working at a level of abstraction that, for some purposes, is already too high.

In addition, research by Zadny and Gerard (1974), Cohen and Ebbesen (1979), and Newtson (1976; Newtson & Engquist, 1976; Newtson, Engquist, & Bois, 1977) indicates that this initial coding can be dramatically affected by the activation of abstract concepts rather than specific instances. So one of the places in which abstract representations are likely to play a major role is simply bypassed in the paradigms Smith relies upon.

These are just a smattering of issues that must be important to any social cognition theorist. Because Smith begins with the conceptual and ends with the substantive, however, there are severe constraints on the types of questions he is able to ask. In fairness, it is also important to keep two things in mind, however.

First, theory development rarely occurs in the classical hypothetico-deductive fashion. Rather, it is an iterative process. Rough theoretical ideas are sketched out and then investigated. However, as the data base becomes more complete and new phenomena are discovered, the theory is revised and, if pursued diligently, grows both broader and more deeply. Notwithstanding the large number of empirical studies that Smith reports, it is important to keep in mind that he is still in the initial stages.

The second point is that not every issue needs to be addressed in one theory, or by one theorist. Our field is one in which individual scientists play an unusually central role. Good researchers are also expected to be good theorists, good theorists are also expected to be good researchers, and theorists who address one issue are often criticized for not also addressing others. This may be the dominant model but it is not necessarily the best model (cf. Sampson, 1977, 1978). Every theory has strengths and weaknesses, and a particular range of convenience, and individual theories can complement each other. So there is nothing inherently wrong or fatal with Smith's approach. By a similar token, however, issues that are ignored or finessed by a theory cannot be ignored or finessed forever. Unfortunately, there is likely to be considerable overlap between the issues that are ignored by applying one theory from cognitive psychology and the issues that are ignored by applying nearly any other theory from cognitive psychology. So the temptation to apply existing theory from cognitive psychology comes at a price, a severe price. And, at least some of the time, the substantive issues need to be considered first rather than last.

DIRECTIONS FOR EXTENSION AND REFINEMENT

As we noted earlier, theory development is an iterative process in which the theory continuously evolves, or at least should. The crucial point is not whether a theory is true or correct, but whether it is detailed enough, and whether its concepts are: (a) specific enough to make precise predictions, and (b) abstract enough to be applied to many different types of data. We believe that developing a theoretical vocabulary at the right level of abstraction is one of the most important challenges a theorist must face.

We also noted that, while Smith's chapter is noteworthy for the large number of empirical findings he reports, it is most impressive when one considers that Smith has really just begun. He has done so much so quickly that one can't help but be optimistic about the long-term viability of the theory. One of the most important challenges at present is to push the theory to its limits, to see where its problems lie, and then to modify the theory accordingly. This can be done in two slightly different ways. First, the internal components of the theory can be refined—definitions can be made more precise, hidden assumptions can be more clearly articulated, internal inconsistencies can be identified and eliminated, and so on; in other words, the theory can be developed more deeply. The second way a theory can evolve is to extend it into areas that have not been discussed previously—to introduce new concepts, develop the logic in new directions, and so on; to develop it more broadly.

In the present section we try to identify several areas that we believe are ripe for extension and refinement. We do not pretend to be exhaustive; our choices simply reflect our thoughts about when we would do next in order to pursue this theoretical line of reasoning.

Avoiding the Tautological

One of the most obvious things about Smith's chapter is that he has an extremely powerful vocabulary. This is a great accomplishment, but it also presents a unique challenge. The challenge is that the theorist must state, as precisely as possible, and on an a priori basis, exactly when a given process will be activated and when it will not. Otherwise the *theory* will become tautological because the vocabulary is so general.

To see this, consider again one of Lewicki's (1986) experiments that Smith relies upon to show the effect of content specificity. Subjects were first insulted by an experimenter. They were than sent to another room to complete a separate task. In the other room were two people, sitting at separate desks on opposite sides of the room; neither was busy. Thus, subjects were faced with an arbitrary choice of whom to approach. Lewicki found that subjects tended to avoid the person who had a hairstyle similar to the original experimenter.

This is fine and Smith's interpretation that subjects avoided the person because he was *similar* to the first experimenter is reasonable. However, suppose that the effect did not occur. Would this disprove the theory? Not at all. The interpretation would then be that the second person was not similar after all.

Similarity plays a very central role in Smith's theory, and we return to his conception of it shortly. For now, however, we simply want to make one point: There is a big difference between having a vocabulary that is flexible enough to *account for* a wide array of findings and an internally consistent theory that *predicts a priori* when a given effect will and will not occur. One of the most important ways for the theory to evolve is to specify in much greater detail the myriad of boundary conditions that must be known to predict a priori any given effect.

Other ambiguities in Smith's conceptualization create similar problems. For example, consider the effects of declarative and procedural knowledge on the processing of new information. A prior experience can, on the one hand, increase the accessibility of concepts that affect the interpretation of later information (i.e., have a *content* priming effect). In addition, however, the experience may activate and strengthen productions, thereby increasing the likelihood of applying these productions again (i.e., have a *procedural* priming effect). As Smith points out, several findings that have traditionally been attributed to content priming (for summaries, see Bargh, 1984; Higgins & King, 1981; Wyer & Srull, 1986, 1989) could, in fact, be due to procedural priming. The model he proposes, however, does not adequately circumscribe the conditions under which each type of priming effect will occur.

In an attempt to distinguish empirically between the two types of priming effects, Smith assumes that the effects of priming semantic concepts are more short-lived (see p. 41). Consequently, he attributes priming effects that persist over time to strengthened productions. Although we recognize the historical roots of this assumption, we are not clear why, on a priori grounds, it is valid in the situations to which Smith applies his model. Higgins and his colleagues (Higgins & King, 1981; Higgins, Bargh, & Lombardi, 1985) have also proposed a decay model of concept accessibility. Other models, however, do not postulate any decay process. As but one example, we have proposed an interference model of memory in which the time interval between activation of a concept and the presentation of stimulus information to which it is relevant is not the critical determinant of the influence of this concept (Wyer & Srull, 1986, 1989). According to this model, semantic priming effects may persist for some time if other applicable concepts have not been activated in the interim. In other words, whether a priming effect is short-lived or of long duration is not sufficient for determining whether it is due to content or procedural priming.

The application of Smith's assumption is made more problematic by his failure to specify conceptually when a particular effect is likely to be due to content rather than procedural priming. The use of a particular production in a test situation is determined, in part, by its accessibility or strength and, in part, by the similarity of its features to the particular situation. But these assumptions do not seem sufficient. Consider, for example, a study by Tulving, Schacter, and Stark (1982) that was designed to distinguish between semantic and episodic memory effects. Subjects were initially presented with a long list of familiar but infrequently used words (e.g., *pendulum, assassin,* etc.) with instructions to learn them. After a delay of either several minutes or several days, some subjects were given a recognition memory test with OLD and NEW items. Others were given a word fragment completion test in which some (but not all) of the to-be-completed words were among those on the study list; these subjects were given no indication that any of the words had been seen before.

Recognition memory was quite high when tested after a short delay. In addition, the presence of words on the study list facilitated subjects' identification of them on the word fragment completion test. The more interesting question was whether either of these effects, or both, would persist over several days. It is reasonable to assume that the productions required to perform the recognition task are more similar to those activated during study than are the productions involved in the word fragment completion task. If this is so, and if Smith's assumption concerning the relative duration of content and procedural priming is correct, the effect of studying the initial word list on recognition memory performance should persist for a longer time than its effect on word fragment completion. In fact, however, the opposite was true. That is, recognition memory decreased substantially over time, whereas the facilitating effect of the study list on word fragment completion persisted.

To account for these results on the basis of Smith's present formulation, one would need to assume that the learning task required procedures that were more similar to those involved in performing the word fragment completion task than those involved in a task that was specifically designed to assess the amount of learning. We recognize that this possibility cannot be dismissed (cf. Roediger & Blaxton, 1987). It would seem more plausible, however, that the effects of the study list on word fragment completion were the result of content priming rather than procedural priming, and that the assumption that the former effects are always short-lived is incorrect.

In any event, unless the conditions under which procedural and content priming are likely to have an effect can be specified on a priori grounds, any inference that is made simply on the basis of their persistence seems tautological. In principle, one must be able to specify a priori the nature of the productions that are involved in different cognitive tasks and establish multiple criteria for inferring that one type of priming effect has occurred rather than another.

Avoiding Too Many Productions

The concept of a production system is powerful and seductive. However, Smith needs to be careful not to imbibe in too much of a good thing. For example, it is noteworthy that Smith postulates production systems at all levels of generality, from the ultra-specific to the very general. By doing this, however, he sometimes appears to reap the benefits of the concept (its explanatory power) without accepting the responsibility associated with its use (telling us the *limits* of its explanatory power, and when the concept *no longer* applies).

Consider an example. What exactly is the advantage of postulating a production that is specific to a particular encoding of a particular word in terms of a particular trait? Why is this theoretical tact preferable to postulating the priming of a trait concept and the use of a more general "trait encoding" production?

Indeed, if a different production is postulated for every trait-behavior combination, the number of productions will soon exceed both the number of behaviors to be encoded and the number of traits that can be used to encode them. For example, imagine that five different traits are applicable for encoding each of five behaviors. A total of 25 separate trait-behavior productions would then be required to account for the set of possible encodings that might emerge. The number of more general productions that Smith postulates adds to this total. Unless Smith can demonstrate that his conceptualization can account for phenomena that a more parsimonious conceptualization cannot, the latter formulation will remain more appealing. Moreover, if a new production must be created for every new task, the cognitive system (and the theoretical description of it) gets so cluttered with productions that the utility of the construct becomes questionable. Its utility is also compromised to the extent that readers are unsure of when *not* to apply it.

Once again, we do not think this is a fatal flaw in Smith's model. And we think the issue will come up naturally as more work is conducted and, especially, as the theory is contrasted with other alternative accounts. We also believe, however, that the issue of putting limits on when the concept applies is one that should not be deferred too long.

How Do We Know IF . . .

As Smith points out, productions are *if, then* or *condition, action* patterns. Up until this point, however, we have only discussed the second half of the conditional. This is due, in large part, to the fact that Smith discusses the "if" part very little in his chapter. To the extent he does discuss it, it is in the context of statements such as: "increased strength increases the speed with which the production will apply on a future occasion *when its pattern matches information in memory . . .* " (p. 28). However, Smith says very little about how these patterns are constructed or what they look like.

It is informative to examine what these "if" statements are like in the context of the paradigms Smith employs. An example at an intermediate level of generality would be (for details, see p. 31):

> IF   the goal is to judge whether ⟨behavior⟩ is friendly and ⟨behavior⟩ has
>   ⟨features of friendliness . . .⟩
> THEN   respond "yes"

Note first of all that the "if" part of the conditional is explicit. What we mean by this is that subjects are explicitly told that their task is to judge the extent to which each behavior is friendly. Note also that the sequence of events is very well practiced; what we mean here is that subjects perform the same operations across many trials. Finally, and most important, note that there is only one objective. That is, subjects are to judge the friendless of the behaviors *and nothing else.*

All of this makes sense within the constraints of the paradigms Smith uses. However, when one begins to think about how these processes operate in a more naturalistic environment, a whole host of additional questions are raised. For example, what is meant by "when its pattern matches information in memory?" A major problem, or so it would seem to us, is that many of the goals in a social environment are vague and diffuse. If this is true, however, it is a major challenge to determine what these "if" conditionals look like. Imagine, for example, that we meet someone and are "smitten" with him or her. (In our dictionary *smitten* falls somewhere between *like* and *love*.) We suppose it is theoretically possible to have a production that reads: IF . . . , THEN become smitten with the person. But what in the world would the "if" part of the production look like?

To make matters worse, we often have multiple goals in social interaction (Srull & Wyer, 1986). Moreover, even those that seem similar on the surface may be very different in terms of the psychological processes activated, and they do not necessarily form a hierarchical relationship. For example, recent research by Devine, Sedikides, and Fuhrman (1989) suggests that "trying to form an impression" and "anticipating future interaction" are two goals that activate very different sets of processes. Moreover, attaining the first goal is not simply a stepping stone in attaining the second.

174

In those cases in which people do have multiple objectives, which takes precedence? Is there a way to determine this on a theoretical basis? If not, is there a principled way to tell after the fact? And what happens in those cases in which there is actual conflict between the two goals? These are questions that we believe will become very salient as the research begins to embrace more naturalistic concerns. Once again, these points should not be read as criticisms, but as possible directions for extension of the theory. In so far as they are motivated by components of natural social interaction, however, they are directions that will need to be followed sooner or later.

Are Other Models Incomplete, Inaccurate, or Irrelevant?

One of the few frustrations we had in reading Smith's chapter concerns his failure to tie his work to other models that have addressed similar concerns. At several points, he says that abstractions are indeed formed and, at least under some conditions, used. But he says very little more than that. We believe there are at least four ways in which the theoretical analysis can be extended along these lines.

First, Smith points out that a great deal of work in social cognition has been devoted to various categorization, prototype, and other abstraction-like models. It was never clear to us, however, whether he considers these models incomplete or inaccurate. When one stops to consider how future theoretical efforts can best be advanced, this not a trivial distinction.

One possibility is that Smith considers these models incomplete. By this we mean that he accepts the processes described, but that he thinks they need to be *supplemented* by something along the lines of what he describes in his chapter. Another possibility, however, is that he believes they are inaccurate in the sense that they are fundamentally flawed and need to be *supplanted* by the type of approach he advocates.

If we accept his arguments and think toward the future, we must choose between adding a little abstraction to the modified ACT* model Smith describes, or adding a little "specificity" to the existing models. We believe this is a very important choice because the end result is likely to be quite different.

This also brings us to our second point. The motivating force behind Smith's chapter seems to have been to convince us that specific instances and procedures are often retained and used to perform certain tasks. We are convinced, and we would guess that most others are as well. But we would have preferred that he also try to specify the boundary conditions associated with each set of processes (the use of abstractions versus specific instances), if not each set of models. In the process of thinking about this ourselves, we have realized what a large challenge this represents. Nevertheless it is a challenge that will need to be met if we are to continue making substantial theoretical progress in the future.

In general, Smith presents his work in relative isolation and, we believe, will need to relate it to other competing models more carefully and productively. To take just one example, Smith refers to several effects of "procedural priming" in support of his model. However, an alternative and very parsimonious account of these effects is provided by the bin model we have recently developed (Wyer & Srull, 1986, 1989). In our model, three types of "memory bins" are postulated: a *semantic* bin (which is essentially a mental dictionary of concepts), *referent* bins (which, in combination, serve as a mental encyclopedia of knowledge about people, places, and events), and a *goal* bin (a depository for goal schemata, or the procedures that are used to attain various processing objectives).[1] The processes that govern storage and retrieval are theoretically the same, regardless of which type of bin is involved. In each case, copies of concepts that are applicable for attaining a particular processing objective are retrieved and later redeposited on top of the bin from which they were drawn. As a result, they become more accessible and, thus, more likely to be retrieved and used again in the future.

Procedural priming in our model is conceptualized in much the same way as content priming. This gives the model a certain degree of symmetry and parsimony. An apparent advantage, however, of the bin model over Smith's is that it permits one to conceptualize both the separate and combined influence of content and procedural priming, and to specify when they occur in the course of: (a) activating a goal schema to attain a processing objective, and (b) the accessing of existing concepts and knowledge that are necessary to attain the objective (for details of this process, see Wyer & Srull, 1986, 1989).

We might note that the goal schemata we postulate (which might be viewed as a set of productions) are seldom instance-specific. Rather, we postulate a general set of goal schemata that operate on a variety of semantic and episodic material. Although future work may ultimately force us to modify this assumption, we have identified no reason to do so thus far.

The important point, however, is that the issues Smith addresses will be expanded, and the interpretations he gives to his data will be constrained, to the degree he also considers other competing models. We see both of these as good things, and the possibility of integrating work from different traditions an important objective of further theory development.

Finally, and perhaps most important, Smith will need to address potential identifiability problems in his future refinements of the model. Whether people are relying on specific instances or abstract representations is often an excruciatingly difficult question to answer. In fact, there may be some situations in which it is logically impossible to tell and our choice of one model over another will need to be made on the basis of other criteria.

---

[1]Incidentally, Smith's characterization of our assumptions about the storage of semantic concepts is not entirely correct. In several places he refers to a concept having its own bin. In fact, however, we assume that all trait concepts, as well as all noun and action concepts, are stored in a single (semantic) bin.

A good place to begin is to recognize that the language of one can often be translated into the language of the other. In other words, instance models can often be constructed to mimic what abstraction models predict, and vice versa. We do not believe this is a hopeless endeavor however. Just because something *can* be done does not mean it can be done easily, or parsimoniously, or in a way that is consistent with a large array of other data.

The next step would then be to find those phenomena that are easily accounted for by an alternative framework, and those in which the translation is much more difficult and cumbersome. This is also likely to be a slow and iterative process. In the long run, however, it will be required if we are to be in a position to prefer some (and reject other) models on the basis of such criteria as simplicity, parsimony, internal consistency, and verisimilitude.

The Lability of Similarity

The concept of similarity is one of the most vexing in psychology and, although Smith relies on the concept extensively, he says virtually nothing about it in terms of making specific theoretical commitments. Eventually he will need to.

The specific instance that is retrieved from memory is said to be based on its "similarity" with some cue. For the most part this cue is some characteristic of the person that is perceptually available. So, for example, a particular person may be avoided because he has a hairstyle that is similar to another person that is disliked, or a woman may be judged to have high math ability because her hair is similar to another women who is known to be a math whiz (cf. Lewicki, 1986). We have no doubt that such phenomena are real or important. But we also believe they are just the tip of the iceberg.

Many of the most important attributes of people are functional or psychological in nature. This means that they are *similar* in a very abstract sense, and we are not convinced that Smith has a theory that is sufficient to account for this type of similarity.

The recent literature on "remindings" is related to many of Smith's concerns. In a manner that is very compatible with Smith's model, theorists in this area suggest that specific instances are retrieved from memory based on their having features that are similar to those of some cue. However, the features that are used run the gamut from the very specific to the very general and abstract. For example, Ross (1984) examined how people learn to use a text editor. Subjects in this study were trained to apply a particular procedure in solving a problem (e.g., inserting a word). This was done by using an example that involved a particular type of verbal material (e.g., a restaurant review). Later subjects were tested by using materials that were either similar (e.g., a second restaurant review) or dissimilar (e.g., a telephone list). Ross found that subjects were much more likely to retrieve their prior experience when working on material that was similar. These are very specific remindings.

Contrast this with an example provided by Schank (1982):

> X described how his wife would never make his steak as rare as he liked it. When this was told to Y, it reminded Y of a time, 30 years earlier, when he tried to get his hair cut in a short style in England, and the barber would not cut it as short as he wanted it. (p. 47)

Here we have a reminding that is also based on two experiences having similar features. In this case, however, the features are similar only in the most abstract sense.

Our point here is that similarity runs throughout Smith's system. Moreover, there is reason to believe that specific instances or episodes can be accessed because they share features with a cue that are very concrete (e.g., X has short curly, black hair), very abstract (e.g., X is a person who trivializes important problems, while intellectualizing the small ones), or anywhere in between. In order for the model to accommodate all these phenomena, Smith will need a conceptualization of similarity that is much more involved than anything we have seen to date. Moreover, because the concept of similarity plays such a central role in his system, this would seem to us to be the type of extension that should be given a very high priority.

CONCLUDING REMARKS

We have tried in our comments to be both critical and constructive. And, primarily because of space constraints, we have consciously avoided pointing to the many places in which we agree with Smith. Let us simply say in closing that we believe Smith's model is one of the most important ever to be developed in the area of social cognition. His arguments are insightful and compelling, and the amount of empirical support he has been able to generate in support of them is truly impressive. In no way is it surprising that he has left some issues unaddressed, or that the model will benefit by extending it in certain directions. We look forward to seeing the model develop further; and, if we are certain of anything, it is that there will be a few surprises along the way. There is no doubt that the next few years are going to be very exciting ones for the field of social cognition, and Eliot Smith's work will be one of the reasons why.

ACKNOWLEDGMENTS

Writing of the present paper, as well as some of the research described therein, was supported by National Institute of Mental Health Grant MH 38585-05A1.

The first author would also like to thank Sharon Shavitt for her anagogic support.

REFERENCES

Bargh, J. A. (1984). Automatic and conscious processing of social information. In R. S. Wyer & T. K. Srull (Eds.), *Handbook of social cognition* (Vol. 3). Hillsdale, NJ: Lawrence Erlbaum Associates.

Brewer, M. B. (1988). A dual process model of impression formation. In T. K. Srull & R. S. Wyer (Eds.), *Advances in social cognition, Volume I: A dual process model of impression formation.* Hillsdale, NJ: Lawrence Erlbaum Associates.

Cohen, C., & Ebbesen, E. B. (1979). Observational goals and schema activation: A theoretical framework for behavior perception. *Journal of Experimental Social Psychology, 15,* 305–329.

Devine, P. G., Sedikides, C., & Fuhrman, R. W. (1989). Goals in social information processing: The case of anticipated interaction. *Journal of Personality and Social Psychology, 56,* 680–690.

Higgins, E. T., Bargh, J. A., & Lombardi, W. (1985). The nature of priming effects on categorization. *Journal of Experimental Psychology: Learning, Memory, and Cognition, 11,* 59–69.

Higgins, E. T., & King, G. (1981). Accessibility of social constructs: Information processing consequences of individual and contextual variability. In N. Cantor & J. F. Kihlstrom (Eds.), *Personality, cognition and social interaction.* Hillsdale, NJ: Lawrence Erlbaum Associates.

Higgins, E, T., Kuiper, N. A., & Olson, J. M. (1981). Social cognition: A need to get personal. In E. T. Higgins, C. P. Herman, & M. P. Zanna (Eds.), *Social cognition: The Ontario Symposium.* Hillsdale, NJ: Lawrence Erlbaum Associates.

Lewicki, P. (1986). *Nonconscious social information processing.* Orlando, FL: Academic Press.

Newtson, D. (1976). Foundations of attribution: The perception of ongoing behavior. In J. Harvey, W. Ickes, & R. Kidd (Eds.), *New directions in attribution research* (Vol. 1). Hillsdale, NJ: Lawrence Erlbaum Associates.

Newtson, D., & Engquist, G. (1976). The perceptual organization of ongoing behavior. *Journal of Experimental Social Psychology, 12,* 436–450.

Newtson, D., Engquist, G., & Bois, J. (1977). The objective basis of behavior units. *Journal of Personality and Social Psychology, 35,* 847–862.

Ostrom, T. M. (1984). The sovereignty of social cognition. In R. S. Wyer & T. K. Srull (Eds.), *Handbook of social cognition* (Vol. 1). Hillsdale, NJ: Lawrence Erlbaum Associates.

Roediger, H,. R., & Blaxton, T. A. (1987). Retrieval modes produce dissociations in memory for surface information. In D. S. Gorfein & R. R. Hoffman (Eds.), *Memory and cognitive processes: The Ebbinghaus Centennial Conference.* Hillsdale, NJ: Lawrence Erlbaum Associates.

Ross, B. H. (1984). Remindings and their effects in learning a familiar skill. *Cognitive Psychology, 16,* 371–416.

Sampson, E. E. (1977). Psychology and the American deal. *Journal of Personality and Social Psychology, 35,* 767–782.

Sampson, E. E. (1978). Scientific paradigms and social values: Wanted—A scientific revolution. *Journal of Personality and Social Psychology, 36,* 1332–1343.

Schank, R. C. (1982). *Dynamic memory: A theory of reminding in computers and people.* New York: Cambridge University Press.

Srull, T. K., & Wyer, R. S. (1986). The role of chronic and temporary goals in social information processing. In R. M. Sorrentino & E. T. Higgins (Eds.), *Handbook of motivation and cognition.* New York: Guilford Press.

Tulving, E., Schacter, D. L., & Stark, H. A. (1982). Priming effects in word-fragment completion are independent of recognition memory. *Journal of Experimental Psychology: Learning, Memory and Cognition, 8,* 336–342.

Wyer, R.S., & Srull, T. K. (1986). Human cognition in its social context. *Psychological Review*, *93*, 322–359.

Wyer, R. S., & Srull, T. K. (1989). *Memory and cognition in its social context*. Hillsdale, NJ: Lawrence Erlbaum Associates.

Zadny, J., & Gerard, H. B. (1974). Attributed intentions and informational selectivity. *Journal of Experimental Social Psychology, 10*, 34–52.

11

Reply to Commentaries

Eliot R. Smith
Purdue University

The commentaries in this volume display a remarkably wide range of perspectives, reflecting their authors' various theoretical preferences and different backgrounds in social and cognitive psychology. They also show a diversity of focus, from a broad consideration of relationships of social to cognitive psychology in general (Ostrom) to a very specific treatment of empirical issues raised in my article (Bassili, Klein & Loftus). I am impressed by the thoughtfulness of all the comments. I am particularly happy to see that the ideas presented in the Target Article stimulated these individuals to cite data, raise criticisms, and express ideas which I in turn have found quite stimulating.

Particularly because of the diversity of the comments, it would not be possible or desirable for me to address each of them point by point. Instead, I will discuss a general theme that I see running through just about all of them, the ambiguity of empirical findings in psychology. I take up this theme at three levels of specificity, which serve to categorize the main emphases of the various comments. They are:

1. Reinterpretations of specific empirical results, with regard to the self (Klein & Loftus), the explicit/implicit memory distinction (Bassili), priming effects (Srull & Wyer), and stereotyping (Hamilton & Mackie, Judd).

2. Broader questions concerning the formal properties of classes of theoretical models, particularly their ability to support clear, testable predictions (Barsalou; Logan; Jacoby, Marriott, & Collins).

3. Questions involving the ultimate value of theory-testing versus "heuristic value" or other goals of research (touched on by several comments including Jacoby et al., Ostrom, and Barsalou).

In this reply I take up these three levels of the general theme in turn. I then give more detailed attention to stereotyping, which received significant emphasis in my target article as well as in the comments by Hamilton and Mackie and by Judd. Stereotyping will be used as a source of examples of what has been learned—or at least become clearer—in this exchange of views, as well as what remains to be discovered. Finally, I briefly draw conclusions as a way of reinforcing a few central points in my target article and the comments.

REINTERPRETATIONS OF SPECIFIC RESULTS

Several comments address specific empirical issues, either giving alternatives to interpretations put forward in my target article, or applying the notion of specific versus general cognitive mediators in new domains. I discuss three of those issues here, while holding stereotyping for more extended treatment later in this reply.

Representation of Information About the Self

Klein and Loftus analyze the self-concept in terms of its incorporation of relatively abstract (trait) versus specific (behavioral) information. In ingenious experiments, they show persuasively that specific behaviors may play a much more limited role in the self-concept than previous theorists had imagined. Subjects can and do make trait judgments about the self without any evidence that they are accessing specific behaviors stored in memory. I applaud their methodological approaches to this issue, and have little reason to question their conclusions. I do not find it troubling to think that self-knowledge might be largely represented in relatively abstract, general form (e.g., as traits) when much of my emphasis in the target article was on the importance of specific memory traces in other types of social knowledge. The self is probably unique among social and nonsocial objects in the extent to which it is a frequent target of thought across virtually all the situations, contexts, and tasks of everyday life. The self-concept would therefore be expected to lose much of the specific and context-bound aspect of the behaviors and episodes that originally contributed to its content.

Explicit and Implicit Memory

Bassili addresses the explicit-implicit memory distinction and my process-specificity framework for interpreting dissociations between various measures of memory. Specifically discussing the experiment of Smith and Branscombe (1988), Bassili provides an alternative "modified activation" account that he believes can account for the results, as well as other findings in related paradigms. Bassili (cf. MacLeod & Bassili, in press) postulates cognitive nodes or logogens, which can be activated in a relatively long-lasting way by exposure to the corresponding stimulus item, and which contain both modality-specific and general components. Logogens are associatively linked to each other, in a network-like structure. A further assumption is that implicit memory tests depend mainly on the activation level of the logogen, while explicit tests, because they involve "deliberate retrieval that is guided by a relevant episodic context" (p. 92), depend more on the associative links among logogens.

The framework put forward by Bassili is plausible in many respects. I note, however, that it constitutes an account of dissociations and other differential properties of *explicit versus implicit memory tests* (p. 93, for example). Explicit tests are said to encourage subjects to traverse associative links as a retrieval strategy, while implicit tests depend on logogen activation. For this reason, this model does not fit well as an account for the Smith and Branscombe (1988) results, which demonstrated a dissociation between *two implicit memory tests,* word-fragment completion and category accessibility. To fit the data Bassili has to adopt the post-hoc assumption that, despite its implicit nature, subjects used deliberate retrieval strategies for the category accessibility test. I find this implausible, primarily because the task in a category accessibility test is simply to name a trait that could be inferred from a given behavior. There are no objectively right or wrong answers (a factor that is stressed in the subjects' instructions), and everyone can perform this task easily even without prior study of a set of target traits. Why would subjects bother to adopt a deliberate retrieval strategy?

This question becomes even more puzzling when one considers that subjects did not—and for purposes of Bassili's account *could* not—do the same for the word-fragment completion test. This test has objective answers, a fact that is obvious to subjects, for if the "right" word is not accessed the fragment cannot be completed. Moreover, the task is difficult: subjects completed fewer than half of the unstudied fragments. Why would subjects *not* adopt a deliberate retrieval strategy for this task, if they do for the easy category-accessibility task? Yet this is the pattern of subject strategies required for Bassili's account to fit the results.

The dissociation between the two implicit tests (word-fragment completion and category accessibility) in my experiment is predictable from the processing account that I prefer, for it constitutes a difference between data-driven and conceptually-driven tests. The data of Roediger and Blaxton (1987) are particularly relevant, for they demonstrate similar patterns of performance on explicit versus implicit memory tests, but dissociations between data-driven and conceptually-driven tests. For empirical reasons like these, I believe that an account that places fundamental weight on the explicit-implicit distinction is less viable in the long run than one that stresses the similarity of processing at study and at test (cf. Roediger & Blaxton, 1987). Bassili's comment does properly caution us that subjects' strategies may affect results, even in conditions that supposedly tap implicit memory. However, experiments by Graf and Schacter (1987) and Hayman and Tulving (1989) suggest that subjects given implicit memory instructions generally will not attempt to use explicit memory strategies.

One other point in Bassili's comment warrants a brief reply. Bassili expresses puzzlement about the specific and long-lasting facilitation of task performance that results from a single trial of the task—even when the general task is familiar and well-practiced. It is quite counterintuitive to imagine that reading a word once should have an effect on someone's ability to read that word again, even days later. Yet precisely such results have been repeatedly obtained (see pp. 38-41 of the target article for citations). Proceduralization in ACT* is supposed to happen in a single trial (Anderson, 1987), and its theoretical properties (e.g., process specificity) match the observed properties of these effects; see Smith (in press) for an elaboration of this argument. Proceduralization should be distinguished from the production strengthening mechanism, also part of ACT*, which would be expected to have slower effects that would become evident only after many practice trials.

Priming: Declarative or Procedural Mediation

Srull and Wyer question my interpretation of long-term priming in terms of the formation and use of trait-specific inference procedures (i.e., as a version of the process outlined in the previous paragraph: Smith & Branscombe, 1987). Their argument involves several points. (1) They question the idea that the activation of constructs in declarative memory necessarily has short-term effects, noting that in their own theoretical system (Wyer & Srull, 1986, 1989) increased accessibility of a construct does not decay over time (though it can be reduced by interference from related constructs). (2) They wonder whether a procedural interpretation of priming actually fits data better than their alternative involving the activation of constructs and of goal schemas in memory. (3) Finally, they raise questions about the theoretical utility of productions in general, particularly because the exact nature of the patterns of significant productions may be difficult to identify. I reply to these issues in turn.

Possibility of Long-term Declarative Priming. Srull and Wyer label as "tautological" my inference that long-term priming effects cannot be mediated by the activation of declarative knowledge structures. They would not make such an inference, for in their preferred model declarative priming can be long-lasting. I don't accept the term tautology: however, it is true that this inference from empirical observations—*like all such inferences*—is theory-dependent. As the Target Article observed (p. 4), though long-term declarative priming is inconsistent with the basic framework of ACT*, and though there are other arguments against the possibility as well (e.g., Jacoby & Witherspoon, 1982, p. 314), those who work within a different theoretical framework will in general draw different theoretical inferences from data. The logical structure is: "Within my general theoretical framework, observation X (e.g., long-term priming) is inconsistent with theoretical conclusion Y (mediation by activation of declarative memory structures)." Of course, under another framework like Srull and Wyer's, this observation is consistent with this conclusion. But such theory-based inferences are not tautological.

Alternative Models of Priming.   Srull and Wyer question whether the formation and strengthening of content-specific productions yields a good fit to data, whether from Tulving, Schacter, and Stark (1982) or from priming studies. They suggest alternative accounts involving the increased accessibility of declarative trait constructs in memory. I cite three types of evidence answering their points and favoring procedural mediation in these contests. First, a number of studies have obtained data patterns suggesting two separate processes resulting from subjects' processing of a stimulus (Humphreys, Besner, & Quinlan, 1988; Ratcliff, Hockley, & McKoon, 1985; Smith & Branscombe, 1987; Smith, in press). One component is large, short-lived (on the order of seconds) and not task-specific; I interpret this as the result of activation of a declarative construct. The second is long-lived *and task specific* (that is, it is found only when the stimuli are processed in the same way during priming and test). It is difficult to see how a single theoretical mechanism, activation of a cognitive representation of the stimulus, can do double duty and account for both types of effects. Moreover, even ignoring the time issue, increased accessibility of a declarative construct in memory cannot have effects that are process- or context-specific (cf. Jacoby, 1983; Roediger & Blaxton, 1987). A construct that is higher in its Storage Bin becomes more accessible for any process that seeks information from memory, not just for repetitions of the same process that originally caused it to become more accessible.

Second, Srull and Wyer cite Tulving et al. (1982) as an example of a situation in which a procedural viewpoint makes incorrect predictions. In that study, subjects read a list of words and were tested with either a recognition or word-fragment completion (WFC) test. Effects of study on the WFC test were longer-lasting than effects on recognition. Srull and Wyer (p. 172) state that there is a better match between the productions used during study and those involved in the recognition test, compared to the WFC test. Hence, a procedural viewpoint should predict longer-lasting effects on recognition than on WFC, contrary to what was actually found.

However, this wrong prediction rests on a wrong assumption regarding the similarity of processes at study and at test. Roediger (e.g., Roediger & Blaxton, 1987), Jacoby (1983), and others describe cognitive processes along a continuum from data-driven to conceptually-driven (cf. Target Article, pp. 33-35). In the Tulving et al. study, subjects read words in a list, without semantic context, so the study processing has a large data-driven component (i.e., it involves accessing a representation of a word from visual cues). Since WFC is known on independent grounds to be a data-driven test and recognition conceptually driven, the study and test processes are a better match for WFC. This framework predicts that if words were studied in a meaningful semantic context they would elicit more conceptually-driven processing (i.e., elaboration; connecting the item with semantically related concepts), eliminating or perhaps reversing the advantage of WFC over the recognition test. Jacoby (1983) tested this hypothesis and obtained results exactly as predicted. I conclude that the Tulving et al. (1982) results pose no problem for the procedural viewpoint, in that data-driven study processing leads to an advantage on a data-driven test; study conditions that encouraged conceptually driven processing would result in better performance on conceptually driven tests.

Srull and Wyer go on to argue (p. 172) that construct priming accounts for WFC performance, but this claim is inconsistent with the results of Smith and Branscombe (1988). That study demonstrated a dissociation between WFC and category accessibility dependent measures, the latter assessing the trait subjects use to characterize an ambiguous behavior. Of course, Wyer and Srull have often interpreted category accessibility effects also in terms of construct activation. Given both of these claims, however, Srull and Wyer may have difficulty explaining how different study conditions (i.e., relatively data driven versus conceptually driven) led to opposite patterns of performance on the two measures in the Smith and Branscombe (1988) study. On the other hand, a procedural view neatly accounts for the dissociation by noting that WFC and category accessibility tests tap data-driven and conceptually-driven processes respectively, so each study condition leads to superior performance on tasks that involve the same type of processing.

I address a final point under this heading by starting with Srull and Wyer's concern that the procedural model outlined in the Target Article may require too many productions. These commentators note that every process that a subject performs (e.g., judging a behavior on a trait dimension) creates or strengthens productions at several levels of specificity. Moreover, judging n behaviors on m traits would result in the formation of $n * m$ productions, one for each pair. This is all true. Contrary to Srull and Wyer's intuition, my own feeling is that this would not make "too many" productions. Indeed, Srull and Wyer's intuition is not consistently applied. In their own model (with the Copy Postulate introduced in 1986), each time a construct (e.g., a trait) is used in judgment a new copy is created in its Storage Bin. Thus, their model would also create $n * m$ new constructs under the same conditions. But the decision as to whether a model involves "too many" theoretical entities should not be a contest of intuitions; fortunately, empirical evidence can be brought to bear.

Srull and Wyer would presumably say that judging a behavior on a trait would render the behavior construct and the trait construct more accessible in memory. This idea predicts that judging behavior #1 on trait #1, and also behavior #2 on trait #2, would leave all four of the constructs highly accessible. Therefore, later judgments of behavior #1 on trait #2 or behavior #2 on trait #1 would be just as fast as repetitions of the original judgments. Any interaction effect (i.e., any advantage of a previously judged *combination* over a novel pairing of an equally activated behavior and trait) must imply the storage of information about the combination over and above the activation of the individual components.

Precisely such interactions have been observed. As noted in the Target Article (pp. 39-41), Smith (in press) had subjects judge behaviors on traits. After subjects judged behavior #1 and many others on trait #1, if behavior #1 was presented a second time (several minutes later), the judgment was facilitated. Other subjects made a similar series of judgment on trait #1, then switched to making judgments on a different trait (#2). If behavior #1 was repeated with the second trait, no facilitation whatever was observed. This pattern of results is inexplicable in terms of main effects for behaviors (i.e., previously judged behaviors can be judged faster when repeated) and traits (a series of judgments on the same trait become faster), for it amounts to an interaction: the repeated behavior is judged faster only when the same process (the same trait judgment) is performed on both occasions. Logan cites similar results showing no facilitation of processing a repeated stimulus item when the subject's judgment task has changed. Empirical observations thus seem to demand the assumption that people store a specific trace (whether a content-specific production or something else) representing each specific judgment they have made, over and above an increase of activation of the individual components that were used in the judgment. Only such a model can predict interaction effects like those observed.

In summary, I believe that three types of evidence weigh against the pure declarative-construct mediation of priming effects that Srull and Wyer favor. Several studies have obtained evidence for two separate effects, one short-lived and one long-lived and process-specific. Results from the Tulving et al. (1982) and Smith and Branscombe (1988) studies using word-fragment completion dependent measures are consistent with the procedural framework outlined in the Target Article, but inconsistent with the construct-activation notion (because different dependent variables, both thought by Wyer and Srull to be mediated by construct activation, show different or even opposite patterns of effects). Finally, long-term facilitative effects of performing a particular process (e.g., judging a behavior on a trait) are specific to repetitions of the same behavior with the same trait, but do not occur if the same behavior is re-presented with a different trait. Therefore, they cannot be interpreted simply in terms of independent, additive effects of accessibility of the behavior and the trait construct in memory, but require the assumption that a trace of *the judgment process applied to the specific item* is stored in memory, despite the supposed nonparsimonious nature of this idea.

Conditions of Productions.   Finally, Srull and Wyer ask a broader question about the utility of productions as a theoretical language in which to describe cognitive processes. What patterns might appear on the condition side of productions that apply in real social interaction; for example, how would a production model account for being "smitten" by someone one has just met? To answer the specific question, I would assume that meeting someone activates a goal of forming an impression of the person, via a production like "IF I am interacting with a new person, THEN set as a goal to form an impression of the person." Because of this goal, various inference productions would then operate, based on the person's physical attributes and observed behaviors, to construct a representation of the person in terms of traits and other attributes. Finally, one can imagine something like "IF this person is physically attractive, intelligent and witty, and warm and responsive to me THEN develop extreme positive affect toward the person" as one possible version of the "being smitten" production. On a more general level, however, it is certainly true that we do not have an adequate typology of social goals, nor much concrete idea of what goals are most important to social perceivers in different situations, a point also alluded to by Ostrom (pp. 157-158). Further development along these lines is important for a production-system perspective as well as for other types of theory in social psychology.

Summary.   As one would expect given their sustained, strongly theoretically driven program of research over the last decade, Srull and Wyer are able to advance alternative viewpoints on several phenomena that I discussed in the Target Article. I have covered their points in some detail here, partly because their comment (p. 176) criticized the Target Article for failing to address the Wyer-Srull model directly and in detail. I continue to believe that these effects are better interpreted in terms of specific-exemplar and procedural mediators than in terms of the Wyer-Srull theory's abstract constructs and their position in Storage Bins. But whatever the reader's own conclusion, it is clear that the juxtaposition of alternative accounts of provocative empirical phenomena is a highly productive means of stimulating fresh hypotheses and theoretical advancement.

EMPIRICAL DISTINGUISHABILITY OF MODELS

In the target article, I used the term "signature" to refer to the pattern of observable effects that would be expected from a particular theoretical mediator. The commentaries raise two questions about this notion. First, is the idea new and different? Second, are "signatures" unique and unambiguous, so that "forgery" is not a possibility? Clearly, the answers to both of these questions are no.

As Ostrom observes, the logic of distinguishing various mediators by comparing empirically observed with theoretically predicted patterns of effects is nothing more than the familiar notion of construct validity. I chose to begin the article with the "methodological principle of specificity" as a convenient frame for the tale I wanted to tell about observations of content and process specificity and their implications for mediation, but certainly this principle itself should not be unfamiliar to any reader.

Several commentaries point out, Bassili and Barsalou perhaps most directly, that any single empirical observation is inevitably ambiguous and subject to multiple interpretations. This is a valid and important point, and for this reason the term "signature" may have been poorly chosen. Theory-testing always rests on (a) multiple observations across diverse experimental paradigms, that (b) serve to rule out competing theories (or at least to require ad-hoc adjustments) rather than directly confirming one's preferred theory. However, the commentaries go beyond this general point about the multiple interpretations of data to make some more specific observations, to which I now turn.

Content Versus Process

As Barsalou notes, one cannot identify the structure or content of a cognitive representation without making assumptions about the processes that use that representation; the converse is true as well. This is a general theme running through this book. At several points in the target article, I noted that the effects of a particular past experience depend not only on the content of the stimulus information but also on how it was processed (e.g., pp. 16, 33-35, 44-47). Logan and Jacoby et al. make similar points. And I believe that this truth is widely recognized; certainly our best and most influential theories in social cognition (e.g., Wyer & Srull, 1986, 1989; Hastie, 1988) involve explicit processing components as well as structural assumptions.

The more difficult question is whether a model containing both structural and processing components can be empirically tested and falsified. Barsalou appears to hold a relatively pessimistic viewpoint on this question. He notes that alternative models can make indistinguishable predictions about categorization judgments if they store the same information, even if it is in different formats (e.g., records of specific exemplars versus attribute n-tuples). Can RT, recall or recognition memory, or other "process-oriented" measures distinguish such theories? Barsalou is doubtful (p. 75). However, we need to be careful here. The question that Barsalou is answering in the negative—probably correctly—and the question that we might want to answer are slightly but importantly different. Barsalou is asking whether *whole classes of models* (e.g., exemplar models or abstractionist models) can be rejected on the basis of empirical observations. A more realistic ambition, however, might be to reject a *specific model* that is an instance of one or the other class. Rejection of specific models might be feasible but it requires theoretical explicitness and specificity. Barsalou's impressive commentary clearly shows the value of the types of formal analysis that can be applied to theories once they are stated fully and in explicit detail.

Barsalou's whole focus appears to be on classes of models. For example, around pp. 68-72 he describes several "fallacies" about properties of abstractionist models, such as the idea that they do not contain idiosyncratic or cooccurrence information. I was very interested to read his discussion, and am struck by the variety of abstractionist models that can be formulated. However, the claims discussed by Barsalou are accurate characterizations and not fallacies when applied to a *specific* abstractionist model, which I referred to as a "prototype" model in the target article and Barsalou describes as the "modal prototype model."

What is a "Prototype" Theory?

At times in the target article, my language may have suggested that I was interested in ruling out entire classes of models (such as "abstractionist" models) on the basis of empirical observations. However, this was not my intention. My major focus was on a specific version of a prototype-based model as a target for conclusions. Pages 8-9 outlined the categorization model I characterized as the "prevailing theory" in social psychology. It involves (a) defining (necessary and sufficient) features for many important social categories, such as gender or race; (b) for other categories, a prototype, defined as "a representation of the average or typical category member, or (equivalently) information about the typical or expected ranges of attribute values for category members" (p. 8). Processing assumptions include categorizing a new stimulus by assessing "its attribute-by-attribute similarity to multiple category prototypes . . . (weighted by the . . . accessibility of each one)" (p. 8) and categorizing it according to the greatest similarity.

Further characterization of this "prevailing" model (pp. 8-9) spells out that (1) only a single prototype per category is stored; (2) similarity is a weighted sum of similarities on the stimulus attributes (i.e., an independent-cue metric, Medin & Shaffer, 1978), perhaps weighted by the variability of the attribute; (3) specific exemplars play no role in categorization; and (4) the prototype is derived from social learning or abstracted from experiences with category members.

The model just outlined is one of those discussed by Barsalou. On p. 62 he mentions "those prototype models that discard exemplar information and that combine characteristic properties linearly (e.g., the models of Posner & Keele, 1968; Franks & Bransford, 1971; also see Reed, 1972)" as being empirically rejected on the basis of Brooks' and Medin's early work. He adds that we can reject "large classes of exemplar and abstraction models that are insensitive to idiosyncratic and cooccurrence information" (p. 84).

My point, therefore, is that the "prototype" model that prevails in social psychology, though certainly not the entire class of abstractionist models, can be rejected as a general model of categorization on the basis of existing evidence. How interesting the reader finds this claim depends on whether he or she agrees with my assertion that it characterizes the modal social psychological model of categorization. Most social psychologists use the term "prototype" in describing category representations and cite Posner and Keele (1968) or Reed (1972). For example, Cantor and Michel (1977) give these citations and state that category representations "may vary from an abstract image, comprised of the average value of each feature pictured in the set of presented items . . . to a collection of the most typical or highly related features associated with a category label" (p. 39). Similarly, Fiske, Neuberg, Beattie, and Milberg (1987) define social categories as "a category label at the top level and expected attributes at a lower level (p. 401)". The core meaning attached to the term "prototype" by social psychologists therefore seems to be information about the average, typical, or expected attribute values for the category; there is ordinarily no mention of the retention of idiosyncratic individual-exemplar information or of information about cooccurrence of attributes. Since this type of model can be empirically rejected, I believe that social psychology has much to gain by turning to more adequate models of categorization (such as the exemplar-based context model of Medin & Schaffer, 1978, or the more adequate abstractionist models covered by Barsalou in his commentary).

I hope that even those who disagree with my assertion that this empirically inadequate model is the prevailing one in social psychology would agree that more theoretical explicitness on the part of social psychologists is desirable, for it is often difficult to characterize theorists' views on categorization.

What is an Exemplar Theory?

It is also important to identify a specific member of the class of exemplar models of categorization. As noted in the target article (p. 26, p. 49), I view the context model (Medin & Schaffer, 1978) and its recent generalizations by Nosofsky (1987, 1988) as a very promising theory. It commands empirical support from a wide range of studies with nonsocial and social stimuli (for the latter, see Medin, Dewey, & Murphy, 1983; Smith & Zarate, in press). The exact assumptions of the context model are outlined in any of the works just cited. At the core of the context model is the very important point raised by Srull and Wyer (pp. 177-178) on the meaning of "similarity": similarity cannot be viewed as an abstract and context-free property of a set of exemplars or stimuli, but depends on the context, the perceiver's goals, individual differences, and the like. The flexibility of the definition of similarity in the context model is particularly evident in Nosofsky's recent work, though only a narrow range of influences on perceived similarity has been explored to date.

A more fundamental question, which also comes up in several commentaries, concerns the nature of "exemplars" that are considered (in the context model) to be stored in memory and used in categorizing new stimuli. And this question again raises issues of content versus process, as Logan and Jacoby et al. have noted. In an experimental situation, it is often convenient to assume that an "exemplar" is equivalent to a stimulus—that is, that subjects encode the content of the stimuli in more or less veridical and unbiased fashion. Experimental procedures (e.g., Smith & Zarate, in press) often expose subjects repeatedly to each of a small set of exemplars, so that this assumption becomes reasonable. However, in general this assumption is inadequate, and in principle it must be recognized that an exemplar is a stimulus *as represented* or *as interpreted* by the perceiver (Logan, p. 142), or what Jacoby et al. (p. 112) term an "episode."

I certainly accept this viewpoint, as many parts of the target article show. (e.g., pp. 16, 33-35, 44-47). However, it has many subtle implications, one of which is prominent in comments by Logan and Jacoby et al.: The intertwining of content and process that is evident in this conception of an "exemplar" may call into question the theoretical distinction between content and process itself. As Logan acknowledges, this distinction is basic to Anderson's (1983) ACT* framework, which I adopt (and also to other frameworks, like Wyer & Srull, 1986, 1989). I have outlined some of ACT*'s advantages elsewhere (Smith, 1984), and some are mentioned by Logan (e.g., p. 148: it permits the representation of knowledge at different levels of specificity). But the clear distinction between declarative knowledge (structure) and procedural knowledge (process) that Anderson (1983, ch. 1) defends may be difficult to trace at the level of specific experiences and episodes, which have effects that are *both* content- and process-specific (cf. target article, pp. 44-47). In effect, Jacoby et al. and Logan question the adequacy of the ACT* framework to encompass such effects via the mediation of content-specific productions. This is a difficult question which only further research will answer. Logan's (1988) instance theory of skill acquisition (1988) and Jacoby et al.'s episodic view of cognition constitute attractive alternatives to the ACT* framework and deserve full exploration.

TESTING THEORY OR SEEKING HEURISTIC VALUE?

Perhaps reflecting a pessimistic view of the possibility of theory testing, several commentaries emphasize the heuristic value of making sweepingly broad theoretical claims (e.g., that all knowledge is specific; Logan, p. 150) even if they are not directly empirically testable. The emphasis is most explicit in Jacoby et al. (pp. 114, 119-120), but is also found in Barsalou (pp. 84-85) and Logan

(p. 149-150), and it is implicit in several other comments. As Logan notes, broad claims are likely to be provocative in challenging intuition, requiring sharp deductions of hypotheses, and inspiring creativity. Even if such a claim is wrong, proving it wrong should be a useful exercise. As Jacoby et al. note, the episodic view leads one to ask questions and formulate research hypotheses that would not arise under alternative theoretical viewpoints. In short, these commentators point out that a theoretical statement does not have to be true, or even narrow enough to be testable, to be useful. I agree with this viewpoint, and in a way took the *Advances in Social Cognition* format as license to be provocative and perhaps overly sweeping in some claims. I am glad that others find this direction helpful.

A second aspect of heuristic value, besides value in stimulating research, is applied value (cf. Jacoby et al., pp. 119-120, and Judd). Even if research findings cannot be used to choose among theories, they may be valuable for applied reasons. For example, it would be useful to have solid empirical generalizations about the conditions under which intergroup contact would lead to a lessening of stereotyping and prejudice. In this spirit, I attempted to emphasize several ideas with immediate applied relevance in the target article's discussion of exemplar-based conceptions of stereotypes, such as their potential flexibility and changeability.

Consideration of possible differences between social and nonsocial cognition (Ostrom, p. 157-160; Srull & Wyer, pp. 166-168) appears to be another potentially fruitful heuristic question. Ostrom argues that social cognition has "primacy" over nonsocial. Though this idea has some a priori plausibility and (of course) some attractiveness, at least to a social psychologist, I see no way to operationalize "primacy" in order to test the claim. The claim therefore becomes—like Logan's suggested claim that all knowledge is specific—a means of generating interesting research questions rather than a specific theoretical proposition. Such questions (e.g., exploration of ways in which object perception might reflect its origins in social perception) deserve attention from Ostrom and other researchers.

It is interesting to contrast Ostrom's and Srull and Wyer's views on the relations between social and nonsocial cognition. I find Ostrom's points (p. 160) on the relationship extremely helpful and to the point. Researchers in social cognition frequently hear the types of criticism Ostrom refers to (e.g., that their work is "merely" derivative of cognitive paradigms and theories), and Ostrom's is the clearest and most concise formulation of a persuasive response that I have yet seen in print. He notes in effect that social and cognitive psychologists study the same entities and processes, though at different levels and with a focus on characteristically different classes of independent and dependent variables.

Srull and Wyer, however, appear to believe that theories and experimental paradigms originating in nonsocial cognitive psychology are *in principle* too narrow to encompass the range of factors that operate in social judgment and interaction. For example, they note that a theorist could begin with a cognitive framework and extend it to include a variety of social influences, or could take a social-psychological framework and make it deeper and more specific to incorporate details of cognitive processes. However, they hold that these two general approaches would not completely converge. Their evident preference is for the latter approach, for it is clear that their model (Wyer & Srull, 1986, 1989) was constructed with issues of social judgment and person memory foremost in mind. Perhaps for this reason, the model does not map well onto those that are most popular in the cognitive literature, for example in its use of Storage Bins (instead of a connectionistic spreading-activation network) to represent declarative memory and goal schemas (instead of production systems) to represent cognitive processes. Of course, these differences do not limit the utility of the Wyer-Srull model within its own domain of application, but I believe that they represent difficulties that will have to be faced in the future if the Wyer-Srull model is to be brought into closer contact with cognitive models of perception, memory, language, categorization, decision processes, and the like.

Researchers will have different preferences between taking as a starting point a theory that is firmly rooted in phenomena of memory and cognitive process (e.g., Anderson, 1983) or one that is rooted in social judgment and person perception (e.g., Wyer & Srull). However, all must agree with Srull and Wyer that numerous enticingly difficult theoretical and empirical issues must be solved before we have a full account of social interaction, intergroup behavior, and the like. In a real sense, attempting to address the full complexity of social life will for the foreseeable future prove our most powerful heuristic guide, giving us painfully clear reminders of issues that have yet to be incorporated into our theories and research.

STEREOTYPING: WHAT HAS BEEN LEARNED, WHAT ISSUES REMAIN?

Continuing a theme in the target article and in the comments by Hamilton and Mackie and by Judd, I briefly discuss stereotyping in person perception as a concrete example of some of the issues raised by a consideration of content and process specificity. First, I summarize what I believe we have learned that may be helpful in eventually arriving at an overall theoretical picture of stereotyping. Then, I review some of the major open issues as directions for future research.

From a considerable body of evidence on both social and nonsocial categorization, I believe we have learned that *exemplars play an important role in categorization*. A past experience with a specific stimulus person, in other words, may well influence the future categorization of the same or similar other persons. As discussed earlier in this reply, we can reject a particular prototype model, apparently common in social psychologists' thinking, that uses a single representation of a category's typical attributes and fails to account for the influence of idiosyncratic information and cooccurrence information on categorization.

Note that the use of exemplars in categorization is not inconsistent with the access and use of group-level knowledge *after* the stimulus person has been categorized. In fact, categorization is logically a prerequisite for the access of category-level knowledge! Judd devotes much of his comment to pointing out (correctly) that how a stimulus is categorized and what knowledge is used to make inferences about the stimulus are separate issues. However, both Judd and Hamilton and Mackie appear to read me as saying that group level knowledge may not be accessed at all, and both of their comments present convincing arguments that knowledge about social groups (i.e., stereotypes by common definition) can be used to make inferences about individual group members (once they have been categorized, that is).

I have no quarrel with this position. The target article contains the suggestion (point (e), p. 50) that specific exemplars as well as category-level knowledge may affect inferences about a target individual, as Lewicki (1985) and White and Shapiro (1987) among others have demonstrated. But of course general knowledge about groups will be likely to be used as well, whether directly (by being accessed once the target person is categorized) or indirectly (by shaping the prior representation of other exemplars in memory, whose attributes become an immediate basis for inferences about the target). As Hamilton and Mackie elaborate in detail, the interesting questions concern the *mix* of category-level and exemplar-based information that will be used to make inferences and form judgments about a target in different circumstances, and I return to this issue later.

Many of the things we know about stereotypes have been contributed by social psychologists. *Judgments about social groups can be made in "on-line" or "memory-based" fashion, depending on the subject's task or spontaneously adopted goal.* This is a particularly relevant version of the general point that what is stored in memory depends not only on what stimuli are encountered but on how they are processed (see earlier comments). Moreover, *a judgment once made is likely to be stored in memory, and retrieved if demanded on a future occasion.* This insight may set an important constraint on theories (e.g., Hintzman, 1986) that say *only* exemplars are stored in memory, as Hamilton and Mackie (pp. 102-103) note. A mixed model, with both exemplars and abstracted information as part of the representation of social groups, will probably prove more adequate for this reason among others, as I suggested in the target article (pp. 11-13, 26).

Social psychological research on stereotyping has also elaborated the *importance of context, perceivers' individual differences, and the social setting* in determining how social categorization and stereotyping will occur. These points imply that an adequate model of categorization and person perception will have to take account of a variety of factors besides the immediate stimulus information itself.

Finally, social psychologists recognize that *much group-level knowledge may be socially learned rather than abstracted from encounters with group exemplars*. This point deserves particular emphasis in the context of formal models like those set out by Barsalou. In the class of abstractionist models that he considers, all group-level information is induced from exemplars. This would be consistent with "grain-of-truth" theoretical approaches to stereotypes, which may have empirical merit in some cases (e.g., Eagly & Steffen, 1984). However, the possibility of group-level knowledge arising from independent sources like social learning, without *any* necessary correspondence with exemplar-level information, also deserves to be taken seriously. It raises fascinating issues (particularly in the case of inconsistency and contradiction between knowledge at different levels), and it will be interesting to see whether the abstractionist models outlined by Barsalou can be extended to take account of such situations.

The commentary by Barsalou demonstrates dramatically that *different ways of representing information can have similar observable effects*. Hard questions about the testability of competing models of stereotype representation and use flow from this demonstration, as discussed earlier. The importance and value of formal analyses of individual models and classes of models is also an obvious lesson to be drawn.

Jacoby's comment contributes *provocative new ideas for research approaches to questions concerning social judgment and person perception*. These include the dual-task methods (pp. 116-118) and the use of subjective experience as an indirect test of memory or judgment (pp. 118-119). I am particularly struck by several implications of Jacoby's comments (p. 116) on the Hastie and Park (1986) distinction between memory-based and on-line processing. Jacoby notes that research on memory-judgment relationships in social cognition has invariably relied on measures of explicit memory (usually recall), which we now know do not tap all that is stored in memory and can potentially influence judgments (Schacter, 1987). Jacoby and his associates and Smith and Branscombe (1988) have considered several types of judgments (e.g., famousness of names, intensity of noise, trait implications of behaviors) as measures of implicit memory, and it might be worth pushing this idea much further. Could all effects of prior information on judgment be conceptualized as implicit memory phenomena? At least two strong parallels between the implicit-memory literature (cf. Schacter, 1987; Roediger & Blaxton, 1987) and the memory-judgment literature (Hastie & Park, 1986) are evident. Both focus on patterns of association (correlation) or dissociation (independence) between explicit memory on the one hand and implicit memory or judgment measures on the other. And for both, the processing performed by subjects when the information was originally acquired (considered along a dimension of data-driven versus conceptually-driven processing, or in terms of on-line versus memory-based processing) are of central theoretical importance in explaining the observed relationships among measures. Developing these parallels further with both theoretical and empirical work might yield extremely useful insights for both areas of study.

Despite all of the above contributions, however, we do not yet have an adequate model of stereotyping in person perception in sight. Some of the major open questions appear be the following.

What is the purpose of categorization in person perception? Many writers on stereotyping (e.g., Brewer, 1988; Hamilton & Mackie, pp. 101-102) assume that one purpose is cognitive efficiency, that categorization allows the perceiver to deal with information overload. I believe that there is substantial reason to question this view, and Medin (1988), Oakes and Turner (in press), and Srull and Wyer (p. 167) make similar arguments. Far from reducing a more-than-adequate amount of stimulus information, categorization allows one to enrich stimulus information, "going beyond the information given" (Bruner, 1957) by adding expectations and inferences based on relevant memory structures.

Of course, it is true (as the results of Rothbart, Fulero, Jensen, Howard, & Birrell, 1978, suggest) that exposure to different amounts or types of information can lead subjects to adopt different processing strategies and thereby make different judgments. However, this is not equivalent to the notion that dealing with information overload is a chief purpose of social categorization, which I believe deserves serious questioning.

What determines the balance of individual-level and group-level knowledge, and which group representation will be accessed, in person perception? Hamilton and Mackie (pp. 103-105) give a detailed discussion of many of these issues, which are related to the general questions about "boundary conditions" of exemplar and abstract-construct effects that are pressed by Srull and Wyer (e.g., p. 173). If we acknowledge the evidence for specific effects (as well as general ones) in person perception and stereotyping and therefore move to a mixed representation incorporating exemplars as well as group-level knowledge, we must specify the ways in which different types of knowledge (about exemplars, and about multiple overlapping groups) interact. Obvious questions include what properties of the stimulus, the context of an encounter, and the perceiver will determine what types and levels of information are accessed and used to characterize the stimulus person. One suggestion (Target Article, point d, p. 49) is that an individual group member might be a more effective cue for past experiences with other individual exemplars, while a verbal group label (e.g., "Black people") may be a more effective cue for abstract, group-level knowledge. As Hamilton and Mackie suggest, we could also investigate *how* group-level information has effects: as a direct source of inferences or expectations about the target, as an indirect source (via its effect on the representation of prior exemplars, which themselves are retrieved in the current encounter), or by constraining what exemplars are retrieved. Note that the latter suggestion implies a multiple-stage process, in which (a) the target is categorized, permitting (b) the access of similar exemplars *of that category* from memory, (c) as bases for making inferences or judgments about the target. As Hamilton and Mackie point out, such category-guided but exemplar-based inference might constitute a mechanism for the self-perpetuation of stereotypes. I find many of these detailed suggestions plausible. In my current research I am exploring the applicability of the generalized context model (Nosofsky, 1987; Medin & Schaffer, 1978) as a framework for dealing with a social categorization, including the application of both exemplar and abstracted knowledge in a way that is sensitive to specific stimulus attributes, the current context and task, and perceiver individual differences.

These are just a few of the many and important unanswered questions about the representations and processes involved in stereotyping. My hope is not so much that the positions taken in my target article will eventually prove correct, but that thinking in terms of content and process specificity will expand researchers' thinking and inspire a variety of new and imaginative approaches to the questions.

CONCLUSIONS

Some of the messages of this volume may be summarized in dialectical form.

Thesis: all interesting aspects of social cognition depend on abstract, schematic knowledge representations. Nobody would endorse this view stated this baldly, but it is not far from the viewpoint that an observer might attribute to the field of social cognition, *based on the content of research that has been conducted to date.*

Antithesis: all interesting aspects of social cognition depend on specific memory traces. Though my emphasis in the target article was clearly toward this side, at several points (e.g., pp. 11, 26) I specifically disavowed this extreme view. It is most interesting to note, however, that Logan explicitly and some other commentators implicitly favor the adoption of this viewpoint as a productive research strategy. For example, one could postulate that the "accessibility of an abstract construct in memory" is actually a summary of the massed influence, depending on their number and similarity, of memory traces of prior episodes that involve the construct (Jacoby, 1983, p. 502). This idea hints that large numbers of specific episodes might be able to play the role that Wyer and Srull (and others) postulate for abstract constructs (cf. Srull & Wyer, pp. 173-174). As another example, it is entirely within the spirit of Barsalou's article to set a similar research question: in what ways can a set of specific memory representations produce effects on categorization that have previously been attributed to properties of abstract, general structures? (See also Hintzman, 1986, pp. 422-423; Smith, 1988, 1989.) To answer this question will require both formal analyses to develop specific predictions from competing models, and focused research to test such predictions.

Synthesis: we need to find ways to test competing theories. The pitfalls in this effort are numerous, and many of them have been aptly pointed out in the commentaries. The core issue is mimicry, the fact that a broad class of theories (e.g., abstractionist models as formulated by Barsalou; or, in a different domain, parallel-processing models) will often contain one or more specific theories with properties that appear on the surface to favor a different class (e.g., exemplar models; serial-processing models). A good example is Logan's (1988) compelling demonstration that at least in some domains the effects of practice on skilled performance, which might most naturally be thought of as due to changes in procedural knowledge (cf. Smith, in press), may actually be mediated by the storage and retrieval of specific declarative knowledge.

I am not sure that the mimicry problem in its broadest form can be solved. Evidently at least some of the commentators are not sure either, for an emphasis on the heuristic value of research instead of its value in testing competing theories amounts to a turn away from the very effort. However, solution of this problem in specific domains may not be impossible. If this is to occur, two trends in research will be essential.

One is *theoretical explicitness*. Barsalou's paper best illustrates the value of this approach, which at times has not been evident to some social psychologists. As Srull and Wyer note, most work in social cognition has not been guided by detailed information processing models. Explicit statements of theoretical assumptions, including both postulated representational structures and processes, are essential for theoretical progress. When authors are not explicit, it becomes impossible to know what phenomena would be consistent with a theory and what would be inconsistent; in a very real sense, inexplicit theories are untestable. For example, Barsalou well illustrates that general statements like "abstractionist models of categorization cannot account for X," are likely to be incorrect. It is likely that *an* abstractionist model can be constructed that can account for X. It is therefore crucial for a theorist who uses such a model to specify its details, so that its properties can be formally derived and its validity empirically tested.

The second aspect that may contribute to solving the mimicry problem is *theoretical breadth*. A theory that makes contact with phenomena in diverse areas (e.g., memory, social judgment, emotion, and intergroup relations) can make good use of empirical constraints from all these areas. For example, alternative theories of social judgment might make predictions in that domain that are empirically indistinguishable. But one theory might be better able than another to account for known results in a different empirical domain (such as the effects of practice on processing efficiency, or implicit-memory phenomena). Many have made this argument that theories of broader scope are more easily tested (e.g., Wyer & Srull, 1986). And Barsalou concludes his comment (p. 85) with a discussion of the possibility that one might look for guidance "outside the category learning literature" to provide additional constraints on models of categorization. He specifically mentions other areas of cognitive psychology, computer science, and neuroscience as sources of constraint, but omits social psychology or social cognition! Social and (nonsocial) cognitive psychology as subdisciplines are coming increasingly to speak the same language, to adopt the same types of explanatory constructs (memory representations, cognitive processes), and even to share specific theories. At the interface of these subdisciplines, then, social cognition is ideally placed to be able to formulate broad theories that can exploit multiple constraints.

As Ostrom comments, the very issues that absorb cognitive psychologists—representation, informational codes, attention, encoding, retrieval—are central to current views of social judgment, impression formation, stereotyping, and the like, within social cognition. Taking theoretical advantage of this common focus (though without negating the benefits of a division of labor) should not be viewed as "mere application" of cognitive principles by either social or cognitive psychologists. Srull and Wyer and Ostrom are right to emphasize that social life and social interaction are rich domains in which new insights into the nature of these fundamental principles can and will be obtained, particularly as social cognition advances in understanding such classic social-psychological issues as affect (Smith & Ellsworth, 1987), social interaction (Gilbert, Pelham, & Krull, 1988), and group phenomena (Mullen, in press). Just as social cognition can benefit from imitating the theoretical explicitness and careful methodology that characterize the best work in cognitive psychology, cognitive psychologists can benefit from the breadth of theoretical insight and the empirical constraints that arise from the best work by social psychologists past and present.

REFERENCES

Anderson, J. R. (1983). *The architecture of cognition.* Cambridge, MA: Harvard University Press.

Anderson, J. R. (1987). Skill acquisition: Compilation of weak-method problem solutions. *Psychological Review, 94,* 192–210.

Brewer, M. B. (1988). A dual process model of impression formation. In R. S. Wyer & T. K. Srull (Eds.), *Advances in social cognition* (vol. 1, pp. 1–36). Hillsdale, NJ: Lawrence Erlbaum Associates.

Bruner, J. S. (1957). Going beyond the information given. In H. Gruber, G. Terrell, & M. Wertheimer (Eds.), *Contemporary approaches to cognition.* Cambridge, MA: Harvard University Press.

Cantor, N., & Mischel, W. (1977). Traits as prototypes: Effects on recognition memory. *Journal of Personality and Social Psychology, 35,* 38–48.

Eagly, A. H., & Steffen, V. J. (1984). Gender stereotypes stem from the distribution of women and men into social roles. *Journal of Personality and Social Psychology, 46,* 735–754.

Fiske, S. T., Neuberg, S. L., Beattie, A. E., & Milberg, S. J. (1987). Category-based and attribute-based reactions to others: Some informational conditions of stereotyping and individuating processes. *Journal of Experimental Social Psychology, 23,* 399–427.

Franks, J. J., & Bransford, J. D. (1971). Abstraction of visual patterns. *Journal of Experimental Psychology, 90,* 64–74.

Gilbert, D. T., Pelham, B. W., & Krull, D. S. (1988). On cognitive business: When person perceivers meet persons perceived. *Journal of Personality and Social Psychology, 54,* 733–740.

Graf, P., & Schacter, D. L. (1987). Selective effects of interference on implicit and explicit memory for new associations. *Journal of Experimental Psychology: Learning, Memory, and Cognition, 13,* 45–53.

Hastie, R. (1988). A computer simulation model of person memory. *Journal of Experimental Social Psychology, 24*, 423–447.

Hastie, R., & Park, B. (1986). The relationship between memory and judgment depends on whether the judgment task is memory-based or on-line. *Psychological Review, 93*,258–268.

Hayman, C. A. G., & Tulving, E. (1989). Contingent dissociation between recognition and fragment completion. *Journal of Experimental Psychology: Learning, Memory, and Cognition, 15*, 228–240.

Hintzman, D. L. (1986). "Schema abstraction" in a multiple-trace memory model. *Psychological Review, 93*, 411–428.

Humphreys, G. W., Besner, D., & Quinlan, P. T. (1988). Event perception and the word recognition effect. *Journal of Experimental Psychology: General, 117*, 51–67.

Jacoby, L. L. (1983). Remembering the data: Analyzing interactive processes in reading. *Journal of Verbal Learning and Verbal Behavior, 22*, 485–508.

Jacoby, L. L., & Witherspoon, D. (1982). Remembering without awareness. *Canadian Journal of Psychology, 36*, 300–324.

Lewicki, P. (1985). Nonconscious biasing effects of single instances on subsequent judgments. *Journal of Personality and Social Psychology, 48*, 563–574.

Logan, G. D. (1988). Toward an instance theory of automatization. *Psychological Review, 95*, 492–527.

MacLeod, C. M., & Bassili, J. N. (in press). Are implicit and explicit tests differentially sensitive to item-specific and relational information in memory? In S. Lewandowsky, J. C. Dunn, & K. Kirsner (Eds.), *Implicit memory: Theoretical issues*. Hillsdale, NJ: Lawrence Erlbaum Associates.

Medin, D. L. (1988). Social categorization: Structures, processes, and purposes. In R. S. Wyer & T. K. Srull (Eds.), *Advances in social cognition* (vol. 1, pp. 119–126). Hillsdale, NJ: Lawrence Erlbaum Associates.

Medin, D. L., Dewey, G. I., & Murphy, T. D. (1983). Relationships between item and category learning: Evidence that abstraction is not automatic. *Journal of Experimental Psychology: Learning, Memory, and Cognition, 9*, 607–625.

Medin, D. L., & Schaffer, M. M. (1978). Context theory of classification learning. *Psychological Review, 85*, 207–238.

Mullen, B. (in press). The phenomenology of being in a group: Integrations of social cognition and group processes. *Personality and Social Psychology Bulletin*.

Nosofsky, R. M. (1987). Attention and learning processes in the identification and categorization of integral stimuli. *Journal of Experimental Psychology: Learning, Memory, and Cognition, 13*, 87–108.

Nosofsky, R. M. (1988). Similarity, frequency, and category representations. *Journal of Experimental Psychology: Learning, Memory, and Cognition, 14*, 54–65.

Oakes, P. J., & Turner, J. C. (in press). Is limited information processing capacity the cause of social stereotyping? In M. Hewstone & W. Stroebe (Eds.), *European review of social psychology* (Vol. 1). Chichester, England: Wiley.

Posner, M. I., & Keele, S. W. (1968). On the genesis of abstract ideas. *Journal of Experimental Psychology, 77*, 353–363.

Ratcliff, R., Hockley, W., & McKoon, G. (1985). Components of activation: Repetition and priming effects in lexical decision and recognition. *Journal of Experimental Psychology: General, 114*, 435–450.

Reed, S. K. (1972). Pattern recognition and categorization. *Cognitive Psychology, 3*, 382–407.

Roediger, H. R., & Blaxton, T. A. (1987). Retrieval modes produce dissociations in memory for surface information. In D. S. Gorfein & R. R. Hoffman (Eds.), *Memory and cognitive processes: The Ebbinghaus Centennial Conference* (pp. 349–379). Hillsdale, NJ: Lawrence Erlbaum Associates.

Rothbart, M., Fulero, S., Jensen, C., Howard, J., & Birrell, P. (1978). From individual to group impressions: Availability heuristics in stereotype formation. *Journal of Experimental Social Psychology, 14*, 237–255.

Schacter, D. L. (1987). Implicit memory: History and current status. *Journal of Experimental Psychology: Learning, Memory, and Cognition, 13*, 501–518.

Smith, C. A., & Ellsworth, P. C. (1987). Patterns of appraisal and emotion related to taking an exam. *Journal of Personality and Social Psychology, 52*, 475–488.

Smith, E. R. (1984). Model of social inference processes. *Psychological Review, 91*, 392–413.

Smith, E. R. (1988). Category accessibility effects in a simulated exemplar-based memory. *Journal of Experimental Social Psychology, 24*, 448–463.

Smith, E. R. (1989). *Illusory correlation in a stimulated exemplar-based memory*. Unpublished paper, Purdue University.

Smith, E. R. (in press). Procedural efficiency: General and specific components and effects on social judgment. *Journal of Experimental Social Psychology*.

Smith, E. R., & Branscombe, N. R. (1987). Procedurally mediated social inferences: The case of category accessibility effects. *Journal of Experimental Social Psychology, 23*, 361–382.

Smith, E. R., & Branscombe, N. R. (1988). Category accessibility as implicit memory. *Journal of Experimental Social Psychology, 24*, 490–504.

Smith, E. R., & Zarate, M. A. (in press). Exemplar and prototype use in social categorization. *Social Cognition*.

Tulving, E., Schacter, D. L., & Stark, H. A. (1982). Priming effects in word-fragment completion are independent of recognition memory. *Journal of Experimental Psychology: Learning, Memory, and Cognition, 8*, 336–342.

White, G. L., & Shapiro, D. (1987). Don't I know you? Antecedents and social consequences of perceived familiarity. *Journal of Experimental Social Psychology, 23*, 75–92.

Wyer, R. S., & Srull, T. K. (1986). Human cognition in its social context. *Psychological Review, 93*, 322–359.

Wyer, R. S., & Srull, T. K. (1989). *Memory and cognition in its social context*. Hillsdale, NJ: Lawrence Erlbaum Associates.

Author Index

Subject Index